A Philadelphia Perspective

Sidney George Fisher. Daguerrotype, c. 1860. Historical Society of Pennsylvania.

A PHILADELPHIA PERSPECTIVE

The Civil War Diary of Sidney George Fisher

EDITED AND WITH A NEW INTRODUCTION
BY JONATHAN W. WHITE

Fordham University Press | New York | 2007

Copyright © 2007 Fordham University Press

All rights reserved. No part of this publication may be reproduced, stored in a retrieval system, or transmitted in any form or by any means—electronic, mechanical, photocopy, recording, or any other—except for brief quotations in printed reviews, without the prior permission of the publisher.

Portions of this book have been adapted, by permission, from *A Philadelphia Perspective: The Diary of Sidney George Fisher, Covering the Years 1834–1871*, edited by Nicholas B. Wainwright (Philadelphia: Historical Society of Pennsylvania, 1967).

Library of Congress Cataloging-in-Publication Data
Fisher, Sidney George, 1809–1871.
  A Philadelphia perspective : the Civil War diary of Sidney George Fisher / edited and with a new introduction by Jonathan W. White.—1st ed.
    p. cm.—(The North's Civil War series)
  "Portions of this book have been adapted from A Philadelphia Perspective: The Diary of Sidney George Fisher, Covering the Years 1834–1871, edited by Nicholas B. Wainwright (Philadelphia: Historical Society of Pennsylvania, 1967)"—T.p. verso.
  Includes bibliographical references and index.
  ISBN-13: 978-0-8232-2727-3 (cloth : alk. paper)
  ISBN-10: 0-8232-2727-8 (cloth : alk. paper)
  ISBN-13: 978-0-8232-2728-0 (pbk. : alk. paper)
  ISBN-10: 0-8232-2728-6 (pbk. : alk. paper)
  1. Fisher, Sidney George, 1809–1871—Diaries. 2. Philadelphia (Pa.)—History—Civil War, 1861-1865—Sources. 3. Philadelphia (Pa.)—Social life and customs—19th century. 4. Fisher family, 5. Ingersoll family. I. White, Jonathan W., 1979– II. Title.
F158.44F55 2007
974.8'1103—dc22

2007009740

Printed in the United States of America
09 08 07   5 4 3 2 1
First edition

CONTENTS

Acknowledgments vii

Editorial Comment | *Jonathan W. White* ix

Preface to the 1967 Edition | *Nicholas B. Wainwright* xi

Introduction | *Jonathan W. White* 1

THE CIVIL WAR DIARY OF SIDNEY GEORGE FISHER

~1860~ 17

~1861~ 71

~1862~ 129

~1863~ 179

~1864~ 211

~1865~ 248

Epilogue 274

Fishers and Ingersolls 275

Countryseats 279

Index 281

ACKNOWLEDGMENTS

I would like to thank the H. B. Earhart Foundation and the Lynde and Harry Bradley Foundation for their support of my graduate education, without which I would not have been able to do this project. I would like to thank Herman Belz and Trisha Posey for commenting on drafts of the introduction. Paul Cimbala, Robert Oppedisano, and Nicholas Frankovich of Fordham University Press have been incredibly helpful and supportive in this, my first book-length publication. R. A. Friedman of the Historical Society of Pennsylvania generously checked the manuscript diary to verify some last-minute details. Lastly, I thank my parents, Bill and Eileen White, for their continual support of my pursuit of a career as a historian.

—*Jonathan W. White*

EDITORIAL COMMENT

When Nicholas B. Wainwright first released the diary of Sidney George Fisher as a book in 1967, he selected passages that covered the broad range of topics, events, and ideas that had interested the diarist. Through this selection process, Wainwright allowed Fisher to tell readers a coherent narrative of his life. When I traveled to the Historical Society of Pennsylvania to check parts of the 1967 edition against the original manuscript diaries, I found, much to my surprise, that Wainwright had transcribed only a very small portion of Fisher's diary. The Civil War years, in their original form, span some twenty-two volumes of large journal books. Perhaps only 5 to 10 percent of the original diary has thus far been released.

This edition of *A Philadelphia Perspective* reproduces the Civil War years of Fisher's diary as Wainwright published them. As stated in his preface, Wainwright corrected punctuation and some minor spelling errors, hoping to release the book as Fisher "would have wanted" it. I have kept Wainwright's alterations, silently correcting a small number of typographical errors. I have also amplified the footnotes, keeping Wainwright's, with some modification, and adding many new notes. In the original diary Fisher did not write the date at the beginning of each entry, as it appears in the text. Wainwright also used ellipses sparingly to indicate omitted portions of the diary. For the sake of readability, I have kept the dates and ellipses as Wainwright published them. I have also retained from Wainwright's original edition the epilogue, genealogies of the Fisher and Ingersoll families, and list of countryseats near Philadelphia.

This edition of Fisher's diary is an excellent abridgment. It should find a place in classrooms from the high-school through the graduate level, as well as on the bookshelves of scholars and of general readers with an interest in American and Philadelphia history. When published in its entirety, Fisher's diary will rival those of George Templeton Strong and Mary Boykin Chesnut for a place among the greatest private journals of nineteenth-century America and the War Between the States.

—*Jonathan W. White*

PREFACE TO THE 1967 EDITION

Because of his writings on political and constitutional questions during the Civil War era, Sidney George Fisher (1809-1871) attained sufficient distinction to warrant the inclusion of his career in the *Dictionary of American Biography*. In that brief and not altogether accurate sketch, his biographer made no mention of Fisher's most noteworthy literary accomplishment—his diary, the existence of which has only recently been made public. Given to The Historical Society of Pennsylvania in 1948 by R. Sturgis Ingersoll, the diary began to appear four years later in *The Pennsylvania Magazine of History and Biography*. Ultimately, it ran through twenty-four issues, but even so the part published was but a small fraction of the original. Subjects of seemingly little interest, repetitions, long resumes of books the diarist read, and much coverage of foreign events were deleted.

Readers were both repelled and fascinated by Fisher's candid exposition of his views. Nothing hitherto published in the *Magazine* attracted more comment, and long before the series came to an end in 1965 the Historical Society was being urged to print the diary in book form. Through the generosity of Mrs. Harry Clark Boden of Newark, Delaware, such a publication has now been made possible. Mrs. Boden is the granddaughter of Mrs. Alexis Irénée du Pont, who was, in turn, the granddaughter of Phoebe George, half-sister of Sidney George Fisher's mother. Phoebe George, who married Moses Bradford, was to have inherited her father's Mount Harmon estate on the Sassafras River, Cecil County, Maryland. However, that property went instead to Mrs. Fisher, and subsequently became part of the inheritance of her son, the diarist.

Mount Harmon was to prove a determining factor in Sidney George Fisher's life. After graduating from Dickinson College in 1827, he studied farming for a time and then became a member of the Philadelphia Bar, but the legal profession did not interest him and in 1834 he turned his attention to Mount Harmon in the hope of finding there a source of income. While his absentee direction of the farm was to prove disastrous, it is pleasant to note that Mrs. Boden has purchased the place and restored the house to the way it appeared in the days of its former glory, when occupied by Sidney George Fisher's grandfather.

In its present form, the diary contains nearly all the material that came out in the *Magazine*, and, in addition, about twenty per cent more appears for the first time. In copying the parts selected for publication, the original document has been followed as closely as possible, with the exception of errors in punctuation and spelling (habitual and peculiarly Philadelphia spellings such as Shakspeare and chesnut remain). The diarist often wrote hastily without the nice regard he paid to his works intended for publication, and I hope my minor changes are what he would have wanted, could he have anticipated the printing of his diary.

Fisher was exceedingly proud of its many volumes. He had "the vanity to think them, in parts at least, well written, and that the various reflections on men and things, books and public affairs are sound and well reasoned." His diary was "a sort of father confessor to me, unluckily without the power of giving me either advice or absolution." From time to time he worried about what would happen to it after his death, but it is clear that he wanted the record preserved. Several times he read over it and tore out passages. In his preparation to leave the world, no task was of greater importance to him than putting his diary in order.

Historians should find many nuggets of information in the pages which follow, but the diary is more than a source of history; it is a document of unique human interest, the unfolding of a life. While the personality of the diarist in his youth was marred by arrogance, his character mellowed under the influence of profound philosophical studies, and a certain gallantry added a bit of lustre to a way of life that few will praise.

According to Fisher, it was Bacon who said "reading maketh a full man, writing an exact man." Cut off from the world of business, and not otherwise actively employed, he devoted his time to reading and writing, with a certain detachment from his surroundings that gave to his conclusions an originality and a stamp of character. And so it was that, by and large, his quiet life was a full one and his insights into "men and things" singularly perceptive. Unworldliness, his desire to live "in learned leisure and contemplative indolence," brought on the disasters which clouded his final years. In his diary for 1860, there is a translation which he made from a verse of French poetry. It seems to forecast his coming poverty, illness, and obscurity.

> Thus do all things change and pass,
> Thus we changing pass away,
> Leaving behind as faint a trace
> Of our transitory stay,
> Of our troubled brief life-dream,
> As a boat leaves in the stream.

Fisher's fear that, in the words of the poem, he would leave behind no trace of his existence is expressed in his diary: "If I do not write, I shall do nothing, for I am unfit for business, and to do nothing in life, to be useless and obscure, to leave no trace behind me that I have lived, is a miserable fate." It was for this reason that he contributed numerous articles to magazines and newspapers, and delivered addresses, which, according to the custom, were published in pamphlet form. Moreover, two small books of undistinguished poetry came from his pen, while the culmination of his political thinking was expressed in another three volumes—*The Law of the Territories*, *The Laws of Race as Connected with Slavery*, and *The Trial of the Constitution*. These writings have served to keep a faint and fading recollection of his name in historical circles. His diary, however, recreates his career as a human being, and more than any other of his literary efforts will prevent his being forgotten.

—*Nicholas B. Wainwright*

A Philadelphia Perspective

INTRODUCTION | JONATHAN W. WHITE

Few published diaries from the Civil War era are as incisive and illuminating as that of Sidney George Fisher (1809-71). Written between 1834 and 1871, Fisher's diary chronicles, in arresting detail, many of the most important political and social events of nineteenth-century America. A prolific and talented writer, Fisher also published numerous newspaper articles, partisan pamphlets, and full-length books about the political and constitutional struggles in America from the Age of Jackson until Reconstruction. The publication of his diary in 1967 generated renewed interest in his work. In it historians found "one of the most remarkable political records of the era" and "an invaluable daily commentary by a member of Philadelphia's elite."[1] The 1967 edition had a limited printing, however, and Fisher's contribution to nineteenth-century historical letters has been insufficiently appreciated. Fisher's diary offers a remarkable portrait of Civil War Philadelphia in particular and of Civil War America more broadly. It is a work that deserves renewed attention by all readers with an interest in the Civil War.

1. William Dusinberre, *Civil War Issues in Philadelphia, 1856-1865* (Philadelphia: University of Pennsylvania Press, 1965), 14; J. Matthew Gallman, *Mastering Wartime: A Social History of Philadelphia during the Civil War* (New York: Cambridge University Press, 1990), 347. For other praise of Fisher's diary, see Catherine Clinton, *Civil War Stories* (Athens: University of Georgia Press, 1998), 114; E. Digby Baltzell, *Puritan Boston and Quaker Philadelphia* (New Brunswick, N.J.: Transaction Press, 1996), 45; Malcolm Bell, *Major Butler's Legacy: Five Generations of a Slaveholding Family* (Athens: University of Georgia Press, 1987), 519.

Sidney George Fisher was a member of a socially prominent Philadelphia family. For most of his life he lived on inherited or borrowed money, rarely working to sustain himself. After graduating from Dickinson College in 1827, he tried his hand at farming, and then law, but neither suited his tastes. Instead, he preferred the more gentlemanly pursuits of thinking, reading, and writing. "Sidney lived in an inner world of ideas, thought, speculation—he was a dreamer," wrote Nicholas B. Wainwright.[2] An aristocratic man of letters, Fisher was a strong and unrelenting critic of democracy and the Democratic party. He detested in particular its revered symbol and leader, President Andrew Jackson. "Old Hickory," according to Fisher, was vile and corrupt—"ignorant, passionate and imbecile, without a striking or estimable trait, the tool of low adventurers & swindlers . . . [and] the chieftain of the lower orders."[3]

Jackson's rise to power caused Fisher to doubt that republican institutions could survive in America. In antebellum Philadelphia he witnessed or heard about numerous instances of mob violence.[4] During a contested election in 1838, Fisher analyzed the actions of a mob that descended on the state capitol: "This is the working of the democratic spirit, which seems increasing in boldness & turbulence every hour." The Democrats, he believed, sought "to overawe the constituted authorities, and to gain success for their party by any means &

---

2. Nicholas B. Wainwright, "Sidney George Fisher—The Personality of a Diarist," *Proceedings of the American Antiquarian Society* 72 (April 1962), 15. "Keeping a diary," according to Wainwright, "supplemented and gave purpose to Sidney's life of contemplation. . . . This diary is, presumably, the most complete and most revealing ever compiled by a Philadelphian, and surely one of the best written ever kept by an American." Ibid., 22, 29.

3. Diary entry, August 6, 1834. All diary entries cited in the text and notes are from *A Philadelphia Perspective: The Diary of Sidney George Fisher, Covering the Years 1834-1871*, ed. Nicholas B. Wainwright (Philadelphia: Historical Society of Pennsylvania, 1967).

4. Some scholars of nineteenth-century riots and class relations have cited Fisher. See, for example, Michael Feldberg, *The Turbulent Era: Riot and Disorder in Jacksonian America* (New York: Oxford University Press, 1980); Noel Ignatiev, *How the Irish Became White* (London: Routledge, 1995), 223; Cindy S. Aron, *Working at Play: A History of Vacations in the United States* (New York: Oxford University Press, 1999), 273.

at any sacrifice. A resort to brute force has now become familiar & expected."[5] One year later he marked election day with the lamentation: "I always vote *against* the popular side on principle. The evil of our government, and a great & pressing one, is the tyranny of the many, the supremacy of numbers over mind; the danger is, the excess of the democratic spirit, which threatens the destruction of all law, order and security. It is nonsense to talk of liberty in this country, where the educated classes must always be in a minority & therefore without political influence or power and subjected, without protection, to the control of demagogues & mobs."[6] As far as Fisher could tell, democratic government led only to "confusion, alarm, distress, violence and fraud."[7] Eventually the system would have to collapse. "Ignorance, imbecility and corruption rule at Washington and will continue to rule until revolution and anarchy bring about a change of principles, of the whole system."[8]

The most divisive political issue of antebellum America was slavery. In 1837, Fisher observed that the "subject of slavery is becoming a very important & exciting one, pregnant I fear with many future disasters." Northern public opinion was becoming increasingly hostile to the South's peculiar institution, and Fisher doubted that wise and prudent leaders would be able "to avert the coming storm." As the abolitionists became more "numerous, powerful, enthusiastic & determined," Fisher concluded "they must in the end prevail or sever the Union."[9] Fisher in part blamed the abolitionists for the opposition they aroused. When a Philadelphia mob destroyed a building owned by abolitionists, Fisher observed that it was difficult to protect citizens who so rashly provoked the rabble. "The cause itself is unpopular & justly so, and the fanatic orators openly recommended dissolution of the Union, abused Washington, etc. Black & white men & women sat

5. Diary entry, December 7, 1838.
6. Diary entry, October 8, 1839.
7. Diary entry, March 9, 1842.
8. Diary entry, February 19, 1859.
9. Diary entry, February 15, 1837.

promiscuously together, & walked about arm in arm," he wrote with disdain. No respectable northerner would defend these "excesses of enthusiasm."[10]

By the mid-1840s, Fisher began to notice how thoroughly slavery was dividing the nation. "The union of the country is factitious, and is becoming less real every day," he wrote during the debate over the annexation of Texas. "Every day the difference between the North & South is becoming more prominent and apparent. The difference exists in everything which forms the life of a people—in institutions, laws, opinions, manners, feelings, education, pursuits, climate & soil." In Fisher's mind, the federal Union was showing itself to be little more than "a paper bond" that lacked any sense of national feeling or identity.[11] The annexation debate only exacerbated these differences and tensions. Ultimately the debate came down to power. The South hoped to carve several new slave states out of Texas to increase Southern representation in Congress and the Electoral College. Many Northerners, by contrast, hoped to reduce Southern influence in the national government. Fisher chastised the South for trying to "govern the country." The North was superior in numbers and therefore ought to govern; if the North did not rule, Fisher believed, civil war was imminent.[12]

More than a decade before Lincoln's election, Fisher correctly foresaw disaster in the future of the nation. Selfishness and the lust for political power, combined with the explosive issue of slavery in the territories, would bring a violent end to national unity:

10. Diary entry, May 19, 1838. Fisher later criticized Senator William H. Seward of New York for going "as far against slavery as the measures of the southern men do in its favor." Fisher complained that there was no national, moderate political party in the country. "The South breaks down the Constitution to extend slavery in the North, where it should *not* go, the North threatens to prevent southern men from occupying new territory in the South, where they & slavery ought in all fairness to be allowed to go. Both are mad & between them they may destroy the Union." Diary entry, March 4, 1858.

11. Diary entry, April 28, 1844.

12. Diary entry, June 11, 1848.

> The management of a great confederacy demands the ability to exercise self-denial, to sacrifice local interest & passions to great & general ends, & the masses are capable neither of comprehending the purpose nor of making the sacrifice. That this Union is to be dissolved I regard as certain. It is a mere question of time. It may last 20 years, or ten or 6 months, but go it must beyond doubt within half a century. I hope, however, it will last my day, for dissolution is synonymous with civil war, anarchy & misery & disaster of every kind. The North could bear it & recover from it speedily, so could the West, but to the South it would be utter destruction & this I think they are beginning to understand.[13]

Despite such despondent forebodings, Fisher took up his pen, hoping to cast some calm, conservative words into the stormy debate over slavery. His public writings in the 1850s echoed his private sentiments. The Southern minority should not rule the North, and the Northern majority should act with moderation, rejecting the radicalism of the abolitionists. Only political moderation and adherence to inherited constitutional principles would save the Union.

Fisher published several essays and pamphlets related to the sectional conflict in America. In *Kanzas and the Constitution* (1856), *The Law of the Territories* (1859), and *The Laws of Race, as Connected with Slavery* (1860), Fisher argued that the Constitution protected slavery in the Southern states but that Congress had the power to legislate regarding slavery in the territories. Fisher wrote these works in response to the outbreak of violence in the Kansas territory following the passage of the Kansas-Nebraska Act in 1854. This law repealed the 1820 Missouri Compromise (which had closed certain territories to slavery), and allowed the territories to decide for themselves whether or not to permit slavery within their borders. But "popular sovereignty" regarding slavery in the territories led to fraudulent and violent elections. Southerners poured into Kansas to vote in a referendum on slavery, carrying the day for the South. Such illegal actions, Fisher warned, would only alienate the South from the North. "Not one in a thousand of the [northern] people cares much whether [Kansas] be a

---

13. Diary entry, March 4, 1850.

slave State or a free State," Fisher declared, "but millions do care, most deeply, whether slavery is to be forced upon it against the wishes of its people; whether the Constitution of their country is to be repealed for the sake of slavery; whether their Government is to be used as an instrument to accomplish the schemes of sectional ambition in violation of the obligations of truth and justice."[14]

Fisher chastised Southerners and their Northern Democratic allies for rejecting the traditional constitutional principle that Congress could legislate regarding slavery in the territories. Only in the Constitution, he believed, would Southerners find protection for their peculiar institution. As it was, world opinion was turning against slavery, and the institution was in danger of becoming extinct. The South, therefore, needed to maintain the friendship of the North:

> [Slavery] is doomed to recede, not to advance; and, finally, to be greatly modified or to perish. Whether this fate is to arrive peacefully and gradually, or suddenly and violently, depends wholly on the action of the South. There is security for the South, living as it must always do by the side of Northern strength, only in the Constitution and the friendship of the North. The Constitution is wise, and every departure from it proves its wisdom. It has shown itself hitherto sufficient for the protection of slavery. The Northern people are loyal to the South. The vast majority yield willingly, zealously, all the constitutional rights of the South. They love the Union and the Constitution and their country, and the South as part of their country.[15]

But the North would not stand by as Southern conspiracies and violence turned Kansas and other Northern territories into slave states. The South must content itself with protection of slavery where it already existed.

Fisher accepted slavery as a necessity in America because he believed it was the only way for whites to control the Southern black population, but he was not an ardent supporter of the institution.

---

14. Fisher, *The Law of the Territories* (Philadelphia: C. Sherman and Son, 1859), 108.
15. Fisher, *Kanzas and the Constitution* (Boston: Damrell and Moore, 1856), 16.

Slavery, according to Fisher, "performs the duty of magistrates, police, prisons, poor-houses and hospitals, for the negro race in the South, without expense to government, and far more efficiently than any government could perform them. Slavery is not in itself a good thing; on the contrary, it is an evil thing, and bears fruit according to its nature. But we have the negro, and therefore we must have slavery."[16] Fisher believed that blacks "must be either free or absolutely and securely slaves." Since the South had flourished with slavery, he argued that things ought to remain the way they were. But Southern politicians were hurting their own cause by their overly aggressive attempts to protect and extend slavery. "The excesses of Southern politicians have also stimulated, encouraged, and inflamed into enthusiasm the Abolitionists, strengthened their cause, added to their numbers, and put weapons in their hands, which they know how to use with skill and effect, and are using." The violence of Bleeding Kansas and Harpers Ferry were the logical results of the Kansas-Nebraska Act, the caning of Senator Charles Sumner of Massachusetts, the *Dred Scott* decision, the Lecompton Constitution, and Northern Democratic acquiescence in all of these Southern aggressions. If the South wished to protect its cherished institution and the racial status quo, Fisher concluded, it ought to maintain the friendship of the North by upholding the Constitution and slavery as they were.[17]

In many ways, Fisher came to believe that Southerners lived in a completely different society and that slavery was incompatible with liberty and Union. "The slaveowners are an oligarchy, who live in dread not only of the Negroes, but of the whites who are not slaveowners," Fisher wrote on December 16, 1859. Out of this fear Southern

---

16. Fisher, *The Laws of Race, as Connected with Slavery* (Philadelphia: Willis P. Hazard, 1860), 48.

17. Fisher, *Law of the Territories*, xiv–xv, xxii. Fisher found the *Dred Scott* decision, and its doctrine that blacks could not be citizens of the United States, particularly abominable. Privately he wrote that the case was "iniquitous, disgraceful to a civilized and Christian nation & impolitic for the South, for its tendency is to make slavery revolting and to strengthen against it the opinion of the civilized world." Diary entry, April 4, 1858.

society naturally degenerated into tyranny. Moreover, as Southern politicians became increasingly vociferous in their defense of slavery, abolitionism became connected "with the cause of liberty, order & civil rights," ideals that "have been destroyed in the southern states for the sake of slavery." Fisher concluded that slavery and the Union could not long coexist. Five days later, on December 21, 1859, he noted that the "moral feeling of the North is setting strongly against slavery & southern politicians are the cause of it."

Fisher's personal opinions about slavery were complex. Although he believed that blacks were intellectually and morally elevated by slavery, his heart still wrenched at the plight of African Americans in bondage. When one acquaintance sent some slaves to a plantation in Georgia and sold others at auction, Fisher witnessed the "terrible distress" the slave families suffered:

> The Negroes here dread nothing on earth so much as this, and they are in great commotion about it. . . . The Negro is capable of strong affection & local attachment. Here these people have lived all their lives & their parents also, for generations. All their friends & relations are here. They regard the South with perfect horror, and to be sent there is considered as the worst punishment inflicted on them, & is reserved for one offence alone by the custom of the neighborhood, an attempt to run away. When to all this is added the separation of husband & wife, parent & child, the case is very hard. But, they are *property*, & [the owner] has a right to do as he pleases with his own. Only it requires a Southern education to enable a man to bring his mind to the point of exercising such a right in such a manner.[18]

When one of his close friends, Pierce Butler, sold his slaves to relieve his debt, Fisher noted that the sale of slaves was "among the many frightful consequences of slavery and contradicts our civilization, our Christianity, our Republicanism. Can such a system endure, is it consistent with humanity, with moral progress? These are difficult questions, and still more difficult is it to say, what can be done? The

18. Diary entry, May 13, 1846.

Negroes of the South must be slaves or the South will be Africanized. Slavery is better for them and for us than such a result."[19]

Despite his misgivings about slavery, Fisher believed the institution ought to be protected where it already existed. If Southern Democratic leaders acted with "moderation & prudence" their way of life would be kept safe.[20] But this was not to be. Moderation and prudence did not guide Democratic politics at the end of the 1850s, and the party split into Northern and Southern wings during the 1860 presidential contest. This division within the Democratic party allowed Abraham Lincoln to capture the presidency that year with less than 40 percent of the popular vote, eventually bringing on disunion and civil war, and setting the stage for the emancipation of four million Southern slaves.

Fisher published his most important political text after the outbreak of the war, releasing *The Trial of the Constitution* in late 1862. Originally intended as a tract on the suspension of the writ of habeas corpus, the book took on a life of its own, ultimately becoming a treatise on the benefits and defects of the American constitutional order. In this book Fisher argued that the Constitution was adequate to deal with the major issues raised by the Civil War so long as it was interpreted broadly enough to respond to political realities and the popular will. "Every government," Fisher wrote, "has and must have sufficient power to satisfy the majority of the people, for the power of the Government is the power of the people." This was a peculiar position for Fisher to take considering his disdain for popular democracy, but the war seems to have taught him that extraordinary times necessitated extraordinary measures.[21] Perhaps, too, Fisher finally saw in the White House a statesman who restored his confidence in American institutions.

19. Diary entry, February 17, 1859.
20. Diary entry, October 13, 1858.
21. Fisher, *The Trial of the Constitution* (Philadelphia: J. B. Lippincott, 1862), 76. To be sure, Fisher still blamed the Democratic Party for the coming of the war, and he remained critical of what he believed were the vulgar expressions of popular mass democracy.

Fisher believed that unwritten constitutions, such as the British constitution, were superior to America's written constitution, because they afforded more flexibility to policymakers and the people. Nevertheless, he believed the U.S. Constitution could be construed to allow for nearly any action necessary to sustain the national government, defeat the rebellion, and restore the Union. Since it was impracticable to amend the Constitution to allow for stronger action by the federal government during the war, Fisher concluded that "surely nothing remains to be done but to arm the existing Government by our support, with all the power that a Convention [to amend the Constitution] would have, that is to say, with the whole power of the people, because nothing less than the whole can be adequate to the crisis."[22] In short, the government possessed the authority to do whatever the people demanded in order to win the war.

Scholars have praised *The Trial of the Constitution* for its insights into the American constitutional order. "Among American analysts of the Constitution produced by the Civil War," wrote Harold M. Hyman, Fisher "was the most quickly critical, most completely perceptive, most constructively aware of the document's defects and strengths."[23] Similarly, William H. Riker commended Fisher for being the first "student of the Constitution who wrote about it the way it actually worked rather than about the way it ought to work."[24] Students of the Constitution across several generations have found Fisher's work instructive.[25]

22. Ibid., 200.

23. Harold M. Hyman, new introduction to Fisher, *The Trial of the Constitution* (1862; repr., New York: Da Capo Press, 1972), xi-xii. See also Hyman, *A More Perfect Union: The Impact of the Civil War and Reconstruction on the Constitution* (New York, Alfred A. Knopf, 1973), 115.

24. William H. Riker, "Sidney George Fisher and the Separation of Powers during the Civil War," *Journal of the History of Ideas* 15 (June 1954): 411.

25. Herman Belz, "The Constitution in the Gilded Age: The Beginnings of Constitutional Realism in American Scholarship," *American Journal of Legal History* 13 (April 1969): 110-125; Arthur Bestor, "State Sovereignty and Slavery: A Reinterpretation of Pro-slavery Constitutional Doctrine, 1846-1860," *Journal of the Illinois State Historical Society* 54 (Summer 1961): 152; Edward S. Corwin, *The President: Office and Powers, 1787-1957*, 4th ed. (New York: New York University Press, 1957), 232, 451-54; Sydney

During the Civil War, Fisher continued to invest time in his diary, and it is an especially rich record of the war between the states. The tone and content of his diary reveal how many Americans grappled with such a long and devastating conflict. On hearing news of an alleged Union defeat, Fisher described the confusion and disillusionment in the North: "The town was full of all sorts of rumors but nothing was considered reliable except the fact of a battle. The night is cold, there is a fierce wind. I can think of nothing but the wounded now lying exposed to the weather on the battlefield. What a scene of suffering & horror it must be, yet in spite of it all, who does not love war & its glory? Such is our mysterious nature that under the excitement of danger and a struggle we court what else we shrink from instinctively, pain and death."[26] Fisher remained a perceptive political observer and critic of the Democratic Party. During the summer of 1863, for example, after describing a near-riot outside the offices of a Democratic newspaper in Philadelphia, he rationalized the anger of the mob: "These Democrats can see in this great war only a party contest. Every victory of the government they lament as a defeat of their party; in every success of the rebels they see a party victory & hail it with triumph. In all possible ways they oppose the administration & thus encourage the enemy to persevere. Their treasonable speeches are republished in the South. They are evidence of a divided North. Division is weakness and our weakness is strength for the

---

G. Fisher, "The Suspension of Habeas Corpus during the War of the Rebellion," *Political Science Quarterly* 3 (September 1888): 454-88; Mark E. Neely Jr., *The Fate of Liberty: Abraham Lincoln and Civil Liberties* (New York: Oxford University Press, 1991), 189, 202; Phillip Shaw Paludan, *A Covenant with Death: The Constitution, Law, and Equality in the Civil War Era* (Urbana: University of Illinois Press,1975), 170-218; Clinton Rossiter, *Constitutional Dictatorship: Crisis Government in the Modern Democracies* (Princeton: Princeton University Press, 1948), 224; Michael Vorenberg, *Final Freedom: The Civil War, the Abolition of Slavery, and the Thirteenth Amendment* (New York: Cambridge University Press, 2001). Paludan's book contains two chapters on Fisher. For contemporary assessments of Fisher's *Trial* see the reviews in the *Christian Examiner* (March 1864), the *North American Review* (April 1863), and the *American Law Register* (October 1864).

26. Diary entry, February 28, 1862.

enemy."[27] In passages such as this, Fisher speaks directly to debates in current historiography over the utility of party competition to the Northern war effort.[28]

As with many Americans, the Civil War had a transformative effect on Fisher's thinking. By late 1862 he was ready to endorse President Lincoln's policy of military emancipation, though he still opposed equality for African Americans.[29] Writing nearly two years after the close of the war, Fisher noted what he saw as an ironic effect of black suffrage in the South:

> Hating democracy, disdaining the mob, they [southerners] yet allied themselves with the democracy of the North for the sake of governing the country in the interests of slavery, thus sanctioning the principle of democracy, which was a lie, and lo! they are now themselves subjected to the power of a viler mob than that of the North. They are forced to meet their former slaves at the hustings, to court them & make stump speeches to them & beg them for their votes, as they are now doing even in So. Carolina, where some of the proudest planters & most conspicuous secessionists, among them Wade Hampton, have on a recent occasion been the orators. This is poetical justice & tho I hate Negro suffrage & all . . . ignorant suffrage as much as anyone, I cannot help a feeling of satisfaction at beholding it, which however does not overcome my sympathy with those who are subjected to so terrible a curse.[30]

With the introduction of black suffrage, Fisher's hatred of democracy merged with his racist tendencies so that he, ironically, felt some sympathy for Southerners after the war.

27. Diary entry, May 8, 1863.
28. See Mark E. Neely Jr., *The Union Divided: Party Conflict in the Civil War North* (Cambridge, Mass.: Harvard University Press, 2002); Adam I. P. Smith, "Beyond Politics: Patriotism and Partisanship on the Northern Home Front," in *An Uncommon Time: The Civil War and the Northern Home Front*, ed. Paul A. Cimbala and Randall M. Miller (New York: Fordham University Press, 2002), 145–69.
29. [Fisher], "The President's Proclamation of September 22," *Philadelphia North American and United States Gazette*, November 29, 1862; "Our Black Army," June 24, 1863.
30. Diary entry, March 21, 1867.

Introduction

When on his deathbed, Fisher spent much time reading his old diaries. He relished in his memories. "Read diary of 1839," he wrote on April 29, 1871. "It brings back those days of youth very vividly." Some memories apparently caused the diarist remorse or embarrassment. He tore out many pages and felt "much inclined to destroy the whole."[31] His final entry, July 22, 1871, concluded, "Very miserable all day. Am losing ground every day." Indeed, he died three days later at the age of sixty-two. But readers today have Fisher to thank for leaving behind such a lucid and insightful account of the American Civil War. We ought to be grateful that he did not "put my house in order" or "destroy what I do not wish to leave behind me."[32] Instead, Fisher left us an invaluable record of the past that has served a generation of scholars, and, with this new edition, will serve many generations more.

---

31. Diary entry, May 3, 1871.
32. Diary entry, May 6, 1871.

*The Civil War Diary
of Sidney George Fisher*

~1860~

JANUARY 1, 1860 | Walked with Bet[1] to church, but did not go in. Indeed, I have never been to our village church, Mr. Davis'[2] conversation giving me no desire to hear his sermons. I think I can employ Sunday as profitably, as *religiously* at home. It is very well for the multitude to have a day consecrated to religious observances, for otherwise the engrossing cares of the world would exclude religious ideas altogether from most minds. But for the thinking man, every day is Sunday, he sees the moral, the divine in truth, and truth governs every day and all things, the most common and familiar. His thoughts are his church.

JANUARY 2, 1860 | Slavery occupies all conversation now. Fisher[3] belongs to what is called the conservative class. For the sake of preserving the Union and peace and order, which in reality means his own property and enjoyments, he is willing to sacrifice the right & the truth, to yield to all the demands of the South and to maintain slavery without so much as asking whether it be not in itself a wrong and a

---

1. Elizabeth "Bet" Fisher (1815–72), daughter of Charles Jared Ingersoll, married the diarist on May 28, 1851. More than ten years before they were married, Fisher wrote: "Talked half the evening to Miss. E. Ingersoll who is always attractive. She has but little beauty, but her manner, voice, grace, & expression make up for the want of it." Diary entry, January 31, 1840.

2. Rev. Thomas J. Davis, rector of the Protestant Episcopal Church of the Resurrection at Broad and Tioga Streets.

3. Joshua Francis Fisher (1807–73), called "Fisher," was a cousin of the diarist.

crime. He denounces such men as Emerson,[4] Wendell Phillips[5] & other leading abolitionists, who have more intellect, knowledge, and sincerity than all the politicians in the country put together, as traitors, blasphemers, incendiarists, &c. So have reformers & those who bear witness to the truth always been treated by the worldly & prosperous. Truth, when it attacks the interests of property or power, is always derided & persecuted, as all history testifies. . . .

The issue that is now in reality and ere long will formally be offered to the southern people is, shall the slaves be emancipated peacefully or forcibly? Disunion would at once decide it in favor of the latter alternative. If the Union can be preserved, material interests are so strong that slavery may be preserved for a time, but its destruction must come at last. Moral truth is of a commanding nature; it will be obeyed. Slavery is a wrong, an injustice. It must either destroy the moral sentiment of the country or be destroyed by it. In this age of thought and free discussion, there is some hope that the destruction of slavery may be brought about by peaceful means. If John Brown had succeeded in his purpose of running off the Negroes in the neighborhood of Harper's Ferry, his success would have been a real failure. His death was necessary to his triumph. . . .

Fisher mentioned today a fact which exhibits one of the most perplexing difficulties of slavery, arising from the mixture of the races. Not only are hundreds who are almost Saxon in blood and who can scarcely be distinguished from the white race held as slaves, but men actually own & sell their sons & brothers. This happens constantly among the best & most refined families in the South. Fisher's story is that George Cadwalader[6] was once at the table of a gentleman on the Eastern Shore of Maryland and noticed a striking likeness between one of his sons and a mulatto servant waiting at dinner. A short time

---

4. Ralph Waldo Emerson (1803-82), of Massachusetts, was a Unitarian minister, author, orator, and leader in the Transcendentalist movement.

5. Wendell Phillips (1811-84), a Boston lawyer, was one of the leading abolitionist orators of the era.

6. George Cadwalader (1806-79), of Philadelphia, a lawyer and veteran of the Mexican War, was commissioned major general of state volunteers in 1861 and of U.S. volunteers in 1862.

afterwards he found this son and the servant in the cars, the latter in *chains*. The son was taking him to be sold in Baltimore, his half-brother, as Cadwalader ascertained. Civilization, liberty, religion cannot coexist where such things are sanctioned.

JANUARY 6, 1860 | Dressed and drove to town, taking Daniel,[7] at 5 to Ashhurst's.[8] Mr. Henry,[9] the mayor of the city, Mr. McCalmont, John Ashhurst,[10] Joshua Fisher, the party. It was very pleasant. Had a great deal of animated conversation. Much pleased with the mayor, whom I never met before. He gave us full particulars of his plans to resist the intended attack by the mob to prevent Mr. Curtis' lecture and his opinions are just and decided.[11] It would be lucky if we could be sure of always having such a man for mayor. Fisher gave me a letter from Mr. Wm. C. Rives, to whom he had sent my Montg. Co. speech and *The Law of The Territories*. Mr. Rives besides being a slaveholder in Virginia has been much in public life, occupying high posts, and is greatly respected in the South.[12] He speaks in very flattering terms of both productions, and agrees fully in the scope and doctrines of the book. This is valuable testimony and as I have now the testimony of the best authorities here, in Boston & in Virginia, I think I may feel satisfied that the work has accomplished its aim, which was to make an appeal to the sound & educated opinion of both North & South.

JANUARY 17, 1860 | Bet told me today that her brothers Charles and Harry intend becoming candidates for Congress at the next election,

---

7. Daniel was a servant who cared for Fisher's carriage on occasions such as this.

8. William Henry Ashhurst (1815-87).

9. Alexander Henry (1823-83), a Republican, was mayor of Philadelphia from 1858 to 1865.

10. Robert McCalmont was a London capitalist whose American affairs were in the hands of Henry Fisher; John Ashhurst was a Philadelphia banker.

11. George William Curtis (1824-92), author and orator.

12. William C. Rives (1793-1868), of Virginia, served several terms as a U.S. congressman and senator between 1823 and 1845, first as a Jacksonian Democrat and later as a Whig; he also twice served as minister to France during that period. On the Southern question, he was a moderate.

if they can get the nomination.[13] Neither are fit for the place and I believe cannot be nominated or, if nominated, cannot be elected. There is no telling, however. Party drill, among Democrats, is very effective. I am sorry they have taken this step, as I am opposed to the principles they support & must therefore, so far as I exert any influence at all, oppose them, and the next election is likely to be an exciting contest.

JANUARY 25, 1860 | The day of southern dictation & supremacy is I think passed. The northern people are roused at length and, as the power of the country is in their hands, they have only to make an effort to gain the control of the government & of the nation. The southern politicians see this and their violence is the rage of desperation. They may thank their own folly for the change. Their excesses and monstrous abuse of power have excited the North & their doom is fixed.

JANUARY 29, 1860 | Henry Gilpin[14] died last night. . . . Another friend of my childhood & whom I have known and been in the habit of seeing constantly all my life is gone. My intercourse with him has always been agreeable and he always showed me the kindness of a relation, made me welcome to his house and expressed sympathy & interest in my life & doings. He was an amiable & worthy man, and performed his duty in all the relations of life. He sedulously cultivated & exerted his talents and acquired reputation & fortune. He was a scholar & a gentleman, and tho his mind was by no means of the highest order, and some things in his public life were open to censure, yet he had many difficulties to encounter in youth and his career was on the whole not only eminently successful, but respectable. He had many friends, was generally liked and will, I think, be much regretted. I shall miss him.

13. Charles Ingersoll (1805-82) and Harry Ingersoll (1809-86) were sons of Charles Jared Ingersoll, and brothers-in-law of the diarist. They failed to obtain the nomination.

14. Henry D. Gilpin (1801-60), a Democrat, had been attorney general of the United States from 1840 to 1841.

FEBRUARY 2, 1860 | At 9½ drove to the 4th St. car to go to Henry Gilpin's funeral. Got to the house[15] at 10½. A very large company assembled, including most of the notabilities (such as they are) in town and filling the three spacious rooms downstairs which form the library. The coffin was placed in the middle room and a part of the funeral service there performed, the rest of it at the grave. He was buried at Laurel Hill, and I noticed in the lot the tombs of his father Joshua & his uncle Thomas, the bodies of both having been removed to that place, no doubt by himself. A comparatively small number, tho still a good many, went out to Laurel Hill. I went in a carriage with Joshua Fisher & Charles Gilpin, formerly mayor of the city & a lawyer, a relation of the Gilpins, tho how near I do not know. The service is always impressive, but the thing itself, death, the past of the person gone, I cannot realize at such scenes. Both are ideas, mysteries, & I cannot get nearer to them. In our drive out & in, we had a good deal of conversation, part of it about passenger railways & their abuses. Not only has the government transferred its powers and duties as to the highways to these corporations, but they rule the government by the system of bribery & corruption now fully and avowedly established & practiced. The charters were all bought from the legislature, & contained therefore just such provisions as the parties interested chose to insert and the City Councils are controlled by the railroad companies, so that any action against their wishes is impossible.

 I have already said all that is needful about Henry Gilpin. His grandfather, Thomas Gilpin, married a daughter of my grt. grandfather Joshua Fisher. His father, Joshua Gilpin, was therefore my grandfather's nephew and my father's first cousin. Henry's character cannot be said to have been of a high order. His intellect was commonplace and, tho sedulously cultivated, was incapable of original thought or of any thought of a kind above the ordinary level, as all that he ever wrote proves. He could not appreciate works of the noblest genius in philosophy, poetry, or art, and had no perception of

---

15. Gilpin's house was at 300 South Eleventh Street.

the beautiful in its highest manifestations. He nevertheless was cultivated & even learned in the ordinary sense of the terms, had been a student all his life and acquired much knowledge. His character partook of the narrow nature of his mind; he was amiable, courteous, well-bred, but wanted depth of feeling, disinterested impulse, magnanimity and high aims. He was successful in life, not by the fair exercise of superior ability, but through the favor of influential men whom he sedulously courted—Mr. Van Buren, Gen'l Cass, &c., &c.[16] By their favor he became Attorney General, an office above his claims, & by their favor also he made his fortune. He was agent for the Mexican claims & received in contingent fees about $60,000. This he invested, by advice of Cass, in lots in some of the growing towns of the West—Milwaukee, Chicago, &c—and they increased so rapidly & greatly in value that his fortune is now estimated at half a million. Fisher told me that he had 40 acres in the heart of Chicago, which must be immensely valuable. I hope he has left his mother & sisters something handsome. Last year only, he enlarged his house to its present size & furnished it. It is very large & handsome. There are three rooms en suite on the first floor, the walls covered with books, and richly furnished, besides the hall and anteroom; on the 2nd floor are three large drawing rooms and a dining room, all decorated with much cost, if not in the best taste. He had great pleasure in this house and now, after a very short enjoyment of it, he has been summoned away. What he is now, what sphere of activity and objects of enjoyment he finds, it is useless to think of, but whilst he was here, he labored diligently at such work as he was fitted for by nature, not without some useful results, and his career, if not guided by the highest motives, was not stained by unworthy deeds. This is not very high praise, but why not tell the truth. Gilpin was a Democrat, a devoted & obedient adherent to Gen'l Jackson and stuck to his party thro thick & thin. He made his

---

16. Martin Van Buren (1782-1862), a Democrat, was a U.S. senator from New York in the 1820s, vice president during Andrew Jackson's second term, and eighth president of the United States. Lewis Cass (1782-1866), a Democrat, was a U.S. senator from Michigan from 1845 to 1857, and secretary of state under President James Buchanan.

fortune & position by partizan politics. All this is proof enough that he had not a high & sensitive moral nature. I never yet saw or heard of or read of a Democrat who had.

FEBRUARY 5, 1860 | I went to Stenton.[17] The estate is now divided by fences into lots and the roads (future streets) between them are open. Turned off from the York Road into one of these and followed it quite up to the house. It is shut up, no one living there now, apparently, tho I suppose there are servants as Mrs. [Gustavus] Logan spends the summer there. Sat on my horse looking at it for some time. There were the trees & the house, as I had known them from childhood, unchanged, but the people I used to see there so often, all passed away. . . . I believe the present owners intend to preserve the old mansion & the grounds immediately around it for public use in some way, which, as it is an historical place, ought to be done.

FEBRUARY 7, 1860 | Went up to Dr. Swann's[18] reception which he has every other Tuesday morning. The four rooms were open and certainly are handsome, but I have lost all pleasure in fine furniture. A lawn with a few trees is far better than the most costly apartments. I prefer plainness & simplicity, but I like also comfort, elegance & good taste. Decorations, also, which are not mere upholstery, but savor of art or works of art, I admire, of course. Swann is adorning his rooms with wood carvings of animals, fruit, leafage & flowers over & on the sides & frames of the doors, which are very handsome. No one was there when I arrived and Dr. [E. F.] Rivinus only came before I went away. Met Mr. Binney[19] in the street. He greeted me very cordially and asked me to come to see him. Had some talk with him about

---

17. Stenton, built by James Logan in 1728, still stands at what is now Eighteenth and Courtland Streets. Owned by the city, it is under the care of the Pennsylvania Society of Colonial Dames of America.

18. Dr. William C. Swann.

19. Horace Binney (1780-1875), a Republican, was a Philadelphia lawyer who served one term in Congress as an Anti-Jacksonian from 1833 to 1834. During the war he published one of the most important pamphlets on the suspension of habeas corpus.

public affairs, of which he spoke with much animation, denouncing the course of the South and of the Democratic Party, which the South has used as its instrument, uniting thus with the rabble in the North for selfish and sectional purposes. He ended by declaring that he would rather vote for the Devil himself than for a Democrat. He is in fine health & preservation, has a good color, a vigorous, alert movement, his voice is clear & ringing, his eye full of fire, he is a splendid old man, physically, intellectually & morally, the result of a superior organization and a prosperous, laborious and temperate life.

FEBRUARY 9, 1860 | The more I think of Henry Gilpin's will, the less I like it. Egotism sticks out in the "Gilpin Gallery" and "Gilpin Library."[20] He has brothers and sisters in very moderate circumstances to whom he should have left his fortune. It would have made them comfortable & happy and kept up his family in a respectable position for one or two more generations, a better monument than "Gilpin" galleries & libraries. Legacies for these purposes, and his fine collection of books would have been properly bestowed, but it was wrong to disappoint just expectations and cruel to withhold happiness from his own blood, when he had the power to bestow it.

FEBRUARY 11, 1860 | This was the day appointed for Craig Biddle's speech on the 75th anniversary of our Agricultural Society. It was delivered at 1 o'clock at the Society's room. The attendance was good and so was the speech. It was an interesting history of the Society from its origin, and also a history of some of the most important improvements in agriculture, expressed in appropriate and graceful

---

20. Fisher had read the provisions of Gilpin's will in the *Germantown Telegraph* the day before. The will provided, after the death of Gilpin's wife and mother and the payment of $100,000 in legacies, that the estate be divided equally between the Historical Society of Pennsylvania, the Pennsylvania Academy of Fine Arts, and the Historical Society of Chicago. Gilpin's will was invalidated because it was made less than a month before his death, and his widow's efforts to carry through its provisions only complicated matters. Following her death in 1874, an agreement was reached with the heirs by which the Historical Society of Pennsylvania eventually received $59,500, a sum much less than Gilpin intended.

language and displaying a knowledge of the subject greater than I supposed he possessed. Altogether it was a very creditable performance and was received by the members with cordial applause. When it was ended, as no one else seemed disposed to do so, I rose and after some remarks in praise of the speech, moved that it be printed in pamphlet form, which was unanimously carried.[21] The portrait of Craig's father, Nicholas Biddle,[22] was hanging on the wall, who with all his shortcomings was a man of fine talents, of varied culture, of liberal mind & high spirit. He did many good things in his life and exerted a powerful influence on public affairs. It was pleasant to me to see the son of a distinguished man also distinguishing himself. I thought of Sidney.[23] How delightful the hope that, when I am gone, he may hold a worthy and eminent position in the world. So I said, before I offered the resolution, that Mr. Biddle had very properly omitted one name among those who had conferred honor on the society; that, altho he had not mentioned it, we had not forgotten it, that the speech we had just heard was worthy of it, and that, when seventy-five more years had elapsed, if the occasion should again be celebrated, the name of Biddle would be remembered with added lustre. At 3 o'clock we had a dinner at the St. Louis Hotel. There were 30 present.

FEBRUARY 15, 1860 | Bought a copy of a little book, just published, giving an account of a trip to Cuba by Mrs. Julia Ward Howe. I knew her many years ago at Newport, where her father had a cottage and where she was a young lady much admired for beauty and talents. Williams Middleton was in love with her and was engaged to her, but

---

21. *Address Delivered before the Philadelphia Society for Promoting Agriculture on its Seventy-Fifth Anniversary, February 11, 1860. By the President Craig Biddle* (Philadelphia, 1860).

22. Nicholas Biddle (1786-1844), of Philadelphia, was the president of the Second Bank of the United States and a chief political enemy of President Andrew Jackson. The painting, attributed to Thomas Sully, currently hangs in the Council Room at the Pennsylvania Horticultural Society.

23. Sydney George Fisher (1856-1927), called "Sidney" in the diary, was the diarist's only child. He later became a renowned historian.

her father prevented the match. After his death, Williams might have come forward with success, but for some reason he did not and she finally married Dr. Howe,[24] a very well-known person, the director of a school for idiocy & blindness, a philanthropist and ostentatious sympathizer with all sorts of Yankee *isms* & lately with John Brown. It is said that his wife has not been happy or had much cause for happiness since her marriage and she is probably a victim of a disappointed feeling and an uncongenial union. She had much grace and attraction when I knew her and is decidedly a woman of very superior gifts, if not of genius. She has written several other works, among them a volume of poems.

FEBRUARY 20, 1860 | My article & Mr. Rives' letter were in a supplement to McMichael's paper this morning,[25] also the proceedings of the Historical Society on the death of Henry Gilpin. Speeches were made by Mr. J. R. Ingersoll,[26] Wm. B. Reed[27] and Mr. Allibone,[28] a man of some literary note, I believe. The speeches were good, tho of course

---

24. Dr. Samuel G. Howe (1801-76), who married Julia Ward in 1843, was a noted champion of people suffering from disabilities.

25. On February 9, the diarist's cousin, J. F. Fisher, sent him a letter by Wm. C. Rives, which had been printed in the *Richmond Whig*, and urged him to supply an introduction for it and print it in Morton McMichael's *North American and United States Gazette*. Although the diarist thought little of Rives's plea for moderation in politics, he placed the letter in the Philadelphia paper, prefacing it with comments, which he signed "S." Morton McMichael (1807-79) was a prominent Republican journalist and politician in Philadelphia. From 1854 until his death he edited the *North American*, a paper that published many of Fisher's articles. McMichael had also been sheriff of Philadelphia in the 1840s, and after the war was the city's mayor from 1866 to 1869.

26. Joseph Reed Ingersoll (1786-1868) was the younger brother of Charles Jared Ingersoll, the diarist's father-in-law. He served one term in Congress as an Anti-Jacksonian (1835-37) and four terms as a Whig (1841-49).

27. William B. Reed (1806-76), of Philadelphia, was a politician and professor of American History and English Literature at the University of Pennsylvania. During the antebellum era Reed was an Anti-Mason and a Whig, but by 1856 he had moved into the Democratic fold. During the Civil War he was an outspoken and virulent Copperhead critic of the Lincoln administration and the conduct of the war.

28. Samuel A. Allibone (1816-89), noted literary lexicographer.

rather too favorable, and the whole affair creditable to the Society and to the person who gave occasion for them. We have not many men here worthy of commemoration and therefore a good deal of fuss is made over one whose claims were by no means of the highest order, tho certainly respectable. Gilpin did nothing likely to be remembered or worthy to be. He wrote but little & that little was commonplace. As the old Abbé Corrére (if so his name was spelt)[29] said of [Robert] Walsh, Gilpin's mind was a reservoir, not a fount.

MARCH 1, 1860 | In the morning read . . . Mr. Seward's speech in the Senate on the question of slavery in the Territories.[30] He is the prominent candidate for the Presidency of the Republican Party and this speech has been prepared with care as an expression of his opinions. He reviews the course of the Democratic Party and declares the object of the Republicans is to restrain slavery within its present limits, not to interfere with it where it exists. There is nothing new in his arguments, but his tone is more moderate than was expected. Extreme opinions would endanger his nomination in the present temper of the country. Indeed he is so much the representative of the abolition sentiment that he will probably be dropped at any rate for some one who can combine the conservative elements of the North & South.

MARCH 22, 1860 | In the evening read an account of the Battle of Germantown etc in Marshall's *Life of Washington*, with interest.[31] These were the heroic days of our country. I am shamefully ignorant of its history and will read some of the principal books on the subject before long. But there is so much to read and history is so dull compared

---

29. Jose Francisco Correa da Serra (1750-1823), botanist and diplomat, served as minister from Portugal to the United States from 1816 to 1821. His *bons mots* were extremely pertinent and should have been recorded.

30. William H. Seward (1801-72), a Whig and later Republican, was governor of New York from 1838 to 1842, U.S. senator from New York from 1849 to 1861, and secretary of state under Presidents Lincoln and Johnson from 1861 to 1869.

31. John Marshall (1755-1835), chief justice of the United States, published the five-volume *The Life of George Washington, Commander in Chief of the American Forces* (London, 1804-7).

with philosophy and poetry, and the charms of fine thought, style & imagery are so attractive that one is induced to postpone the effort to read merely for the sake of acquiring knowledge.

MARCH 23, 1860 | At 3 went with Bet up Germantown in the passenger car to call on Mrs. Geo. Carpenter (Thomas Fisher's daughter).[32] They live in a snug little cottage on his father's place. This place[33] & the buildings are a very conspicuous object in Germantown and it would not be easy to find anywhere ignorance, pretension, bad taste, and wealth more forcibly expressed in unconscious and innocent wood, stone, trees, & shrubbery. The house is very large, of Grecian architecture with an Italian tower, numerous outbuildings of every kind and variety, with Doric porticos and Gothic spires, hideous and clumsy statues of wood and marble are scattered in all directions without meaning or purpose about the grounds,[34] rose bushes and shrubbery are planted on the lawn among noble Norway firs, pines, oaks, and beeches, the winding walks are unkept and littered, the extensive greenhouses and conservatories are dirty and disorderly, everywhere carelessness, cost, ostentation and vulgarity are plainly visible. Behind the house stretches a farm of 300 acres and a beautiful, wide and wooded landscape. The land itself is a large estate at present prices. Mr. Carpenter is said to be worth several millions and as the young man is worthy & gentlemanlike in his manners, and Mary chooses him, the match is good enough for one who might claim more than Thomas Fisher.[35] We walked with the young couple about the grounds for half an hour & got home at 5 to dinner. In the evening read some chapters in the last volume of Bancroft's *History of the U. S.*[36] It is poor

32. Mary Fisher, daughter of Thomas R. Fisher, had married George Carpenter on February 1, 1860.

33. Phil Ellena, 5510 Germantown Avenue.

34. Stan V. Henkels's catalogue of the George W. Carpenter auction of June 1893 lists an extraordinary amount of statuary at Phil Ellena. Much of it had been acquired at the Joseph Bonaparte sale at Bordentown. Included also were seven of William Rush's wood carvings, four of which were life-size figures.

35. The diarist had a poor opinion of his cousin Thomas, an ineffectual man who had lost most of his money in business.

36. George Bancroft's *History of the United States* ran to ten volumes.

stuff, filled with unnecessary details, without just thought, interesting narrative or breadth of effect, commonplace, vulgar in feeling, factitious in sentiment, weak, tawdry & diffuse in style. A miserable performance truly. The 7th vol. is out and he has only got to the Declaration of Independence. He spins it out because he sells it by the volume. It may be useful as a book of reference, but for nothing else. The history of the Revolution is yet to be written.[37]

APRIL 2, 1860 | Went to see Mr. Chas. J. Wister[38] to talk to him about the Germantown School [*for which Fisher was preparing a centennial address*] of which he was for thirty years an active trustee. He told me that he left it in 1835 or 36 because of a change made in its constitution. Before that time the trustees were elected by the contributors, who paid each 40 shillings annually. But James Gowen, a low Irish radical politician, got a change made in the Charter, by which the trustees were elected by all the people of the village on the ground that the former law was aristocratic and created an invidious distinction. In this way, after approved democratic fashion, the means of knowledge were placed under the control of ignorance. As a consequence the school fell into the hands of the Baptists & speedily lost the character it had maintained under the old trustees who were for many years the most prominent gentlemen of the place, and who, when the change was made, either resigned or were turned out. I did not know this before, or I would have refused to write the address.

APRIL 3, 1860 | We dined at Brookwood.[39] After dinner, Henry gave me an account of his business operations, which are so extensive as to alarm me. They amount to millions, and if an unexpected revulsion in business, such as happens in this country periodically, should occur, he would be ruined. He considers himself worth a million,

---

37. Perhaps the diarist's son Sydney agreed with this sentiment, for he was to write *The True History of the American Revolution* (Philadelphia, 1902).

38. Charles J. Wister (1782–1865).

39. Brookwood was built by Charles Henry Fisher, the diarist's brother, in 1851 on Green Lane and County Line. The house was torn down in the 1930s.

clear of all liabilities. But then he owes an immense sum and is engaged in hazardous speculations. It is the old story, habits formed, gambling excitement becomes a necessity, temptation constantly alluring to new adventures, an extravagant establishment, and then the final catastrophe perhaps, destroying the work of a lifetime in an hour and leaving the decline of life and a family unprovided for, where custom has made luxury essential to enjoyment and devotion to business has deprived the mind of all other resources.

APRIL 6, 1860 | Mrs. Edward Burd died yesterday. She must have been very old and was solitary as her husband & children died many years ago. In former days, I knew the family well and visited constantly at the house, a large & handsome one at the corner of 9th & Chesnut Sts., S. W. corner, the scene of constant & very elegant hospitality. At a ball at that house in 1833 I was first introduced to my dear wife and danced with her. I remember it well & the very spot in the library where she stood & the impression she then made on me, which time confirmed. Mrs. Burd's death will liberate and distribute a large estate and the fine old mansion will no doubt soon be pulled down & stores & shops be erected on its site. It is of a simple style of architecture, symmetrical & in good taste, looking like the house of a gentleman, and in the rear is a spacious garden, filled with large trees. In a short time all this will have disappeared as completely as the owners have.

APRIL 14, 1860 | Worked at speech in the morning. At 2 drove up Germantown to get the last minute book of the school and to see some of the Trustees about the arrangements, as next Saturday the speech is to be delivered. They have printed the tickets, on which is a picture of the schoolhouse. Went up to Cliveden. First time I ever was there. It is a fine, large, old-fashioned mansion, built in 1765 by Benj'n Chew, Bet's gr. grt. grandfather.[40] It is now for sale in lots, except the

---

40. Chief Justice Benjamin Chew (1722-1810) was the father of Mary Chew, who married Alexander Wilcocks. Their child, Mary Wilcocks, married Charles Jared Ingersoll and was the mother of Elizabeth Ingersoll, who married the diarist.

house and one or two acres retained by Miss Ann Chew, who lives there with her nephew, whom she has adopted.[41] She received me very kindly, showed me the relics of the battle, marks of shot on walls, &c. Her brother-in-law, Mr. Mason,[42] Senator in Congress from Virginia, was there with Andrew D. Cash, who manages the sale of lots. Had some talk with them. Miss Chew lent me a memoir of her grandfather, Benj'n Chew, published in the *Portfolio* for February 1811. Home to dinner after a pleasant visit.

APRIL 20, 1860 | Worked at speech and finished it in the morning. It has cost me a good deal more trouble than I anticipated because I was obliged to hunt up facts and dates from various different sources. It is to be delivered tomorrow evening at the Town Hall in Germantown and the occasion seems to excite a good deal of interest. The writing of it has given me very pleasant occupation, revived some old recollections of Aunt Logan & Stenton and led me to acquire some interesting knowledge of the early history of the State. I find that there is no enjoyment like work, especially intellectual work.

APRIL 21, 1860 | Started at 6¼ and drove up, with Daniel, to the Hall, a large brownstone building, standing back from the main street, a little above the toll gate. Mr. [Charles P.] Bayard, one of the Trustees, met me at the gate. Went with him to an anteroom, where others were assembled. When the company had arrived, we went on the stage. The first performance was a long extemporaneous prayer. Then followed an ode, *sung*, the composition of Mr. John S. Littell, a conceited, empty fellow enough, but very prominent as a manager of the ceremonies. He was at the school when I was there, and I had never seen him since, till this evening, but I did not like him at school. When the ode was ended, Mr. Littell made some very stupid remarks on the

---

41. Anne Chew (1805–92) was a granddaughter of the chief justice; her nephew was Samuel Chew (1832–87).

42. James Murray Mason (1798–71), a Democrat, represented Virginia in the U.S. Senate from 1847 until he was expelled on March 28, 1861, for supporting secession. His wife was Elizabeth Margaretta Chew.

occasion and introduced me. I then read my speech with care and it occupied just an hour and a quarter. The room was large & crammed full, and I was told there were some hundreds outside who could not get in.[43] I noticed among the crowd some familiar faces, Joshua Fisher & his daughter Helen & the Misses Francis, Mrs. Ashhurst, Eliz'th Fisher,[44] Sarah Wister, Pierce Butler,[45] &c. The attention was unbroken and the applause frequent. They seemed to be interested and willing to listen. When it was over, I went down & spoke to Mrs. Ashhurst, Fisher, &c. Mr. E. H. Butler invited me, with Wm. Wister, over to his house opposite to take a glass of wine. We went. He has a fine large house in a spacious and, so far as I could judge in the dark, very handsome lawn. We sat for an hour. They said they considered the speech a triumph.

APRIL 23, 1860 | Saw Mr. [Jabez] Gates, one of the Trustees of school, by appointment about the printing the speech. He said they intended to print it in the best style and 3000 copies. That it had given universal satisfaction.

MAY 10, 1860 | I sometimes almost resolve to make my diary strictly personal and to say nothing of public affairs, for if I noticed all and expressed about them what I thought and felt, I should do nothing but write what would be less a diary than a contemporaneous history of politics. But public events, both from the great interests and the great principles they involve, necessarily occupy much of the thought

---

43. It was estimated that fifteen hundred people attended.

44. Elizabeth Rodman Fisher, sometimes called "Elizabeth Fisher" and sometimes called "Betty," was a cousin of the diarist.

45. Pierce Butler (1806-67), born in Philadelphia, was the heir of a large fortune in plantations and slaves. In 1834 he married Frances Anne "Fanny" Kemble (1809-93), the English actress. Butler and Kemble divorced in 1849 over their irreconcilable differences on the slavery issue. In the 1850s Butler fell into financial distress and was forced to sell off much of his property, including many of his slaves (see the introduction for Fisher's views on the sale). In 1861, after a trip to Georgia, he was arrested for treason; he did not return to the South until after the war.

of anyone who thinks at all and, therefore, the record of a life, however sequestered, would be incomplete without some allusion to them. On the 23rd of April a convention of the Democratic Party met at Charleston, S. C., to establish a platform of principles and to nominate a candidate for the Presidency. In a week they separated without doing either one or the other. It was soon found that the principles of the party were contradictory, wholly inconsistent with each other, that harmonious action was impossible therefore, that there were in fact two parties, a northern & southern. When this became apparent, the southern members seceded, left the convention and formed another assembly, claiming to represent the South. The Democratic Party is therefore sectionally divided, the strength is with the North, the South is powerless & must remain so, unless it can form an alliance with some party in the North, yet to be constructed. This it can never do except by receding from its extreme doctrines and pretensions. My predictions are thus realized by the event. Northern strength governs, the democracy is turned against the South, which by its excesses has alienated the feelings of the North, and now finds itself isolated and friendless.

It generally, perhaps always happens, that in every opinion, steadily advocated by numbers of men, there is some truth. The mistake they make is in supposing their opinion to contain the whole truth, a very common error, even where interest and passion have no influence. Reflection begins with analysis. One part or branch of a subject is the object of thought at a time. It occupies the mind and if circumstances give it special attraction or importance, it occupies the mind exclusively and further reflection stops. If the process of reasoning went on, it would lead to synthesis, after the investigation of each portion of a subject. Very few, however, get that far, because very few, either by training or talents are capable of following out a chain of logical deduction and then surveying all parts of a subject as a whole. If sectional, sectarian, partizan, or personal motives or passions are connected with one of the series of truths which constitute a system or an argument, that truth or doctrine immediately absorbs the attention of its own advocates, who cannot see it in its relation to the whole, but magnify it into the whole.

The principles of law relating to the Territories are numerous. Together they form a harmonious system. Separately they are partially true only. Each party has seized on one of those principles to suit its purposes and each claims that to be the whole truth. In my book I have endeavored to show how they all harmonize and form what has always been regarded as the law on the subject, until mutilated by the Kansas & Nebraska bill and other innovations of the South. The important question is, what will be the consequences of this sudden breaking up of the Democratic Party.

MAY 17, 1860 | The convention of the Union Party at Baltimore nominated Mr. Bell of Tennessee for President, and Mr. Everett of Boston for Vice-President.[46] Good names both of them, men of cultivation, experience in affairs, talents and character. Too good, indeed, to inspire any strong feeling in the masses, who cannot comprehend the qualities and merits by which these two gentlemen justly claim confidence and respect. They are not distinguished in the way that fixes the gaze of the people and want those positive, prominent, striking points of character necessary to attract the notice & rouse the spirit of the multitude. And yet their merits are the only argument the convention offers in their favor. They do not represent an old party, drilled, organized and accustomed to work together, but a new one, yet to be formed. Neither do they represent any definite principles or opinions, but the convention purposely avoided making a platform, declaring that its members supported & relied on the Constitution. As each party says the same thing, this assertion amounts to nothing. The overwhelming and exciting subject now before the country is slavery, out of which grows the question of the relative power of North and South. By its side all other issues are insignificant. How can a party which passes this question by hope for success. It is true, that its views

46. John Bell (1797–69) was a U.S. congressman from Tennessee from 1827 to 1841, and a U.S. senator from 1847 to 1859. In 1860 he was the unsuccessful candidate for president on the Constitutional Union ticket. His running mate, Edward Everett (1794–1865), was a former governor of Massachusetts, U.S. congressman and senator, and president of Harvard University.

on the subject are known to be moderate, that it represents the sober judgment of both northern & southern people, and that everyone opposed to the extreme opinions of the Democrats and of the Republicans may safely join this party. Nevertheless, a public declaration of its doctrines and the reasons on which they are founded would have been more satisfactory and calculated to give support and coherence to the party. The truth, however, in my judgment is that the members had no definite opinions and that it would have puzzled the wisest among them to draw up a system or program of principles & reasons for them, harmonious, just, and satisfactory.

MAY 18, 1860 | Met Mr. Ryan on the road. He told me news had just come to town that the Republican Party had nominated a Mr. Lincoln for President. I never heard of him before. But it has happened more than once that a new man, previously unthought of, has been selected because the prominent candidates could not be elected, the friends of each refusing to unite with those of any rival. The great point is that Seward is *not* nominated. He represented the extreme opinions opposed to slavery and the South, and the selection of his name would have exasperated the southern people and alarmed conservatives throughout the North. He has been for many years the candidate of the Republican Party and leader of abolition opinion and his rejection is in itself evidence of the influence of moderate and national sentiments. It will calm many fears, allay much animosity and inspire hope of better times throughout the country, whoever Mr. Lincoln may be.

MAY 21, 1860 | Called to see Meredith.[47] He regrets that Seward was not nominated. Says he would, if elected, have been prudent, cautious & safe, that Lincoln is a Western "screamer," represents Western coarseness & violence. The papers say he was fond of horse racing, foot racing, etc., and that when he spoke at Republican meetings in New York, the tickets were *sold* for his benefit. Such is democracy. These very qualities, connecting him in sympathy with the masses,

---

47. William M. Meredith (1799-1873), a Republican, was U.S. secretary of the treasury from 1849 to 1850, and attorney general of Pennsylvania from 1861 to 1867.

favor his success. Education, refinement, the birth & breeding of a gentleman would be against him. Mr. Ingersoll told me today that there is a "strong movement" in town to send me to Congress. *I won't go.*

JUNE 4, 1860 | Saw at Wilmington Mr. Harry du Pont, who told me of a manure which he uses with success. It is the refuse of the powder works, is composed of several substances, common salt, potash, ammonia, &c. He sells it for $7 per ton, about 5 bus. is applied per acre and the cost is 22 cts. per bus. Shall inquire more and try it. Harry du Pont married, about 25 years ago, a sister of Ben Gerhard.[48] Since her marriage I have only seen her once, till today. She came up in the cars with her two daughters, girls of 13 & 15 years old, apparently. She has a son at West Point 22 years old.[49] I talked with her all the way up to town. She is a very charming woman, still handsome, very intelligent, soft, gentle, feminine, and her manners thoroughly ladylike & refined. I was surprised & highly pleased. The du Ponts are an old family & have been settled on the Brandywine for two or three generations, where they have extensive powder mills. They own a very large landed estate there and are very rich. The different families of them, eight in number, all live on the property and have handsome establishments, forming a little community, and all share in the business and its profits which are held in common.

JUNE 11, 1860 | Looked over my annual "summaries of accts" for the last ten years. By what infatuation, indolence, recklessness, want of energy, will and prudence I could have suffered my property to dwindle away, when an effort might have saved it, is to me now inconceivable as well as shameful. I had then $1,700 a year beside my farm.

48. Henry du Pont (1812–89) was graduated from West Point in 1833, but resigned from the Army in 1834 to join his father in the manufacture of gunpowder. In 1850, he became head of E. I. du Pont de Nemours & Co. During the Civil War he was a major general of Delaware Volunteers, in command of the Home Guard. In 1837 he married Louisa Gerhard.

49. Henry Algernon du Pont (1838–1926), soldier, industrialist, and U.S. senator, graduated at the head of his class at West Point in 1861. In 1875, he resigned from the U.S. Army to enter the family business.

Had I resolutely said I will live on $1,700, which I might easily have done, unless & until the farm pays more, I should have had all that now. Now, however, I have only the farm, and I consider that morally mortgaged for my debt to Henry. Two ideas led me astray; one was the expectation of making up deficiencies of income from practice at the bar, which I hated, for which I was unfit, and to obtain which I did not take the ordinary means; another was expectation always of income from the farm, disappointed every year. I had unfortunately a facility of borrowing from Henry, hoping that each year would be the last of borrowing.

JUNE 13, 1860 | An unemployed day, a day thrown away without result, is waste. Yet what to do is the question. To do small things seems unworthy, to do great things is beyond my scope. I read Emerson, or Tennyson, and despair. Even for what they do, how slight is the appreciation, the recognition. The noisy, foolish multitude knows nothing of them. The smaller mob, that considers itself the cultivated, the refined, is equally ignorant. The scanty number who have the slightest sympathy with genius, or power to comprehend & value works of philosophy or poetry, is surprising.

JUNE 15, 1860 | Went to the Library of the Historical Society in the Athenaeum building.[50] I was elected a member last year. First time I ever was there. Mr. [Townsend] Ward, the librarian, asked me for copies of my Germantown Academy address to send to different societies with whom ours corresponds.

JUNE 25, 1860 | The Democratic convention at Baltimore separated into two parties as they did at Charleston, and by one of these Douglas was nominated, by the other Breckenridge, now the Vice-President.[51]

50. The Historical Society of Pennsylvania occupied rooms at the Athenaeum of Philadelphia on Washington Square from 1847 to 1872.
51. Stephen A. Douglas (1813-61) was a U.S. congressman from Illinois from 1843 to 1847, and U.S. senator from 1847 to 1861. He was the unsuccessful candidate for president of the Northern Democrats in 1860. John C. Breckinridge (1821-75), was a U.S. congressman and senator from Kentucky, and vice president under President

There are now four candidates in the field. Of these, two, Lincoln & Douglas, will be supported almost exclusively by Northern votes. Bell is the nominee of the conservative, moderate, union-loving party, North & South, which is respectable and national, but is thought to want those positive qualities which secure popular support. His friends are called the "old gentleman's party," refuse to adopt the extreme views and opinions either of the Republicans or of the Southern "fire eaters" and do, in truth, constitute, whether by reason of their principles or the high character of the men selected, Bell & Everett, the only sound & safe party in the country. For that very reason their defeat is predicted and it is common to hear men say they prefer Bell & Everett, but to vote for them would be useless. Breckenridge is the candidate of the seceders, of the extreme South, of those who threaten to destroy the Union if southern rights are not respected, that is to say, if they cannot govern it. It is for the most part composed of the southern section of the Democratic Party, the northern portion of which, represented by Douglas, has been driven away by the dangerous doctrines and exorbitant demands of the slave interest. Slavery is thus isolated. The probability is, it will have the whole North against it. As to disunion, it is a measure so desperate, so obviously destructive to the South, that I think it will not be attempted, notwithstanding the arrogant threats of southern men. It would be madness, unless the southern states could be united in favor of it, which cannot be. It is not likely, moreover, that anything will occur to afford even a plausible justification of such a step. The Republican Party, should it triumph, will do nothing to injure the rights & interests of the South.

JUNE 29, 1860 | This evening tried for the first time the coal oil, now so much used. Much pleased. It is much more brilliant than common oil or candles, cleaner & cheaper.

JULY 10, 1860 | At Henry's[52] office saw Mr. Marsh, who used to keep the hotel at Schooley's Mountain when I was there as a child and until

James Buchanan. During the Civil War he served as a general in the Confederate army, and later as the Confederate secretary of war.

52. Charles Henry Fisher (1814–62), called Henry, was a brother of the diarist and the family millionaire who built "Brookwood" and married Sarah Ann Atherton.

some twelve years ago. He is now a rich man, is connected with railroads, &c., and has much influence in New Jersey, deservedly, because of his ability and good character. He still owns the Heath house, so named from the first owner, whose daughter Marsh married & whom he succeeded as head of the establishment. The house he tells me is well kept now and much enlarged. My mother for many years went to Schooley's Mountain every summer, driving up in her own carriage, as was then the custom before railroads had enabled everyone to travel. We were in the habit of meeting many families there every year. The Dickinsons & Cadwaladers of Trenton, the Salters, the Roosevelts of N. York, Alexander Henry, &c. Algernon Logan, the Chancellors, Tom Cadwalader, &c came up also to shoot. All brought horses & servants. My recollections of those days & scenes & persons are very vivid & very pleasant, and the beauty of the scenery, the rides & walks over the hills & the free life I led there, renewed from year to year, have had, no doubt, much influence in forming my character and tastes.

In the paper this morning read Mr. Breckenridge's letter accepting the nomination of the *seceding* portion of the Democratic Party. He represents the extreme southern opinions. His letter repeats the dogma invented last year by southern politicians as a formula to express their opinions, viz: that it is the duty of Congress to *protect* the property, whether slaves or other, of all citizens in the National Territories, whether from the North or the South. Therefore southern men may take their slaves to the Territories and Congress is bound to pass laws to protect this property, but cannot pass laws to prohibit it. The fallacy of this specious statement is in supposing a government is bound to protect property against its own action. Government regulates property, protects it from violence & fraud and illegal invasion, but not from the government itself. Government may declare what is & what is not property & how & on what conditions it may be possessed and enjoyed. A government that cannot do this is no government at all, and it is absurd to say that Congress has power to *protect* only.

JULY 15, 1860 | Dr. Wister had a son born to him yesterday morning at 5 o'clock.[53] No one was in the house at the time but himself and a

---

53. Dr. Owen J. Wister and his wife Sarah Butler thus became the parents of Owen Wister (1860-1938), the novelist.

servant girl. All that had to be done was therefore done by him. Moreover, no clothing had been provided for the baby. This is a state of things inconceivable to me. There is an old saying that blacksmiths' horses and shoemakers' wives are worse shod than those of other people, but how it was that neither Sarah herself nor his mother nor any of her female friends should have had the forethought to make preparation for such an event, I cannot understand. They say that Sarah was fractious and odd & would do nothing. Mother & child are, however, well.

JULY 29, 1860 | Received yesterday a notice that I had been elected a member of the American Philosophical Society. I suppose I should consider it an honor.

AUGUST 4, 1860 | At 12$^{1}/_{2}$ drove to Stenton. Saw Dickinson & Sarah Walker, who are staying there. Cousin Maria[54] in a very sad condition. She had an attack of gout in the stomach, but when that was over she remained exceedingly weak & nervous and so continues. She is 77 years of age, so that it is unlikely that she will recover entirely. The conduct of Gustavus is no doubt a more powerful cause of her present state than bodily disease. He has abandoned his family and is living in town with a mistress or at his estate in Delaware, whither he takes her. He never goes near his mother, his wife or children. Yet there is nothing radically bad about the fellow. He is a mere, good-natured animal, wholly uneducated, with a large estate. His parents allowed him, or rather encouraged him, to grow up a working farmer and sportsman. He was the companion of laboring men and his pastime & passion were dogs & horses, of which he has a large collection. No attempt was ever made to give him the accomplishments & manners or habits of a gentleman or to cultivate his mind. He married a woman socially much beneath him, and having strong passions & no self-control, insensible to the restraint of public opinion, or any opinion indeed, & with plenty of money, he determines to do as he pleases.

54. Maria Dickinson Logan, widow of Albanus Charles Logan and mother of Dr. John Dickinson Logan, just mentioned, and of Gustavus Logan, about to be mentioned.

Dickinson studied medicine & this probably is the reason why he is respectable, for he has no decided talents, is uncultivated, has no taste for intellectual pursuits and is devoted to shooting & farming. He is a good & worthy fellow, however, domestic in his habits and gentlemanlike in manners and character. He has an estate of 1500 acres near Dover, in Delaware, which belonged to his grandfather, John Dickinson, which he is managing, and he has at Stenton a large establishment for his dogs, with a man to take care of them, also a large farm in the West somewhere, Michigan, I believe, which he keeps for a shooting ground and to which he goes every year. All this is very well. I spent an hour talking with him and looking around the old place, which seemed very homelike and familiar to me, associated as it is with the scenes and persons of early life, of childhood and boyhood. Every room & every piece of furniture and every tree recalled the past, from the time I used to go there with my mother until my school days, when I was received always with the utmost kindness by Aunt Logan and Algernon and usually dined at Stenton once a week. All these persons seemed to rise before me and their voices to sound in my ears, at the sight of the material things among which I saw them so often.

We walked down the old avenue of hemlocks to the graveyard where they all lie, Dr. George Logan, Aunt Logan, Algernon, Albanus, and, last, Miss Sally Dickinson. I was at the funeral of each. There is at each grave a marble stone with name & date of birth & burial & the ground is enclosed with a stone wall & kept in neat order. So, indeed, is the whole place & the house, and I never saw it look better. It is a large, substantial building of brick, well proportioned & picturesque. There are 4 good-sized rooms downstairs in the main house and a hall paved with brick. The walls are all wainscotted, and the house is so well built that it is in perfect preservation now. It was built in 1727. It is situated near the centre of the estate, which is well wooded, with numerous clumps & groves, so that, as no fences are in sight, it looks like a park. The grounds immediately around the house are neat & that is all. Their aspect is rather farmlike than villalike. There is no "high keeping," no well-rolled gravel roads, nicely cut edges, parterres of flowers & no "glass." These are all modern luxuries and Stenton belongs to the last century. The grass is mowed, not shaved, and the lawn front & back is shaded by noble forest trees, hemlocks, oaks, chesnuts, &c. There is no view. In front is a field, with clumps scattered at wide intervals, & so large that the road cannot be seen from the house or the house from the road; in the rear is a green slope on which is a noble avenue of hemlocks, very large & massy. There are seven on each side, 40 feet apart each way. At the end of it is the family graveyard.

On the walls in the house are some family portraits, James Logan,[55] William Logan,[56] George Logan,[57] the old lady,[58] and Algernon, also one of Isaac Norris, the emigrating ancestor of the Norris family, a copy which Dickinson had made from a picture by Sir Godfrey Kneller. It is a striking face, full of character & admirably painted. All the others as works of art are very inferior. There are not many places in America like Stenton. It has the prestige of time and the associations of one family attached to it, together with some historical recollections of interest. In the impression it makes on everyone's mind and in the feelings it inspires among the family who own it or are connected with it, may be seen by one who has eyes to see the source of an aristocracy, how it is founded in nature and how it is necessarily connected with the hereditary ownership of land. No other property remains safe thro long periods of time, nothing else can visibly connect generations of a family together, the present with the past.

AUGUST 13, 1860 | Some weeks ago there was in London a meeting of a scientific association at which Prince Albert[59] was chairman and Mr.

---

55. James Logan (1674-1751), the founder of the family, was painted by Gustavus Hesselius. This portrait was bequeathed to the Historical Society of Pennsylvania in 1939 by Miss Maria Dickinson Logan.

56. William Logan (1718-1776), son of James Logan.

57. This portrait by Gilbert Stuart was presented to the Historical Society in 1931 by Miss Maria Dickinson Logan.

58. "The old lady" was Mrs. George Logan.

59. Prince Albert (1819-61), married Queen Victoria in 1840 and was an important force behind the Great Exposition of 1851.

Dallas[60] a guest. One of the members of the society, then present, was a Negro from Canada, whether of the whole blood or not, was not stated. In the course of the proceedings, Lord Brougham[61] called the attention of Mr. Dallas publicly & pointedly to the fact of the presence of this "colored gentleman," as he called him. Mr. Dallas said nothing. He received the speech as an insult to himself and his country & no doubt let his sentiments be known, either by his manner or subsequent remarks, for afterwards Lord Brougham sent a friend to him to apologize, but Mr. Dallas declared that the apology must be as public as the offense. Lord Brougham then called himself, but was not received, getting the same reply as his friend. At the next meeting of the society Lord Brougham accordingly made an apology, which is not considered very satisfactory, is thought instead to be sarcastic & even worse than the original offense. He said that he meant nothing disrespectful to the U. S., that he merely called the attention of Mr. Dallas to an interesting statistical fact, just as he would, had he thought of it at the moment, have called to the same fact the attention of the Minister of Brazil or of Spain, both of them slaveholding nations. The affair has excited some comment here & in England, and as we are very thin-skinned and always looking out for slights, particularly from England, a good deal of indignation has been expressed on the subject. The other day Mr. J. R. Ingersoll was here, & he & Mr. C. J. I.[62] were much excited about the matter, denouncing the conduct of Lord Brougham as an outrage and censoring also, in no measured terms, Mr. Dallas for not making on the spot a fitting reply to vindicate the dignity & honor of his country. I said that I did not believe any insult was intended, that Lord Brougham was well known to be fond of sarcasm & so reckless that no one cared much about anything he said,

60. George Mifflin Dallas (1792–1864), a Democrat, served at nearly every level of government, including mayor of Philadelphia, attorney general of Pennsylvania, U.S. senator, minister to Russia and Great Britain, and vice president under James K. Polk.

61. Henry Peter Brougham, Baron Brougham and Vaux (1778–1868), lord chancellor.

62. Charles Jared Ingersoll (1782–1862), father-in-law of the diarist, and a Democrat, was a U.S. congressman from Pennsylvania from 1813 to 1815 and again from 1841 to 1849.

and that to take offense would be to acknowledge ourselves wrong on the subject of slavery, which we do not admit and which, in fact, is not true.

AUGUST 19, 1860 | Went to Brookwood to dinner. Wm. Waln & a Mr. Jackson from Jersey there. The latter is the president of some railroad and has a project for making another that is to be a rival of the great "Camden & Amboy," which has ruled New Jersey for so many years. This man talked all the time and talked nothing but railroads. They seem to absorb his whole being. He divides mankind into those who are for & those who are against Camden & Amboy.[63] Yet he was not without intelligence. He came, no doubt, to recommend his scheme to Henry, and I was pleased to see the masterly clearness & force with which Henry discussed the subject. The reason why he is so generally consulted about large business affairs was plain enough.

AUGUST 25, 1860 | Called to see Meredith. The persevering disease has redeemed its power over him. He looks wretchedly & suffers terribly from difficulty of breathing and palpitation of the heart. He bears it all calmly, however, & complains only that the process is so slow, & that he lingers so long in pain. He is cheerful, eager and animated as always and interested in general topics, saying nothing about himself except in answer to my questions. He liked my Dallas speech.[64] When I entered his office, Henry C. Carey was sitting with him, who immediately congratulated me on the speech and praised it in the highest terms. Carey is an active, zealous member of the Republican Party. Yesterday, I met Mr. Fred Fraley,[65] a prominent Democrat, who was also warm in his praise of the speech, saying it would get a thousand

---

63. John P. Jackson later in the year issued a pamphlet on this subject entitled *A General Railroad System for New Jersey* (Newark, 1860), which he called "an examination of the alleged monopoly of the Camden and Amboy Railroad Company."

64. Aroused over the Dallas-Brougham incident, Fisher wrote a speech such as Dallas might have made in reply to the Englishman. This was published in the *North American* on August 18, 1860. Signed "Cecil," the article was headed "Mr. Dallas and Lord Brougham."

65. Frederick Fraley (1804-1901), Philadelphia lawyer and business leader.

votes for his party. It seems, therefore, that I have been lucky enough to please all parties, and I believe the reason is that I have sought only, without bias or prejudice, to find out the truth and to tell it. The truth lies on this subject between the extremes, and most men can see it when it is presented to them, and are also honest enough to accept it.

AUGUST 27, 1860 | At 7½ in the evening went in the car up Germantown to pay a visit to Mrs. Kemble at Dr. Wister's. Saw her & Mrs. Wister & spent a very pleasant evening with them. Always liked Mrs. Kemble. She is a woman of genius & of noble impulses & kind feelings. Too much will & vitality & force of character, however, to be very happy in domestic life, more especially with such a man as Butler, her inferior far in all intellectual endowments, but her equal in firmness & strength of character. She is not a person to be governed by force. They could not live together and, after much unhappiness, were divorced. Her manners & conversation this evening more quiet than they used to be and she was very cordial, easy & pleasant. We talked of books, authors, politics, English country life, &c. Sarah put her oar in, too, & always with effect. She has much of her mother's talent & character & looks very well, tho somewhat thin & pale after her confinement.

SEPTEMBER 19, 1860 | Received a letter this morning from [James] Canby, asking me to deliver an address for the New Castle Co. Agricultural Society on the 17th of next month. After some hesitation determined to accept and so wrote him.

SEPTEMBER 22, 1860 | Met Mr. Boker[66] in the street. He is the author of several volumes of poetry, not without merit. He tried at first to publish them here, but they failed entirely. He then got them published by Ticknor & Fields in Boston and he says several editions have been sold. He says one might as well bury a book in the ground as publish it in Philada.

66. George Henry Boker (1823–90), playwright, poet, and diplomat.

SEPTEMBER 23, 1860 | Mr. J. R. Ingersoll is very enthusiastic for Bell & Everett and very active in his exertions in their behalf, making speeches at public meetings, &c. He has just returned from a canvassing and "stumping" tour in Virginia and was much pleased with all that he saw & heard there. He says that Bell will carry the state. The support he receives in the South is a good sign. It shows the existence of moderate, conservative sentiment where it is most needed and least expected. Mr. Ingersoll looks well and is animated & in good spirits. Work does not hurt him. He shows energy & activity and as his efforts are wholly disinterested & his opinions correct, the course he takes is worthy respect and imitation. Most men of his position, age & fortune prefer their ease & dignity to active labors.

OCTOBER 6, 1860 | The state election comes off next Tuesday & the controversy waxes hot. Mr. J. R. Ingersoll has made himself prominent for Bell and in his speeches & articles for newspapers has committed serious blunders & indiscretions that have exposed him to severe attacks.[67] The vote of Pennsylvania at the coming election will, it is said, be decisive of the election of President in November. Consequently, the politicians on both sides are active. Money is spent like water by each party. Town meetings, stump oratory, torchlight processions and all other means of excitement are rife throughout the state, in every county. The people, however, seem in good humor and no violent or dangerous feeling appears to be roused, tho the leaders & demagogues abuse each other with much bitterness. Standing aloof as a spectator, I enjoy the scene. On the whole it is satisfactory. The people are intelligent, prosperous and happy, as no other people are, they are consulting about their affairs, discussing them warmly indeed, but not in an angry, quarrelsome spirit, and, notwithstanding many abuses to regret, republican institutions work well, particularly in the country. It seems to be generally expected that Lincoln will be elected. It is desirable that he should be, not merely because he is a

---

67. Ingersoll favored the election of a "radical" Democrat as governor of Pennsylvania and denounced the "Black Republicans." This course turned the heavy artillery of the influential *North American* against him.

safe man and the principles of his party are, if not entirely correct, by far the best of any other party, but because, if he be not successful, the election would be thrown into the House, probably into the Senate, in which a candidate representing a small minority of the people and that minority a southern faction might be chosen. The wishes of the great majority of the people would be defeated, which would be a very dangerous thing. I shall therefore probably vote for Lincoln, if I vote at all.

OCTOBER 9, 1860 | Voted at the Rising Sun,[68] this being election day, for Curtin, the Republican candidate for governor.[69] The only candidate on the other side is Foster, a Democrat, and of course I would vote against him.[70] I know nothing of either.

OCTOBER 10, 1860 | I have employed young Terry, son of Terry Mahoney, who lived at this place for 20 years before we came, to copy my essay on Race, as I wish to print it without delay and must now finish my speech. . . . The Prince of Wales arrived in town last night and is at the Continental Hotel.[71] He came from Washington where he was the guest of the president. He has been received with distinction everywhere in the United States and tho the crowds of gazers who throng around him have often been annoying & no doubt in some cases disgusting in their manners, yet he has been greeted with real good will as the heir of the British throne and a very proper and liberal sentiment has been exhibited by the people. His frankness,

---

68. The Rising Sun Inn was located at the intersection of the Germantown and Old York roads, near the home of the diarist.

69. Andrew G. Curtin (1817-94) was Republican governor of Pennsylvania from 1861 to 1867; following the war he was elected to the U.S. House of Representatives as a Democrat.

70. Henry D. Foster (1808-80), a former congressman and the cousin of John C. Breckinridge, was the unsuccessful Democratic candidate for governor of Pennsylvania in 1860.

71. Located at the southeast corner of Chestnut and 9th Streets, the Continental Hotel was the largest in the city and perhaps the newest, for it had opened for business on February 16, 1860.

manliness & affable manners, his youth & good looks, have won favorable opinions. The papers chronicle his slightest movement & word and he is followed by a crowd of reporters & sketchers. He travels under the care of the Duke of Newcastle & has a numerous suite of noblemen, gentlemen and servants. Tonight he attends the opera at the Academy of Music and tickets are sold for $25. I have a stockholder's ticket, Henry having placed some stock in my name & therefore I might have gone. I should like very much to see the Prince & his companions, specimens of a class that an untravelled man does not often see. But the bore of a crowd & of coming out of town late deterred me.

OCTOBER 11, 1860 | At 12 started to go up to Andalusia to dine with Craig Biddle and the Farmers' Club. Had a pleasant drive as the country is now assuming the exquisite colors of autumn, that most delightful period of our year. It is a luxury to breathe and to gaze. Reached the house a little after 2. Found that the gentlemen were out on the farm, so I, not seeking them, walked about the grounds. The lawn slopes to the river and around the house are several acres judiciously planted with groups of trees, now grown to be of large size. There are many fine Norways & other evergreens. The place shows want of keeping, tho it is not neglected or slovenly. It would be very expensive to maintain such a place in high order and the buildings and house, inside and out, tho comfortable & neat, would be improved by renewal & repair. At 3 we dined. The company were Merrick, McMichael, King, Freas, Blight, Harrison, Dr. Jno. Biddle, Dr. Peace, McCrea, Mr. Connell, & Charles Biddle.[72] The conversation was not very interesting, tho animated. I came away at 6 and got home at 8. Terry had been here and finished copying my essay on Race. Bet was

72. Samuel V. Merrick, Morton McMichael, Dr. Charles R. King, Philip R. Freas, George Blight, Charles W. Harrison, Dr. John Biddle, Dr. Edward Peace, Dr. James A. McCrea, and Wilmer Connell were all members of the Farmers' Club. Charles J. Biddle, Craig Biddle's brother, was a guest. Charles J. Biddle (1819–73) was a veteran of the Mexican War and a colonel in the Pennsylvania Reserve Corps during the Civil War. Biddle, a Democrat, was a U.S. congressman from 1861 to 1863, and chairman of the Democratic Party in Pennsylvania in 1863.

waiting tea for me. Some of the company had been to the opera last night and described the scene as very magnificent. The boxes were filled with ladies in full dress and when the Prince entered his box the whole audience rose and the band struck up "God Save the Queen."[73] Several anecdotes were told of his affability & ease of manner and all spoke of him with cordial good will. This is gratifying and it is because of the sympathy of race. The people seem almost to think he is their Prince and the reason is that he is an English Prince. As I said at the dinner, and all agreed with me, we would never have the same feeling or given such a reception to a member of any other royal family of Europe.

OCTOBER 13, 1860 | Finished correcting the essay in the morning. Took it to Hazard. He introduced me to his brother Willis, who, tho almost withdrawn from business, still publishes occasionally. He agreed at once to publish the work on fair terms. I shall thus have the advantage of the book's being sold by S. Hazard, whose shop is now fashionable in town.[74] In the paper this morning, the letter of the London correspondent states that on the 29th of last month my Dallas speech was republished in the London *Times*. Went to the Exchange and there saw it in the *Times* of that date. Henry sent it to Chas. Morrison, who wrote that he had given it to a friend of his who is intimate with one of the editors, and asked him to try to have it published. So it is no great compliment to me, tho I suppose it would not have been reprinted unless they had thought well of it. There were some editorial remarks in the same paper on the subject, referring to & quoting my article, which, in another part, was printed in full, but no criticism of it. I think I will print it along with the essay. I told Hazard I would take him the mss. on Monday. In the evening revised it again. I must now finish my speech which is to be delivered next Wednesday.

73. Escorted by the mayor, the Prince of Wales and his suite had attended a gala performance of the opera *Martha* at the Academy of Music.
74. Samuel Hazard Jr., whose bookstore was at 724 Chestnut Street.

OCTOBER 17, 1860 | Got up at 5, breakfasted at 6, started at 7 & drove to the station at Prime and Broad.[75] Got to Wilmington at 9$^1/_2$. Found Mr. Wales at the station & a carriage waiting for me. We drove out to a farm, which the New Castle Co. Society has just purchased, hoping to found an agricultural school & model farm. It is about two miles from Wilmington, contains 150 acres of good land tho rough and entirely out of order, land and buildings. There is, however, a stone barn and a farmhouse which by some repairs may be made sufficiently comfortable. The situation is beautiful, commanding a fine view over a richly wooded and hilly country. The price was $150 per acre. I was welcomed by Canby, who is the president of the Society. I was to speak at 1$^1/_2$, so had time enough on my hands, which I spent pleasantly in walking about the grounds, looking at the stock, &c.

At 12$^1/_2$ we had lunch in the farmhouse at which some 6 or 8 members of the Society were present. These were all that had the appearance of respectable people at the exhibition, altho there was a large multitude assembled. The great majority were evidently an inferior class, attracted not by the objects interesting to a farmer of education, but by the race track, an attraction which has recently been introduced on these occasions for the express and avowed purpose of making money and which will destroy agricultural societies if persisted in. Prizes are offered to fast trotters, a mob is assembled, gambling is necessarily excited and the whole affair degraded & demoralized. Other meretricious attractions are permitted also for the same purpose, to draw a crowd who pay for admission. On this occasion, there were several tents where humbugs & catchpennies, dwarfs, deformed women, &c, were to be seen. Two or three vendors of quack medicines were haranguing gaping crowds about the grounds, and all the time scrub races, free to all comers, were going on.

At 1$^1/_2$ I went with some of the members to the platform. I saw at once that beyond a few around me there were none present who cared a farthing about anything I could say or felt the smallest interest in agriculture or any topic connected with it. I requested that the races on the track and the harangues of the vendors of quack medicines, &c,

---

75. Depot of the Philadelphia, Wilmington, and Baltimore Railroad.

might be stopped. Then ensued an amusing scene. The horses were with difficulty withdrawn, but not the crowd around the course. About 50 feet to the left of me was a man addressing an admiring audience on the virtues of a wonderful kind of blacking he had for sale, & blacking boots with it to prove its excellence. At the same distance on the right, another orator was holding forth on the virtues of his quack medicines, which he exhibited in boxes and vials. His eloquence had a great effect on the crowd, which numbered I should think about 200, & they greeted him with laughter & applause. I watched him when the officers went to him to request him to stop. He immediately turned round & pointing to me, went on: "I am told, gentlemen, that an address is now to be delivered about agriculture from that stand. Of course, I am willing to give way, that is parliamentary you know. I, gentlemen, am also an admirer of agriculture," &c, &c, for about five minutes longer.

When he ceased, however, his audience did not gather round my stand, but dispersed over the ground. In front of me were only about twenty persons, one half of them boys in their shirt sleeves. I said to Canby: "It is absurd to read an address to these. This is really no audience at all." He then went forward, "Gentlemen," said he, as loud as he could, "I wish to introduce to you Mr. Sidney George Fisher. He will deliver an interesting address about agriculture; he is himself a practical farmer." Even this appeal produced no effect. It was clear no one there cared either for the orator or his topic. Poor Canby was excessively mortified & so were the other members. Seeing this, I said, "Well, gentlemen, I will read my address to you & the few on the ground." Accordingly, I began & read 6 or 8 pages. I then skipped 8 or 10, & read a few more, finally I skipped to the part near the conclusion which notices the proposed school & model farm & then ended, occupying, I suppose, about 15 minutes. The members were profuse in thanks & regrets, but I treated the whole affair as a good joke, for so it really seemed to me. I did not fail, however, to point out to them how this was an illustration of the bad policy they were pursuing by using means to attract a vulgar crowd for the sake of making money & thus degrading their Society and defeating its purposes. I was then introduced to a reporter for one of the Wilmington papers, who requested me to let him have my manuscript that he might make an abstract of it for his paper. I objected to this as I knew by experience what sort of work reporters make by such attempts. He, however, & the members urged the matter so strongly that I said if he would come with me to the President's room, he might look over the mss. for an hour only, as I was obliged at 3 to go home. So we went & I threw the mss. on the table. He gave it a look of despair & said it was impossible for him to read & digest it in an hour. I told him then that I would write the abstract for him, at which he seemed much relieved. I wrote a short statement of the principal matters & he was profuse in thanks.[76] One of the members then drove me to town. The country around Wilmington is very picturesque & delightful views abound in all directions. Pretty cottages & countryseats adorn the neighborhood and the town itself thrives and grows rapidly.

OCTOBER 19, 1860 | Met old Dr. Meigs[77] in the street yesterday. . . . The Doctor advised me to sell Mount Harmon now for what it would bring, as he said the Union would be dissolved & we shall have Civil War in less than six months. He thinks the South will not stand the election of Lincoln. Today, I was told that the *New York Herald* makes the same prediction and that the southern papers are very violent. The people in the South have been made to believe that the Republican Party are abolitionists. This is so far true, that the spirit, the animus of that party is undoubtedly aversion to slavery, tho I believe it is the intention of its leaders to pursue a very moderate course to the South and respect all its Constitutional rights. Nevertheless, it is true that the North has become hostile to slavery, it has also become united

---

76. By order of the Society, one thousand copies of this speech were published at a cost of $45—*An Address Delivered before the Agricultural Society of New Castle County by Sidney George Fisher of Philadelphia* (Philadelphia, 1860).

77. Dr. Charles D. Meigs (1792–1869) was born in Bermuda and raised in Connecticut and Georgia. In 1809 he graduated from the University of Georgia; he then took a medical degree from the University of Pennsylvania in 1817. After two years of practice in Georgia, Meigs returned to Philadelphia, where he practiced medicine and taught at Jefferson Medical College until 1861.

on this subject, and when the North is united it must govern the country. Consequently, the South will be governed by its enemies. The enmity, too, partakes of the nature of moral enthusiasm on a point about which the South is very sensitive and naturally, as everything valuable to them is involved in it.

OCTOBER 25, 1860 | Dined at Brookwood. The view from the piazza magnificent. Mr. & Mrs. Purviance there.[78] Henry says there is but one subject talked about in town, and that is the chances of disunion. That the fear is universal. The crisis is indeed important and not without danger, yet I believe that much of the agitation is really confined to the press and the demagogues, who exaggerate all signs of danger to influence the elections & that the contest once over, quiet will be restored. Yet the result may be different, and then the trouble & misery in store for us are not to be calculated. Home at 10 by moonlight.

OCTOBER 26, 1860 | Went to Hazard's. Got a copy of the essay,[79] which will not be ready till tomorrow. There is a panic in the money market because of the threats of disunion by the South. Henry in a state of great excitement. He is afraid my essay will increase the panic, altho, in fact, the argument justifies slavery. Gave him a copy.

OCTOBER 27, 1860 | Henry said so much about my essay & the injury it is likely to do if published at this time, that I consented to consult Mr. Harvey on the subject.[80] He is the Washington correspondent of McMichael's paper and a clever man for such a post. He is southern by birth and knows southern men in Washington. I went to McMichael's office & saw him. I told him that to please my brother I wanted his opinion on one point only—the effect the book would have on the

78. George D. Purviance and his wife, Emily Atherton Purviance, who was the sister-in-law of the diarist's brother, Charles Henry Fisher.

79. *The Laws of Race, as Connected with Slavery*, an erudite plea for white supremacy based on the acceptance of slavery.

80. James E. Harvey, a South Carolinian by birth and education, was Washington correspondent of Morton McMichael's *North American* from 1844 to 1861. In 1861, President Lincoln appointed him minister to Portugal.

South. I read him parts of it, in which he saw nothing objectionable but the contrary. Whilst we, with McMichael, were talking, Henry came in. He pointed out what he thought the dangerous passages. The result was that I left the book with Harvey to read, saying that it should not be published till Monday, but that then I would hear what he had to say & form my own judgment about it.

Was not pleased with the interview. Henry assumed the air of a dictator to these men & pretty much told McMichael that he must not print anything in his paper not agreeable "*to us*," meaning the clique of businessmen whom he represents. McMichael borrows money from Henry, depends on the patronage of "businessmen." He is therefore their slave. Harvey writes for McMichael for a salary. Of course, whatever Henry says is a law for them. In this way money controls the press, as it does the elections, the legislature, &, in some cases, the judiciary. It is the old story, exemplified in history & everyday life also, of truth governed by expediency, of temporal interests rising up to forbid the free expression of opinion on the most important subjects. I understand Henry's motives perfectly. There is a panic in the money market which affects his interests, as disunion would be disastrous to them. My essay, which is a philosophical argument, temperate in language, perfectly free from party feeling or sectional bias and which, in fact, advocates many southern views of the subject, nevertheless tells some truths not agreeable to the South about the dangers of its position. These Henry thinks will increase the excitement. But I think differently.

The essay is the first that has been written, which, taking the northern ground of opposing the increase of slavery, at the same time justifies and advocates slavery. The thing the South fears is abolition, and my argument condemns abolition. I think its effect in the South will be to conciliate & inspire confidence, in the North, to inspire moderate views among the Republican Party whose triumph by an overwhelming majority seems probable, & which therefore requires restraint & repression. The excesses of southern & northern Democrats have created the Republican Party. It has become, as I predicted it would, the party of the populace & therefore liable to be influenced by blind and ignorant popular passion. It is as likely to go to extremes as the other side was. My book will have a tendency to moderate extreme sentiment & discourage fanaticism.

OCTOBER 29, 1860 | Tom Stewardson[81] came here at 10 o'clock. He had passed the night at Brookwood and came at Henry's request to talk to me about my essay & try to persuade me to repress it. This is too ridiculous. I heard what he had to say, which he had evidently carefully prepared, and the whole amounted to this, that altho the whole scope and tenor of the argument are calculated to conciliate the South and repress northern fanaticism, there are some passages that might offend & might be misunderstood. Because of these, he thought the book had better be withheld in the present excited state of the country. In other words, sacrifice a positive good to a slight contingent evil. Henry no doubt sent him on this foolish errand & told him what to say. There is a panic in the money market produced by exaggerated statements of the passions & purposes of southern men, for the double purpose of affecting the New York elections & speculating in stocks. Henry is a "bull," that is, it is his interest that stocks should not fall, but rise. He is therefore very nervous at anything printed on the subject. . . .

I laughed at Stewardson a good [deal] about his fears & Henry's instructions, and told him that truth should not be sacrificed to expediency of any kind, far less to the schemes of the stock market. We went to town together. As I am very glad to relieve Henry's mind, altho I feel sure that his apprehensions are ill-founded, I went to see Mr. Harvey to ask his opinion after reading the essay. He spoke of it in high terms of commendation, said that it takes a new & important view of the subject, and that its influence is calculated to allay excitement, not increase it. Told all this to Henry & left him Harvey's note, which at my request he addressed to me, stating substantially as above. Went to Hazard's & told him to publish the work at once. Directed copies to some friends & institutions, Phila. Library, Athenaeum, Am. Philosophical Society, &c. Hazard neglected to take out

---

81. Dr. Thomas Stewardson (1807-78), of Philadelphia, earned a medical degree from the University of Pennsylvania in 1830.

a copyright, so that if the book succeeds anyone may print it. I do not think, however, it is likely to have such a run as to tempt cupidity.

NOVEMBER 5, 1860 | Tomorrow is election day, when the various passions and opinions of the people will find expression. It is a crisis no doubt of immense importance, for it *may* involve the fate of the Union, *may* be the signal for discord, destruction & bloodshed. The excitement is violent at the South and demagogues & agitators busy in the work of mischief. Reason is silent when passions are inflamed and designing, ambitious, reckless men may easily precipitate action that would destroy in a moment all hope of peace. On the other hand, even in the South, there is a strong force of opinion against extreme measures & the hopeless nature of a contest with the North, of weakness with strength, of 8 millions with 18 millions, must have its influence even with the most violent.

NOVEMBER 6, 1860 | In the morning walked with Bet & Sidney to Maupay's to get a few trees to plant here.[82] Maupay much alarmed at the prospect of the times. He says his orders from the South have fallen off $4000 a month in consequence of the fears there of disunion....

Today is election day. I did not vote. I do not entirely like the animus of the Republican Party. There is too much of hostility to the South in it. The antislavery party has become the party of the multitude. It has become so, indeed, because of the madness & crime & folly of the South, but there is danger of its going too far. I think that it will be prudent and conservative and I am glad to hear that it is to triumph, but I do not wish it to triumph by too great a majority. If the spirit by which it is animated were simply to restrain slavery within its present limits, but heartily to maintain it within those limits, I would vote for Lincoln. But it is leavened largely with a different feeling, a blind, reckless & enthusiastic hatred of slavery, without regard to the character of the Negro race, or to the consequences of

---

82. Samuel Maupay's nursery on Germantown Avenue north of Ellwood Lane was not far from Fisher's Forest Hill.

abolition. How far this spirit may govern it remains to be seen, but its influence will be powerful & difficult to resist. How indeed can it be otherwise. Slavery is hateful in itself. The animating principle of all our institutions, the ruling passion of our race, is liberty. How can a people at once love liberty and love slavery. They must hate slavery, unless they are placed in circumstances, as the southern men are, to make slavery a necessary thing for their own safety. But to realize such circumstances, to appreciate the reasoning by which slavery is justified because of them, is a process requiring too much thought & logic for the mind of the masses. They stop short at their hatred of slavery & act on that. But this is a very dangerous point for them to stop at. It involves the destruction of the Union & of the South. I wish to preserve both. I hope both may be preserved under Lincoln, but he has a difficult task before him, requiring much firmness, prudence, large views and courage to resist powerful influences.

NOVEMBER 7, 1860 | The electric telegraph makes known now the result of an election all over the country. The majorities for Lincoln are even greater than was anticipated. Penna. gives 60,000, New York, 50,000. He is elected by the overwhelming voice of the northern people. It remains now to be seen what the South will do. Will they dare forcibly to oppose their pigmy strength to this formidable array of power and opinion?

NOVEMBER 8, 1860 | At 4 went to town, to a dinner of the Historical Society at the Continental Hotel. About 100 were assembled in the large & handsome drawing room. Among them there were not twenty that I ever saw before. The dinner was in a large & splendidly lighted hall, and was itself good & well served, tho not particularly elegant or choice. I sat opposite Ben Gerhard & next to Chas. Biddle. On the other side of the latter was a friend of his to whom he introduced me, Judge [John R.] Donnell of North Carolina, a gentleman of large estate, whose mild, gentlemanlike manners & intelligent conversation pleased me much. We had some talk on the position of affairs in the South. He said that North Carolina would, he thought, undoubtedly sustain the Union, spoke of the folly of disunion and of the evidence which he saw everywhere that the northern people were as a whole friendly & loyal to the South. I listened to two dull speeches & then came away & got home before 10 o'clk. The company was by no means distinguished in appearance, tho entirely respectable. Many certainly were not entitled to be members of a literary society.

NOVEMBER 21, 1860 | At 3 drove, with Bet, to Brookwood where we dined. After dinner had some talk with Henry about the state of business affairs produced by the secession threats and movements in the South. He says the panic is as great as it was in 1857, that money cannot be got at any price and that if relief does not come in a few days bankruptcy & confusion will ensue. That the banks will probably suspend, which would mitigate the pressure and enable those who owed money & had property to obtain the means of paying debts. He said also that his own position is very critical and that he may very possibly break, tho he thinks he can get thro. That he has paid $750,000 within the last two weeks, has abundant securities, which are unsaleable, & could draw on England to any amount, but bills of exchange cannot be sold, so that it will be difficult to meet his engagements. This was no pleasant news, tho a thing I have always looked forward to for Henry.

NOVEMBER 22, 1860 | Went to town in no small anxiety at 11. The banks of the city suspended at 12, which relieved my mind as to Henry, for he has most ample means, if he can only make them available, which this measure of the banks will no doubt enable him to do. Various reasons induced the suspension—a threatened run, which would have drained them of their specie, the suspension of the banks of Charleston, Virginia & Baltimore, and the desire to relieve the business community here & prevent sacrifices. The banks are strong, the merchants are strong, the country never more prosperous and full of wealth, but there is a panic, which at once withdraws money, specie, from circulation. The means of making exchanges are thus suddenly curtailed, consequently debts cannot be paid without ruinous sacrifices of property to obtain those means. By suspending, the banks furnish a temporary currency. The measure was wise & prudent &

will be safe as the banks will probably resume in a few weeks, unless things at the South become worse.

NOVEMBER 23, 1860 | Bet has a sewing machine which is a great pleasure to her now that she is able to work it with skill. How these inventions come, one after another, to facilitate labor & multiply & cheapen the comforts & accommodations of life. This ingenious little machine performs in an hour as much work as could be done with a needle in a day, and it is very pleasant employment to use it—many ladies become very fond of the occupation & prefer it to a piano. Then there is the air-tight coal stove which gives abundance of heat at very slight trouble or expense. Coal oil, now very generally burned in lamps, is another late discovery. It is half the expense of common oil and, I suppose, a 10th that of sperm candles. My lamp gives as much light as four candles and burns twice as long.

NOVEMBER 24, 1860 | At 2 I drove up to Alverthorpe to dinner.[83] It was very cold but I went in the farm wagon which has a standing top and curtains, and with fur gloves, thick overcoat & blanket was comfortable enough and enjoyed the drive. I had scarcely got seated in the library when we all began to talk on the absorbing topic of disunion, they introducing the subject, as they said it had become too interesting to refrain. Our talk was only interrupted by dinner at 4, and I staid till 7. During dinner the subject was dropped because of the presence of the Negro servants in attendance.

Harry Middleton and I discussed the subject almost exclusively, the rest listening to us, and I must do him the justice to say that he was sensible in his views, fair in argument, perfectly gentlemanlike and good-humored. The ground he took was that the election of Lincoln by large majorities in all the northern states proved that the North was more powerful than the South, that it was united in hostility to southern institutions and interests, that the South held & must always hold an inferior position in the Union & be governed by an

---

83. Alverthorpe was built by Joshua Francis Fisher in 1850–51 on Meeting House Road near Jenkintown. The house was torn down in 1936.

outside and unfriendly power and, therefore, it was the policy of the South, both as matter of interest and of honor, to secede now, form a new and independent empire united by the interests of slavery and to govern itself. That the hostile feelings of the North were exhibited not merely by the sectional vote for Lincoln, but by legislation intended to obstruct the execution of the fugitive slave law, by the permitted efforts of the underground railroad societies, and by the haranguing & writings of avowed abolitionists.

He said, moreover, that the southern states, if united, had resources, wealth, and population enough to form a powerful and independent nation, more especially as they produced exclusively the great staples of commerce which made all nations tributary to them. He said also that the avowed policy of the North was to restrict slavery to its present limits, to hem in the states where it exists & subject them to the burden & danger of a rapidly increasing Negro population, without the possibility of expansion, either by occupying national territory or by acquiring new territory over which to spread an inferior race whose numbers would in time become an inconvenience & a peril. That the South had equal rights with the North to the territories & to exclude southern men from them was an insult as well as an injury. That for all these evils and dangers, a great southern confederacy, which could, at its pleasure, extend its sway over adjacent tropical regions, over the West Indies, Mexico, & Central America, with slavery as its foundation & cotton, sugar, rice, & tobacco as its sources of wealth & prosperity, was the true remedy.

To this I replied that if it be true that the election of Lincoln did, in fact, indicate a general and settled hostile purpose & feeling on the part of the North to the South, a secession and a united southern confederacy would be a policy dictated at any rate by honorable feeling and if it could be effected, by interest also. But, in truth, the election of Lincoln proves no such state of opinion in the North. That, in the first place, both Breckenridge & Douglas had a large vote in the northern states, & that both of these were representatives of southern interests. That slavery, tho the chief, was by no means the only issue in the late election, but the tariff and the corruptions and excesses of the administration were very influential in producing the result. That the fact that Seward was dropped & Lincoln selected was in itself a proof of the moderate views of the Republican Party. That the great masses of that party were perfectly loyal to the South and would at once disapprove & resist any measures intended for its injury. That Lincoln himself could do nothing, even if disposed, without the consent of Congress, and that the South had for its protection the Senate & the House of Representatives, in both which there was a majority in its favor, so that possessing thus ample Constitutional means of defence, it was madness to seek that defence in revolution, which could only be justified when all Constitutional means had been exhausted. As to the exclusion of the South from the territories, the doctrine & practice of the government had been that Congress had supreme control over the territories & ought to govern them & had governed them for their own good, either prohibiting or preventing slavery according to the exigencies of soil & climate & the wishes of the inhabitants. That this practice had never been departed from except in the case of Kansas, when the South attempted to force slavery on a territory in defiance of the express wish of nine-tenths of its people, out of which attempt had grown all the present troubles & the success of the Republican Party. The laws of the northern states obstructing the execution of the fugitive slave law were the consequences of that excitement. That most of them, if fairly examined, were, in fact, nothing more than the expression of a natural & just northern sentiment—aversion to slavery in the abstract but a willingness to permit the general government to perform its Constitutional obligations by executing the law by its own officers.

I do not know that what I said produced much effect, for it was evident to me that in him, as in the South generally, the real grievance is the being obliged to give up power after having exercised it so long. Stopped to see Henry on my way home. The suspension has relieved his fears for the present. I told him I thought he and all men should prepare for the worst.

NOVEMBER 25, 1860 | My last volume closed with an account of the alarm caused by prospects of disunion. The South is enraged by the election of Lincoln, which is regarded there as evidence of a settled hostility to slavery and of a design to exercise the powers of the government to the injury of the southern people. That this opinion is really entertained by many is, no doubt, true. Much of the passion displayed, however, is the result of defeat, of loss of power. The southern people are arrogant and self-willed. They have been accustomed generally to govern the country, always to have large influence in the government. They cannot bear to lose power, and to submit to the control of the North, of a party composed in part of abolitionists, exasperates their pride. How far they will carry their opposition remains to be seen. The indications are very gloomy. Revolutions are brought about by passion and passions are now greatly excited. It is by no means improbable that I shall be obliged to record in this volume the destruction of our government.

NOVEMBER 26, 1860 | Southern news more unfavorable, public meetings & violent speeches in Charleston, Georgia, Mississippi & Alabama, secession resolutions passed by legislatures & recommended by governors of those states, a blaze of excitement everywhere. Drove Bet up Germantown to pay visits at the Ben Rush's and at Cliveden.[84] Rush lives in a cottage at Mount Airy. Left cards. Got in at Cliveden & had some talk with Miss Chew. It is a fine, picturesque old mansion with large rooms, but house and grounds woefully out of repair.

NOVEMBER 28, 1860 | There has recently been delivered in Georgia a very conservative speech by Mr. A. H. Stevens,[85] a gentleman of some note in Southern public life. It is thought a good indication & to afford some hope of a proper feeling in Georgia & the South. Some gentlemen here thought a good effect would be produced if an answer to it, responding to its just opinions, were written & published here. They asked me to write such a letter. Went with Henry to see Mr. Mercer,

---

84. Benjamin Rush was the eldest son of Richard Rush and had served as secretary of legation for his father when the latter was minister to England.

85. Alexander H. Stephens (1812–83), a Whig and later Democrat from Georgia, was a U.S. congressman from 1843 to 1859, and again following the war from 1873 to 1882. During the Civil War he was vice president of the Confederacy. From 1882 until his death he was governor of Georgia.

pres. of F & M Bank, on the subject.[86] He suggested my name to the others. Agreed to write the letter by Friday. Went to see photographs taken of Mr. Ingersoll and of Sidney some days ago. Both good, Sidney's particularly so. Mr. Ingersoll's looks too old. Home at 5 to dinner. In the evening began the letter.

NOVEMBER 30, 1860 | Took ink & pencil mss. to town at 12. A number of gentlemen met in Henry's office. Read the letter to them. They all say it is too long and that it goes so much into detail of argument on disputed points that it would be impossible to get a proper number of persons who would agree to all parts of it & be willing to sign it. Some would object to one part, some to another. They were right. At their request, I agreed to write a shorter one, avoiding doubtful points. Home to dinner. In the evening wrote another letter. The argument amounts to this. Secession, whether the right to make it be Constitutional or not, is an extreme remedy equivalent to revolution. Revolution is a step which cannot be justified unless grievances be real & serious and unless all legal & peaceable means of redress have been tried & have failed. Now, the fact is that at this time the country is in the enjoyment of universal & unequalled prosperity. It is also true that up to this moment slavery has been safe & has flourished as it never did anywhere else. These two facts decide the question so far as revolution is concerned. By their side, all alleged grievances of the South, supposing all charges to be true, are insignificant. To overturn a government in the midst of prosperity and for the sake of an interest, which, under the protection of that government has constantly grown & expanded, would be folly. These arguments may have some effect on the public opinion in the South, which it is hoped may control the madmen who are driving the country to ruin.

DECEMBER 1, 1860 | Took letter to town. Read it to several at Henry's office who approved it & decided that it should be printed in a shape to be signed. Took it to Sherman who agreed to have 100 copies ready by 5 o'clock.

86. Singleton A. Mercer, president of the Farmers' and Mechanics' Bank.

DECEMBER 3, 1860 | Not many had signed the letter, as everyone could not agree to every point & expression in it. The Democrats thought it not sufficiently respectful to the South, the Republicans not sufficiently so to Mr. Lincoln; one would not say that this government had always sustained slavery, another would not agree that slavery suited the Negro race, &c., &c. A good many names, however, were signed. I told Mr. Mercer that I would not alter the letter but that he & the gentlemen with him might make any use of it they pleased.

DECEMBER 4, 1860 | Congress met yesterday. Members seemed all in good humor. Some propositions looking to a compromise have been made. The opinion, however, seems to be that disunion is inevitable and the only question is whether it shall be peaceful or accompanied by civil war. Coercion however is impossible and as that seems to be admitted, in my judgment, the North should now offer a law to permit any state to withdraw that decides to do so by a vote of 2/3rds of its people. I believe that none except So. Carolina would avail themselves of such an offer. I have thought of this plan before and the more I think of it the more I am convinced that it presents the only path of safety. It is plain that the government should determine either to put down & punish rebellion by force, or should make secession a legal act, for otherwise the law is defied & dishonored. Should the former course be resolved on, it would at once unite all the southern states, at least so everyone thinks. The civil war of a very dreadful character would follow, the consequences of which no man could foresee, for even if the government should succeed, the whole character & value of this union, which should rest on consent, opinion & mutual benefit, not on force & terror, would be destroyed. The North moreover would be by no means united in such a war.

DECEMBER 6, 1860 | The great point just now is to gain time, so that deliberation may be had, passions cool, and the sound opinion which undoubtedly exists in the southern states have an opportunity to form itself & find organs for expression. It is now kept down by a system of terrorism and by the overpowering influence of an oligarchy which assumes the right to dictate. The immediate danger seems narrowed to the risk of a hostile collision between the government & the people of that passionate, factious, headlong, impracticable little state of So. Carolina. If its people should make an attack on Fort Moultrie, which they threaten, or if they should forcibly resist the collection of the revenue, then the risk is extreme that the fire of civil war would be kindled & would spread into such proportions that the question would become, which shall conquer, North or South.

DECEMBER 7, 1860 | My Stephens letter has been numerously signed and was sent to him today.

DECEMBER 12, 1860 | Went to see Fisher in town. He has published a pamphlet on the times, entitled *Concessions & Compromises*. He has had 4000 printed and was in great excitement, directing them for the post office as they are to be widely distributed. He seemed evidently to think he had discovered a remedy for all our troubles and his manner was not a little amusing. He gave me some copies to distribute. Read it when I got home. Some of the suggestions are sensible enough, others impracticable & ill-considered, much excitement visible in the style. Altogether it amounts to nothing, tho it may do good as it is short, quite well expressed and practical. What he says about the fugitive slave law is very well worth considering.

DECEMBER 13, 1860 | A pamphlet was sent me yesterday by the author, Mr. Stephen Colwell,[87] whom I do not know, but am told he is a very worthy & intelligent merchant, by birth a Virginian. It is well written and its object is to show that the South & slavery can only be safe in the Union & under the Constitution, that the only foundation or excuse for slavery is the good of the Negro race and that secession would be destructive to every interest of the South. These are the opinions I have always advocated, but I begin now to think that tho the Union can alone protect slavery, it cannot protect it long. The

---

87. Stephen Colwell (1800–71), political economist and iron manufacturer of Conshohocken, Pa., published *The Five Cotton States and New York; or, Remarks upon the Social and Economical Aspects of the Southern Political Crisis* in January 1861.

opinion of the civilized world is against the institution and tho cotton is king, it is only king on the Exchange. Morality is progressive, its progress is reflected & stimulated by literature and the moral & enlightened sentiment of mankind is too strong for material interest. Civilized nations are governed not by force but by opinion, northern opinion is averse to slavery, is becoming more hostile to it every day, & this hostility is constantly increased by the outrages of the South. These outrages have at length reached the point of attempted revolution for the sake of slavery. The late election was a protest against southern dictation, it was a protest against the corruption & abuses of the Democratic Party, it was to a great extent an expression of hatred to slavery itself, and it was a declaration that power resides, not with weakness, but with strength, and that it is an attribute of power to govern. Strength & power are with the North, weakness and slavery are with the South. The utmost that the South can expect in the Union is toleration of slavery, not hearty approbation and support of it. The agitation of the subject must therefore go on & will always necessarily form a question of party politics. Now this discussion and excitement are dangerous things for slavery. It inspires the Negroes with the idea & desire for freedom, it assures them of sympathizers and friends and tends directly to revolt & servile war. When this spirit reaches a certain point, the sense of security is destroyed, business loses energy, capital disappears, decay commences, & finally society is so weakened that emancipation, voluntary or forcible, must be the result. Southern men instinctively feel this and hence their desire to separate from this dangerous North, which must govern them and even while giving them protection, must also, by a fatal necessity, undermine the institution on which their social system is founded. But how can they separate? That is the difficult question. Suppose the North says, as by right & law it may, separation is treason and you shall not go. The result would be a civil war, and the first gun fired in such a war would sound the knell of slavery.

DECEMBER 16, 1860 | At 3 drove up to Henry's. He says that Mr. Henry Ward Beecher, a noted abolitionist, is to deliver a lecture in town on Friday for a literary society and that trouble is anticipated.[88] The Democrats are likely to make a riot and the Republicans declare they will organize to defend him. This is another indication of the danger of attempting to coerce the southern states. It would produce a civil war not only between sections but between parties throughout the country—civil war with anarchy, in short. It shows too the nature of democracy & how surely it leads thro popular violence to military despotism. The South has destroyed liberty of speech and of the press for the sake of slavery at home; the adherents of the South are attempting the same thing here. It is a dangerous thing, people say, to permit lectures and speeches about slavery at such a time; they add to excitement, they irritate the South, they may even tend to stir up the Negroes to revolt; therefore they should be frowned down according to some, or hissed down or knocked down according to others. Last year Mr. Curtis came here, about the time of John Brown's attempt in Virginia, to deliver a lecture on the times. He was threatened with violence, but he was protected by the mayor on the ground that liberty of speech must be maintained. The lecture was delivered, the building was surrounded by a shouting, hooting mob, but the presence of a strong police force prevented serious violence, otherwise there would have been a fearful riot, as Mr. Henry told me himself.

DECEMBER 21, 1860 | The convention of South Carolina passed an ordinance yesterday declaring the state to be no longer a member of the Union, but a sovereign & independent nation. In the debate which ensued, some of the difficulties of the new position became apparent. They could give no clearances to vessels leaving their ports. Consequently, all commerce was at once stopped, as a vessel without a clearance would not be received at foreign ports & would be without protection on the high seas, having no flag or national character. They have no post office, & without mails all business must cease. It would

---

88. Henry Ward Beecher (1813-87) was a minister at Plymouth Congregational Church in Brooklyn, New York. An advocate of woman suffrage, temperance, and the abolition of slavery, Beecher was also very active in Republican Party politics in the Civil War era.

really seem as if these very obvious difficulties had never suggested themselves to the minds of the actors in this tragi-comic scene, for the speeches are marked with trepidation & conflicting counsels on subjects in relation to which some definite course of action ought beforehand to have been determined on. One member declared that they were homeless & houseless & that the ships would rot in their ports. After much floundering, the only conclusion they arrived at was that Mr. Buchanan *being their friend,* he would no doubt allow them to use the officers of the U. S., both of the custom house and post office, until the arrangements of the new nation could be perfected. That is to say, they appeal to the government for aid to enable them to break up the Union. This is cool certainly, and not very consistent with "the honor & dignity of So. Carolina," about which they talk so much. Such has been the first formal step in the course of events which may turn out to be either a farce or a mournful tragedy.

DECEMBER 25, 1860 | Christmas. Delightful winter weather. Therm. 32. Of course, a stocking was hung at Sidney's bed last night, filled with pretty things and he went to rest, entirely convinced of the reality of Christkinkle and full of hope. At dawn he was awake and the first thing he said was, "Has Kriskinkle been here & has he brought me anything, if he has, I shall be *so* pleased." As soon as the light permitted, he examined the stocking and was in raptures at its contents and at the toys on a chair by his little bed. This was all very delightful to witness and I think we were more pleased than he.

The perilous state of the country occupied my thoughts, and my plan of legalizing secession, of making it easy & safe, since secession is to be, appeared to me the only proper remedy. I determined to write an article on the subject, as strong convictions naturally seek expression and one cannot help thinking that what seems to him true will convince others and thus produce a good result. Accordingly, began the article & worked at it morning and evening.

DECEMBER 26, 1860 | Henry and Pierce Butler here for a few moments on their way to Brookwood. Butler is eager for secession & has just returned from Georgia, where he says there is no difference of opinion. He said that he came here only to *buy arms* and intends to return immediately and join the army. He will take his daughter Fanny with him and has bought a rifle for *her*, too, for he says even the women in the South are going to fight. What madness, yet one cannot help admiring the knightly spirit these southern men are displaying. They rush recklessly on fearful odds & fearful dangers and talk like men insane. Yet is there not reason for the wild excitement they exhibit? Is it not really terror, the instinctive dread of approaching peril which they think they can baffle by fronting and defying? The power of the North is overwhelming if it should be used against them.

DECEMBER 28, 1860 | The news is that the people of Charleston have taken Fort Moultrie. There are two forts in the harbor, Moultrie and Sumter. The first is so situated that it could not be defended at all by Captn. [Major Robert] Anderson's small force—the 2nd could be made impregnable by that force. The orders of the President were that he should defend the fort, yet he was refused reinforcements when he demanded them because the President feared that the sending them there would increase the excitement in So. Carolina & lead to a collision. Captn. Anderson has, it seems, on his own responsibility, rather than sacrifice his men and a position which he could not hold if attacked, removed to one, Fort Sumter, that he can maintain. He spiked the guns when he went and soon after a body of troops from Charleston took possession of the fort. This event has produced much feeling everywhere. The commissioners from So. Carolina, sent to Washington to treat with the President, now demand that the President shall withdraw the force from Fort Sumter, and it is thought that he will do so.

DECEMBER 31, 1860 | The article "Legalized Secession" was in the paper this morning.[89] Mr. [John Buchanan] Floyd, Secty of War, has

---

89. Fisher published this article in the *North American* over the name "Cecil." Since secession appeared inevitable, he thought it best to give it legal status by passing certain laws. "Let us therefore open the door wide to our southern friends, and say to them, 'depart in peace, we will not detain you against your will.' . . . To cry Union when there is no Union, is like crying peace, peace, when there is no peace. If the

resigned, because at a meeting of the Cabinet it was resolved that Captn. Anderson should not be remanded to Fort Moultrie as required by the commissioners of So. Carolina. This decision & his withdrawal inspire hope at Washington that some firmness will be shown by the government to vindicate its dignity. Genl. Scott has expressed very decided opinions and advised the President from the first to reinforce all the southern forts.

Union be broken, we should acknowledge the fact and on that build our arguments and policy."

~1861~

JANUARY 3, 1861 | Felt so weak and miserable this morning that I sent for Wister. He came at 6 o'clock. Thinks I have a slight disposition to intermittent, excited by gout. Ordered 2 pills tonight & some powders tomorrow, what they are I do not know. We swallow blindly what the doctor gives, as some people do what the priest or the demagogue gives.

JANUARY 14, 1861 | States are one after another going out of the Union and nothing is done to prevent them. The plan of the government seems now to avoid anything that will irritate the South and bring on civil war. But what ultimate object is proposed is not easy to see. Are these states to be allowed to stay out? I suppose so, for they can only be brought back by force & coercion, which everyone agrees will not be attempted. Why not then say so, legally and officially at once? The *Brooklyn* did not enter the harbor of Charleston, but met the *Star of the West* coming out, and Major Anderson says that he requires neither stores nor reinforcements, so that it will not be necessary to do anything at present to "irritate So. Carolina."[1] The forts of all the seceding states have been seized, yet the President makes no effort to retake

---

1. The *Star of the West*, a merchantman, was chartered to carry reinforcements and supplies to Maj. Robert Anderson at Fort Sumter. When she entered Charleston harbor, the *Star* came under the fire of Confederate batteries and withdrew, being met by the *Brooklyn*, a sloop of war sent to her assistance but with orders not to cross the Charleston bar.

them, tho he declares it to be his duty to protect the public property. The authority of the government is thus brought into contempt. The great point now is to prevent the secession of the border states. An effort to coerce the others would precipitate them into the same movement and then the evils of disunion would be vastly increased. The seceders would possess Washington & would be powerful enough to form a great confederacy. The present policy of the government therefore seems the only one that can be pursued.

JANUARY 17, 1861 | Fisher paid us a visit. He says they have heard nothing for some time from S. Carolina & he thinks the reason is that secession is working very badly & they do not like to confess it. The state has already been obliged to have recourse to stay laws, paper money and forced loans. Severe exactions are made on individuals; for example, 18 Negroes belonging to his friend Sinkler were drafted from his plantation & sent 150 miles away to work at the fortifications, liable, of course, to brutal treatment & to demoralization.[2] He said he had a conversation a day or two ago with Mr. Page. Page has been obliged to go to Mississippi on pain of being treated as an absentee. He writes that everything there is *"going to Hell."*

JANUARY 18, 1861 | The news today rather favorable. It seems probable that Louisiana, Arkansas & North Carolina will refuse to secede. The border states still hold to the Union tho they are wavering. Very moderate concession would secure them. Curtin, our new Governor, has sent commissioners to Maryland. In the morning read the *Federalist*, which, besides being an excellent commentary on the Constitution, is a good work on the philosophy of government. In the evening began an article in relation to the position of the border states in the present crisis.

JANUARY 30, 1861 | Clear & cold. Finished copying the article. It is entitled "The true interest of the border states." Went to town at 12,

---

2. Eutaw Plantation on Eutaw Springs Creek, about sixty miles from Charleston, was owned by William Sinkler, who also owned the adjoining plantation of Belvidere.

driving to the 4th passenger car. Took the article to McMichael, who said it should appear tomorrow.

FEBRUARY 2, 1861 | It is indeed a threatening state of affairs; the seat of government garrisoned, six states in arms against its authority, sectional hatred raging in half the nation, to such an extent that neither the President-elect nor any conspicuous member of his party could visit that section without the certainty of personal indignity and imminent danger of his life. It shows how completely the whole structure of our government has been undermined when it thus falls to pieces at a touch. What prospect is there of filling up these rents & gaps, of subduing these animosities, of restoring peace? I can see none. And yet the dispute is really about nothing of practical importance, and two sensible men ought to be able to settle it in an hour. Take away from it the misrepresentations & the exaggeration, the selfish ambition of individuals, the obstinate dogmatism of parties, and the excited passions of both, and nothing remains that ought to produce discord, much less revolution.

FEBRUARY 6, 1861 | Went to McMichael's office. They have struck off on a separate sheet a large number of my last article for distribution. It seems to have been generally read & approved, if I may judge by what many have said to me about it. At McMichael's were Chas. Gibbons & Mr. Carey, both leading Republicans, & Mr. [Samuel Morse] Felton, pres. of the Wilmington & Baltimore Railroad. He says there is reason to think a plot has been formed in Maryland to *assassinate* Mr. Lincoln on his way to Washington. The supposed plan is to burn a bridge 6 miles this side of Baltimore & then attack the train. All precautions have been taken; Felton has bought 100 revolvers to arm the conductors and the governor of Maryland, Mr. [Thomas H.] Hicks, has been written to and his assistance asked. The seat of government is a camp; the President-elect has to be guarded on his way to the capital and could not show his face anywhere in one half of the so-called Union without risking his life. This dispute may be patched up for the present, but the battle has yet to be fought between slavery & liberty.

FEBRUARY 11, 1861 | Rose at 5—breakfasted at 6 by candlelight with Bet who always insists on getting up too. Therm at that hour 20. Started at 7 [*for Mount Harmon*] and drove to the Prime St. Station. Mr. Felton, the Pres. of the Road, in the car as far as Chester. He told me the details of the plot mentioned before for attacking the train & murdering Lincoln on his way to Washington. The facts were communicated to him by persons of entire respectability, of course in confidence as to names. He said moreover that within a few days past he had an interview with General Scott, in reference to the arrangements to be made for Lincoln's journey. Scott informed him that he had unquestionable evidence of a plan by the conspirators to attack & capture Washington, to put to death Lincoln & all the prominent members of the Republican Party.

FEBRUARY 13, 1861 | Mr. J. R. Ingersoll & Miss Wilcocks came. His deafness spoils all pleasure of conversation with him, more especially as he does not like you to indicate by raising your voice that you think him deaf. So that as Bet says, he is irritated if he does not hear you and still more irritated if he does.

FEBRUARY 15, 1861 | The convention of the seceded states is in session at Montgomery, Alabama, and is going on with its work of organizing a new nation. Jefferson Davis[3] of Mississippi has been elected by the convention President and A. H. Stephens of Georgia, Vice-President. The forces of the U. S., however, still occupy some of the forts within the territory of the new confederacy, the customs are still collected for acct. of the U. S. & the U. S. is "permitted" to furnish mails to the people, so it is not yet quite independent. It is generally thought that it contemplates a return to the Union on terms satisfactory to its leaders. Meanwhile, both parties are watching with anxiety the action of the border states. The elections have shown the sentiments of their people

---

3. Jefferson Davis (1808–89), from Mississippi, served several terms as a U.S. congressman and senator, as well as secretary of war, in the 1840s and 1850s. During the Civil War he was president of the Confederacy.

to be in favor of the Union and there is no doubt they can be retained if certain concessions are made.

FEBRUARY 17, 1861 | Rode around by Butler's lane to Germantown & so home. As I passed Wm. Wister's gate, went in to look at the house [Belfield], which I had not seen since the alterations made in it last year. The roof has been raised & another story added, it has been stuccoed, a piazza built, new doors & windows, all in cottage style and the woodwork painted a good stone color. The whole appearance has been altered & it is a handsome house now. Inquired & found there have been several cases of smallpox in the neighborhood.

FEBRUARY 22, 1861 | Clear, pleasant weather. Therm. about 42. This is Washington's Birthday and at 6 o'clock this morning a new flag with all the stars on it was raised with appropriate ceremonies over Independence Hall. Mr. Lincoln was present and himself hauled it up to the peak of the staff. At 9 o'clock he went off by special train to Harrisburg. The day was celebrated in town by civic & military displays & enthusiastic demonstrations for the Union.

FEBRUARY 23, 1861 | Sally Ingersoll,[4] adopting all her husband's opinions, or rather partizan passions, for he has no opinions, is violent for the South & secession; so also is Mrs. Fisher, very naturally, for she is a Carolinian and her brothers, relatives, & friends are all involved most unfortunately in this unhappy contest. She therefore is excusable and I always speak to her on the subject with great forbearance. Mrs. I. talks in her excited way, but, as she knows nothing whatever of the subject, I no more think of speaking with her about it seriously than I would with a child, or with her husband! Bet, however, has her convictions & can think & is a good deal excited about the outrages of the South, so they all got discussing the matter this morning more warmly than was necessary. One of the evils of civil dissensions is that they produce discord between families & friends &

---

4. Sarah Emlen "Sally" Roberts married Harry Ingersoll.

great care should be taken to avoid disputes which may cause ill feelings to arise.

FEBRUARY 24, 1861 | Went up to Brookwood on horseback. Saw them all, the girls out of mourning & in bright blue dresses & Henry in good spirits, so I suppose his affairs are going on well. He told me some startling news. Mr. Lincoln went to Harrisburg at 9 on Friday morning, was received by the legislature with addresses, &c., & in the evening had a reception at the hotel. He, however, left Harrisburg that night & came to Phila: by special train, with one companion, & then took the 11 o'clock train to Baltimore & thence to Washington, where he arrived at 6 o'clock yesterday morning. His departure was kept a secret until a telegram announced his arrival in Washington and all the preparations for his reception in Baltimore & elsewhere became useless. His plan, as made known, was to go to Baltimore on the railroad from Harrisburg at 9 o'clock on Saturday, and a committee from Baltimore was in Harrisburg to accompany him. The reason of his sudden change of route was that a plot had been discovered to stop the train on its way to Baltimore & assassinate him. Men of influence & social position were said to be engaged in this foul conspiracy and the information was communicated by Genl. Scott[5] & Mr. Seward. Mr. Lincoln at first insisted on going as was originally intended, but finally yielded to the entreaties of his wife and the advice of his friends. Henry says that he has reason to *know* that the evidence of the existence of the plot is conclusive, and Lincoln and his friends must have so regarded it, or they never would have taken a step so open to injurious comment as a clandestine journey to the Capital. It accords entirely with what I heard from Felton and afterwards from Robt. Hare some weeks ago.

MARCH 2, 1861 | Today is my birthday. I have now reached the mature age of 52. It seems to me very strange & hard to realize that I am so

---

5. Winfield Scott (1786-1866), of Virginia, was a veteran of the War of 1812 and the Mexican War. In 1852 he was the unsuccessful Whig candidate for president. Scott was a brevet lieutenant general in command of the Union armies at the beginning of the war but requested retirement on October 31, 1861.

old, that I am no longer a young man. It is mortifying, too, that being so old I have done so little. I have wasted time, talents and money, all which, well employed, would have placed me now in a very different position from that which I occupy. Nevertheless, I have had so far on the whole a happy life and I trust, in what may be left, in some measure to retrieve the past. I have not much time before me and ere long this familiar scene, with its work, its hopes and enjoyments, will pass away and perhaps be exchanged for a freer and larger existence. I enjoy it now, this sense of moral and intellectual being, this communion with the great mind of nature, and cannot conceive that I shall not, somehow or other, enjoy it always. This feeling of the present, this fore-sense of the future, fills my days with deep satisfaction & lifts me above the external things of life. I care not for wealth, I am not eager for reputation or position, it suffices that I live & think & feel and that I shall always do so. My worldly desires are confined to leaving a comfortable independence to Bet & Sidney, to educating him & at least starting him in the right path.

MARCH 5, 1861 | The description of the ceremonies of the inauguration and the speech of Mr. Lincoln were in the morning paper. The crowd was immense, the military & police preparations ample, and the whole affair passed off quietly. The speech in my judgment establishes Lincoln's character as a man of talents and honest purposes, and is calculated to conciliate hostile feeling & inspire confidence. Candor, native good sense, generous & elevated sentiment, and simple sincerity are its characteristics. It displays the firmness of purpose arising from strong convictions and a sense of duty, rather than strength of personal will. He declares that there can be no such thing as secession in the eye of the law, and that he has no power to recognize it, but was elected to execute the law. That it is his intention to do this, not to make war on the seceding states, and that if there shall be war, he will not be the aggressor. In discussing the various doctrinal points of dispute between North & South, he disposes of them with terse, pithy remarks that in a few words cover the whole argument & show that he can think clearly. He evidently appreciates his position, its duties and powers, and I shall be disappointed if he does not prove equal to either. There is not a word or sentiment in the speech offensive to anyone, but it is animated throughout by a feeling of good will and patriotic love for the whole country. Some of his remarks are worthy of a statesman. "No organic law can be framed with a provision specifically applicable to every case that may occur in its practical administration. No President can anticipate nor any document of reasonable length contain express provisions for all possible questions. Shall fugitives from labor be surrendered by national or state authority? The Constitution does not expressly say. May Congress prohibit slavery in the Territories? The Constitution does not expressly say. Must Congress protect slavery in the Territories? The Constitution does not expressly say. From questions of this class spring all our Constitutional controversies and we divide upon them into majorities and minorities. If the minority will not acquiesce, the majority must, or the government must cease. . . . Plainly, the central idea of secession is the essence of anarchy. A majority held in restraint by Constitutional checks and limitations and always changing easily with popular opinion is *the only true sovereign of a free people*." These sentences show that Mr. Lincoln is not ignorant of the philosophy of government.

". . . In your hands, my dissatisfied countrymen, not in mine, is the momentous issue of civil war. The government will not assail you. You can have no conflict with that without being yourselves the aggressors. You have no oath registered in heaven to destroy the government, while I shall have the most solemn one to 'preserve, protect and defend it.' . . . The mystic chords of memory, stretching from every battlefield & patriot grave to every loving[6] heart and hearthstone all over this broad land will yet swell the chorus of the Union, when again touched, as surely they will be, by the better angels of our nature." This fine sentiment and beautiful image concluded the speech. He who wrote it is no common man.

6. Fisher's transcription of Lincoln's speech is not wholly accurate. This word, which should be "living," is the most notable mistake.

MARCH 9, 1861 | The southern confederacy have sent commissioners to treat with Lincoln. They claim to be received officially as the representatives of an independent power. It is said that he will refer them to Congress, which he is soon to convene. Will Congress receive them at all? What will they demand? Doubtless recognition for their government, terms of separation, partition of the public property, treaties of commerce & for the rendition of slaves, &c. In other words, the issue is changed and the question to be met now is the Constitutional right of secession. If Congress denies this right, the laws must be enforced. If this right be yielded, it is giving up to the South a doctrine which has always been steadily maintained by the North and is a virtual abdication of the powers of government.

MARCH 11, 1861 | Met Bet in the street. Went with her & got the daguerre[7] of her. Had it put in a miniature case. It is too precious to hang up on the wall exposed to vulgar eyes. The likeness is admirable

MARCH 13, 1861 | Went to see Barnum's exhibition of human curiosities, albinoes from Madagascar, a bushwoman from South Africa & two specimens, male & female, of what is said to be remnants of the Aztec race in Central America. The albinoes have white hair and pink eyes, but their faces are so intelligent & European that I doubt their being African. The bushwoman looks like a mulatto dwarf. She is about 4 feet 3 inches high, stout & strong and 24 years old. The Aztecs were extraordinary creatures, heads very small, forehead & chin receding, idiotic expression, inarticulate cries, animated movements, brutified humanity, painful to look at. These, then, are lower states of what I am. Man in a state of arrested development.

MARCH 14, 1861 | How wonderfully scenes & people, even ourselves, vanish irrevocably from us. We thus die daily and yesterday is as much lost to me as the hour of my birth. The future is not, the past is

7. The daguerreotype, a nineteenth-century photograph on a copper plate, was developed in France in the late 1830s and popular in America through the 1850s.

not. What then is life? Recollection, hope and the present, fleeting, infinitesimal moment. But recollection & hope or expectation are thought, spiritual acts. The consciousness of the present, what is it? Most of it is mental also, and how much of what we call sensations is also subjective, how much of what appears to be the not-me is really the me, we cannot tell. This minute point of time then is life. Take away the ability to think of the past or the future & what remains? The ability to be conscious of the present. What then is death? The cessation of that consciousness. So that there is no such thing as life except such thought & no such thing as death except inability to think. If the ability remains after death, death is continued life, not more wonderful than our earthly continuous life thro successive changes from infancy to age. If the power of memory be destroyed, death is a new birth, the continuity is broken, and all of our past on earth is as much lost as the things we cannot remember of life here, which are much the larger proportion of what has happened to us. So that whilst life is thought, there is for us, as Plato says, no such thing as death, for if the mind lives after the dissolution of the body, that is not death but life; if it dies with the body, we shall be unconscious of death. Why then do we dread it? Because we shrink from the idea of annihilation if the mind really dies, and because we dread unknown changes if it does not. We love life, therefore we hate its opposite. We have desires & hopes & feelings which this world does not satisfy. It is a painful thought that these shall never be satisfied. We have a profound sense of the dignity and worth of our own souls, and cannot bear the thought that they are of so little worth as to perish utterly & be cast among "the wastes of time." Moreover, we love not life in the abstract only, but this earthly life, this beautiful world, this familiar scene, wife & child & property, our work and plans and thought, and change, even for continued life in the unknown, is terrible to us.

MARCH 23, 1861 | Wm. Gilpin has been appointed Governor of the Territory of Colorado, organized by Congress at the last session.[8] This

8. William Gilpin (1813–94) was a participant in John C. Fremont's 1843 expedition through the West and a veteran of the Mexican War. In 1861 Missouri governor Frank Blair recommended Gilpin to be governor of the Colorado Territory, a position he held

territory includes the Pike's Peak gold region, is a country of great fertility and beauty, emigrants are crowding to it and it is likely to become of great importance. The place suits William exactly & he suits it. I suppose he would rather have it than any the President could give him. He has been accustomed to and likes the hardy adventurous life of the far west and the study of its geography & resources has been his great occupation & pursuit for many years.

MARCH 24, 1861 | Jno. Field came here this morning. He returned from New York yesterday. He talked exuberantly and told me a great deal about the literary men whom he had seen & known during the winter in Boston—Holmes, Longfellow, Emerson, Agassiz, Norton, Felton, &c.[9] He said that they all had read and approved *Race*, and those who did not agree to its opinions praised its execution. Among others, Emerson had spoken kindly of it and of me. I feel particularly glad of this last compliment.

MARCH 25, 1861 | Went on to Brookwood, where I dined. Henry said every sort of business is prostrated and that there is small hope of speedy revival, as the result of the present posture of affairs cannot be foreseen. A painful sense of disaster, of a stern and irresistible course of evil impending over the country and over all private interests, oppresses men's minds. Disaffection seems to spread everywhere, respect for law and love of country, and confidence in the government, and loyalty are so weakened that we can scarcely be said to have a government at all and seem to be approaching the rule of no rule. There is no King in Israel.

MARCH 26, 1861 | Called at Fisher's. Saw him and Eliza. She is going tomorrow to Charleston and takes with her Sophia and George. Her

---

until he was removed from office in 1862 for issuing illegal treasury notes, an action he had deemed necessary to sustain the Union troops in Colorado.

9. Oliver Wendell Holmes (1809-94), a physician and highly regarded poet, was the father of the Supreme Court justice; Henry Wadsworth Longfellow (1807-82); Ralph Waldo Emerson (1803-82); Jean Louis Rodolphe Agassiz (1807-73); Charles Eliot Norton (1827-1908), Boston literary light; and Cornelius Conway Felton (1807-62), president of Harvard College.

escort is to be Pierce Butler, who will be accompanied by his daughter Fanny. Odd changes sometimes occur in people's relations to each other, and that Mrs. Fisher should travel with Butler is one of the oddest. She is an intimate friend of Mrs. Kemble & Fisher is the trustee of the latter, and both Fisher & his wife were not long ago loud in the denunciations of Butler, & Mrs. Fisher even went so far as to refuse to speak to him. But about a year ago, Fisher wished to invite Mrs. Owen Wister to a party, for her mother's sake chiefly. He did not like to do this without also asking Fanny Butler, and he could not ask her without including her father. So he left a card for Butler & invited him. Butler went to the party and as he well knows how to do, if he pleases, made himself acceptable to Mrs. Fisher. The acquaintance being thus renewed, secession I suppose has proved a bond of sympathy and when Butler heard that Mrs. Fisher was going to Carolina, as he also wished and intended to go to Georgia about the same time, he offered to be her escort & this offer was accepted. She expects to be absent a month, thinks that most probably it will be her last visit to her family & friends in the South, and that she had better go now, before affairs get into a worse state to render her going at all inconvenient or impossible.

APRIL 1, 1861 | Was obliged to go to town to get sweet potato seed, &c, for Mount Harmon. Called at McMichael's. He says he thinks the administration has no plan and, such is the position of affairs, can have none. He thinks the border states will all go. He saw Mr. Chase,[10] a member of the Cabinet, a few days ago, who told him the only thing left now was to call a convention of the people & let them decide how the Union was to be divided, and that they would have to adopt the plan of recognizing secession as a right & provide a legal mode by which a state might secede at pleasure. In other words, as McMichael said, my plan of legalized secession. But to call a convention of the

---

10. Salmon P. Chase (1808–73), a Free Soil Democrat and later Republican from Ohio, served in the U.S. Senate and as governor of Ohio before the war. In 1861 Lincoln appointed him secretary of the treasury, and in 1864 he became chief justice of the United States, a position he held until his death.

people & throw open the question of combination into one or more confederacies, is nearly equivalent to authorizing anarchy. Every section, every leading politician would have a separate plan.

APRIL 10, 1861 | Gov. Curtin has sent a message to our legislature advising that the state be put on a war footing & that $500,000 be appropriated to arm the militia. The message is very temperate in language & sentiment. It is said that it will be immediately responded to by legislature & that even the Democrats will not venture to oppose the measure. Other northern states will no doubt follow the example and an array of strength will soon be presented by the North which may perhaps prevent bloodshed by showing the utter folly of resistance.

APRIL 13, 1861 | The news from Charleston is that yesterday Genl. Beauregard, in command there, by order of the authorities of the Confederate States demanded the surrender of Fort Sumter. Major Anderson replied that the demand was one with which "I *regret* that my sense of honor & my obligation to my government prevent my compliance," adding verbally, "if you do not batter us to pieces, we will be starved out in a few days," an answer which looks very suspicious if true. The Secy. of War telegraphed from Montgomery that if Anderson would name a time for evacuation and agree not to use his guns till then the attack would be postponed. He refused to accede to this. The firing by the southern party commenced at 4 o'clock yesterday morning & continued all day. The Union fleet had not arrived. The result at the latest date was that two guns of Sumter were silenced & a breach made in the wall. A few on the secession side were wounded, none killed. Anderson has a very small garrison, only 75 men, not enough to work all the guns. The other side has 7000 men at the forts & batteries.

Henry brought out the afternoon papers which had later intelligence, as telegrams come every hour. He also got a despatch with the news up to 6 o'clock. The accounts are various; the firing had continued all day; the ships had not arrived; they had arrived & were taking part in the fight; Fort Sumter was in flames; Anderson was firing hot shot on Charleston and the city was burning; Anderson had surrendered; and, the last, the Palmetto flag was flying on Fort Sumter. Immense crowds block up the streets in town at the newspaper and telegraph offices and the excitement is intense.

APRIL 15, 1861 | No doubt Fort Sumter is taken and its surrender has roused the war passions of the North to a fearful pitch. From all quarters come accounts that the people are arming, and the danger now is that they will go too far. The South has sowed the wind and is likely to reap the whirlwind. The President has issued a proclamation calling for 75,000 troops. He could get ten times as many. It is to be hoped that this demonstration of force will keep the border states quiet and especially Virginia, in which case the cotton states cannot long maintain their present position. Went to town at 12. Found the city in a state of dangerous excitement. Several well-known persons, who had openly expressed secession opinions had been assaulted in the streets. At the office of an obscure newspaper at the corner of 4th and Chesnut, the editor had been foolish enough to hang out a Palmetto flag. The office was attacked by the mob & only saved by the mayor & police.[11] The mob then visited all the newspaper offices & insisted on their showing the American flag. Prominent individuals known to sympathize with the South are threatened.

APRIL 18, 1861 | Went to town with Bet at 12. The streets are all of a flutter with flags, streaming from windows, hotels, stores, &c. The passenger cars are all decorated with them. Indeed, they are necessary to protect the houses of persons suspected of "secession" opinions from insult by the mob. Fortunately, the sentiments of the people are so generally loyal to the government that, tho we are to have the curse of civil war, we are not likely to suffer from the greater evil of partizan war among ourselves. It is a war of sections, and if the border states

---

11. This paper, advocating secessionist principles and called *The Palmetto Flag*, had just been started at 337 Chestnut Street. It suspended publication after the visit of the mob.

should join the South, as now seems probable, it will become a war between two powerful nations and all the more bitter, bloody, & obstinate, because they are of the same race. Went to Henry's office, who is overwhelmed with affairs, and to McMichael's, where I met Captn. du Pont of the Navy and Mr. Henry Winter Davis of Maryland, a very prominent Republican politician during the late presidential campaign.[12] du Pont,[13] who lives near Wilmington, says the Union feeling in Delaware is perfectly sound. Mr. Davis does not speak with confidence of Maryland, tho he thinks there is not much reason to fear. The Eastern Shore is generally secession. Strange to say, the men of business are so likewise, tho two thirds of the trade of Baltimore depends on the North. He says that the government must occupy Maryland by military power if necessary, as communication of Washington & the North must be kept open. The town is more tranquil, tho in an excited state. It is at the risk of any man's life that he utters publicly a sentiment in favor of secession or the South, and many persons, particularly southern men living here or persons with southern property and connections, are in a painful position. We live under a democracy & mob rule and, tho the Democrats are quiet now & most of them are zealous in support of the government, the party nevertheless chafes at defeat and will take advantage of any turn in affairs to create trouble. They hate Lincoln and the Republicans cordially and they know how to rouse & direct the brute force of society to serve their purposes. Called to see Chas. Ingersoll & had a long talk with him. He is greatly excited and his opinions are most extravagant & absurd. If he were to utter in the street one half what he said to me, he would lose his life. His father is still more violent. I feel by no means easy about them.

12. Henry Winter Davis (1817–65), of Maryland, served in the U.S. House of Representatives as a member of the American party from 1855 to 1861, and the Unconditional Union Party from 1863 to 1865.

13. Samuel Francis du Pont (1803–65) was a veteran of the Mexican War and a member of the board set up to organize the Naval Academy at Annapolis. He spent nearly fifty years in the Navy before resigning in 1863 after his failure to capture Charleston, S.C.

APRIL 20, 1861 | The news of the day is that the Massachusetts regiment fought its way thro the streets of Baltimore & had reached Washington,[14] that the bridges of the Wilmington & Balto. railroad are burnt below Havre de Grace,[15] that Hicks[16] has declared the U. S. forces shall not march thro Maryland to subjugate the South, and that the state will probably secede & join the South. It is not easy to describe the feeling this news produced in town. Everyone I saw, with the exception of two or three Democrats, is filled with rage and resentment. The cry is now for a war of extermination on the South. It is declared that Baltimore will be burnt to the ground if it attempts to resist the passage of troops.

Went to Mr. C. J. I.'s. Had a most painful conversation with him which I will not repeat. All his party passions are enlisted for the South. I fear he may make himself the object of popular resentment & thus draw injury upon some connected with him. Drove with Bet to Brookwood in the evening. Mr. & Mrs. Purviance there. They came some days ago & started to return to Baltimore today, but were obliged by the burning of the bridges to come back.

APRIL 22, 1861 | The town is in a wild state of excitement. Everybody is drilling. I feel that I ought not to remain inactive, but as I am never free from gout & constantly liable to severe attacks of it, I would not be a very effective soldier. I could stand, however, and pull a trigger. Went to Wm. Wister and told [him] I thought of offering to join the home guard forming in Germantown. He said he thought it folly to do so as there were plenty of young & vigorous men eager for such work.

14. The 6th Massachusetts Regiment was mobbed while en route to Washington. Three soldiers and eleven civilians were killed.

15. On the night of April 19, 1861, the railroad bridges of the Philadelphia, Wilmington and Baltimore Railroad and of the Northern Central Railroad were burned by Marylanders to prevent the passage of northern troops through Baltimore. The bridges were soon repaired.

16. Thomas H. Hicks (1798-1865), was governor of Maryland from 1857 to 1862. Following the governorship he served in the U.S. Senate as a Unionist, from 1862 until his death.

APRIL 23, 1861 | In the afternoon some men called on me, asking me to subscribe to a paper calling for the formation of a home guard at the Rising Sun and to attend a meeting there this evening. I consented to both. Went to the meeting. Mr. [Charles] Magarge was made chairman, Mr. [Samuel] Maupay & myself vice-presidents, and I stated the object of the meeting, which was, as I supposed, to form a home guard for the defense of Phila: to act under the orders of the same kind of guard organized in the city. According to the directions of that authority, this force is to be composed of two classes, those over the age of 45 and those under, the former to be considered a reserve to be called on only if necessity requires it. Dickinson Logan was there. Most of those assembled were laboring men. It was not very pleasant work, but there is no help for it. There must be a force created and, tho I think there is very little probability of its being needed to defend the city from southern invasion, it may be needed to preserve order at home.

APRIL 27, 1861 | The slaves are running away from Maryland in great numbers, whole families at a time. It is stated that 500 have gone within the last two weeks. They can go now without risk of capture here. No one, I fancy, would venture at this time in any part of Penna: to attempt the execution of the fugitive slave law.

APRIL 29, 1861 | Went to town. Met Wm. Gilpin in the street. He is on his way to Colorado, of which territory he is governor. . . . He speaks highly of Lincoln. He says the state of affairs in Washington at the time of the inauguration was fearful. The plans of the conspirators had been made so long and deliberately that every subordinate officer in the departments was a traitor in active communication with the enemy, and even the servants in the White House were spies. That the people of the District were disaffected and the army demoralized, the officers being chiefly southern men. The President thus found himself in the midst of traitors armed with official authority. His task was therefore most difficult. It was some time before this could be found out. When discovered, a remedy could not be immediately applied without disturbing the routine business of the departments by displacing experienced subordinates. The work of reorganization & preparation was necessarily slow. Gilpin said that but for the destruction of the arsenal at Harper's Ferry, about two weeks ago, the arms would have been seized by the enemy and Washington would undoubtedly have been taken. He does not even now consider it safe & says that to make it so it must be garrisoned by at least 50,000 men. He considers the power of the South very formidable & says the war will be a long & expensive struggle requiring an army of half a million of troops. He talks rather wildly, I think, for I cannot imagine that the South has resources for a long war or even a short one.

MAY 1, 1861 | The news today continues favorable. No abatement of the war spirit in the North, troops hurrying forward to Washington & opinion changing in Maryland in favor of the government. The finest troops sent are from New England, as might be expected, as there the Saxon blood is most pure and civilization, as a consequence, highest. All the papers speak with admiration of the Massachusetts & Rhode Island regiments, their drill, their dress, the martial bearing, handsome well-cut features, athletic forms and pleasant manners of the men. The Rhode Island regiment is commanded in person by the governor, a man under 30 years of age & worth 5 millions of dollars.[17] They take with them artillery and arms of the best description. Thus do we see the qualities of race display themselves. New England is far superior to the rest of this country in its moral and intellectual standard, in its industry & wealth, in morals & literary culture. The rapid progress of New York & the Northwest arises from the spirit & enterprise of the men of New England by whom they were settled, and by whom they are now governed. New England is a small region, sterile & cold, but it governs this country, and, in like manner, old England, a bleak island, colonizes & governs half the world.

MAY 7, 1861 | Henry has failed. I met him on the steps of his office. "How are you," I said. "I am alive," said he, "& that is all. It is over."

---

17. William Sprague (1830–1915) was elected governor of Rhode Island in 1859, and again in 1861. He served in the U.S. Senate from 1863 to 1875.

"Well," I replied, "there are worse things than losing money." "I cannot talk now," he said, "it will unnerve me and I have much to do." We parted. He looked very badly. After some hours, I went back. He was sitting with George Smith.[18] Now that the strain of effort & uncertainty was over, Henry seemed calmer than he has been for weeks. He said that for a long time he had not slept except by use of anodynes. That when he made his situation known this morning he had met with the utmost sympathy & kindness. That he had now to go to work to support his family. That six months ago he was worth a million. After George went, he spoke of the money he had lent me. That he should never claim it or want it & that he did not anticipate the possibility of his creditors doing so. That it now amounted to $20,000. I told him that as I had always considered it a debt, I should, of course, do so now, more than ever. But that I regarded it as a debt of honor as he had always told me it was [a] gift. That for his sake, & my own too, it must now be so considered, for I would not consent to its being assets for his creditors, as I had not accepted the money on such terms. He replied that he should be very glad so to consider it, but that it was unfortunately on his books and he could not take it off them. And such is just the position of the matter, which I thought of some months ago, when he first told me of his danger. I did not speak to him about it then, as it was as much too late as it is now, for a release of the debt in prospect of insolvency would have been invalid & legally a fraud. The difference it makes to me is that if I have time I can expect to work down the debt from my business at Mount Harmon and that the restoration of peace & prosperity will restore the value of the property. The farm & stock 6 months ago were worth 40 to $50,000. A forced sale now would be ruinous. The difference it makes to Henry is that the debt belongs to his children, which may be important to them. I suppose, however, that even if the creditors should claim it, I could find some way of preventing a sale, unless they were very hard & inexorable, which is not probable. These seem strange words—creditors, sales—to use about Henry, for many years

18. George R. Smith, a friend of the diarist.

so successful, so rich, so lavish and generous that he seemed the favorite of fortune & born not only to enjoy but to dispense her favors. The disclosure of this morning was no shock to me, for I had been prepared for it by previous intimations and my thoughts had been busy with all its consequences. Indeed, for many years I have looked forward to it as a probable event. I believe in the government of this world by moral laws which act with as much uniformity as the laws of matter, and when I saw profuse & extravagant expenditure accompanied & supported by heavy speculations in stocks, my mind foreboded the result. . . .

I know nothing of the details of Henry's affairs, but the fact is about this, that all his securities are pledged for borrowed money. That the fall in prices of stock of all kinds has been so great that these securities, if sold now, would not realize a sum sufficient to pay the amount for which they are pledged. But will they be sold now? Will those who hold them force a sale at a time when the whole community stands on the verge of bankruptcy and mutual forbearance is the interest of all? I cannot think it possible, and if delay is granted, with a restoration of confidence, prices would rise & the debts be paid. On the other hand, who can tell when confidence will be restored? We are on the eve of a civil war, which may last for years and the results of which no one can foresee. Besides these pledged securities, Henry has much valuable real estate, houses in town, ground rents, and his place at Brookwood, where there are now over 300 acres of land. The wine & silver in his house must be worth 30 or $40,000.

MAY 11, 1861 | Saw Henry for a few minutes. He seemed in better spirits and says that his failure is only a suspension, that he will have the entire control of his affairs & hopes that he will have something handsome when they are settled. The sentiment of the public from what I can hear is altogether favorable to him. He was considered at the head of the business community, was very useful & public-spirited, very generous & liberal to all men in business relations, and has so many friends and well wishers that I think no very serious evil can result from what has happened.

MAY 12, 1861 | Dickinson Logan walked home with Bet from church. He said that an officer who had lately visited Camp Curtin, near Harrisburg, told him that it was a most shocking scene of filth, discomfort and disorder. The importance of the commissariat department is not recognized by a people not accustomed to war, nor of proper discipline either. Dickinson said that the men had scarcely sufficient food, no comforts, and were fast becoming dissatisfied & demoralized. The military force of this state is sadly in need of a head. Neither Govr. Curtin nor Genl. Patterson[19] have the requisite ability and moral influence.

MAY 15, 1861 | Called to see Mrs. Page, my old friend Celestine Davis. Her father was a very rich planter in Mississippi who lived here some years before his death & whom I knew very well. He left Mrs. Page a large estate of land & Negroes, a cotton plantation in Louisiana worth $300,000. Found her in great trouble as Page had been sent for & had gone to Louisiana. As he is a Union man, tho a Virginian, I do not think him very safe or the estate either, and his wife is very uneasy about him. Met Morris Waln[20] in the street. He told me that those best acquainted with Henry's affairs say that he will yet be a rich man when his estate is settled.

MAY 16, 1861 | Finished in pencil & partly copied an article on the position of Maryland in the present crisis. No news of much interest in the papers. I have so much gout or rheumatism in my knees & hip that I walk with pain. I have not been entirely free from it since the attack last winter & for a week or two past it has been very unpleasant.

MAY 17, 1861 | Two persons, correspondents, one of them for the *New York Times*, the other for the *Phila. Inquirer*, have had the impudence to use my signature Cecil, so that I do not care to employ it again.

19. Robert Patterson (1792-1881), an Irish immigrant who came to the United States in 1799, was a veteran of the War of 1812 and the Mexican War. In 1861 he reentered military service, but after showing himself an unsuccessful commander, was honorably discharged on July 27, 1861.
20. S. Morris Waln, shipping and general commercial merchant.

I am very sorry that [R. Patterson] Kane is to marry Lilly [Fisher].[21] She is a lovely, excellent girl and I have not much faith in him. He is clever & designing & I fear will exert an evil influence not only on her happiness, but on Fisher and his wife. I think he will govern the family for his own ends. They are a remarkable race, these Kanes. The father, Judge Kane, had ability, acuteness, some learning, plausibility, but he was without moral principle. He was unscrupulous as a politician and was a demogague even on the bench. His manners were agreeable, kind & cordial, his conversation intelligent, flowing & genial, yet it was easy to perceive that he wanted truth & sincerity. His sons are like him. They have talents, accomplishments and courage, indeed a spirit of daring adventure. Elisha made himself famous by his expedition to the Arctic regions. Yet it is now believed that many things recorded in his account of that expedition are positively false. Tom Kane many years ago accompanied the Mormons on their celebrated march from Nauvoo to Utah and wrote a most interesting description of it, which is little better than a romance as he himself, I was told, acknowledged. Not long ago, when there was difficulty with the Mormons, he was sent by Mr. Buchanan to negotiate with them. It was a difficult & hazardous journey & he performed it with ability & courage. He is now living in one of the mountainous & interior counties of this state, called the wild cat region, where he has land. He has enlisted a company of 300 "wild cats" for this war. He is a little, weak, boyish, sickly looking fellow, as was his brother Elisha, and no one would suppose him a fit leader for a company of "wild cats." Yet his

21. Robert Patterson Kane (1827-1906) was the son of U.S. District Judge John Kintzing Kane (1795-1858), a Democrat who had been appointed by President James K. Polk. Patterson's brother, Elisha Kent Kane (1820-57), was a naval surgeon, a Mexican War veteran, and an explorer whose exploits took him to China, the Philippines, West Africa, and the Arctic. Elisha described the adventures that Fisher found unbelievable in *The U.S. Grinnell Expedition in Search of Sir John Franklin: A Personal Narrative* (New York, 1853). Thomas Leiper Kane (1822-83), another of Patterson's brothers, was an abolitionist, Union general, and advocate for the Mormons, publishing several books on the religious sect. Elizabeth Francis "Lilly" Fisher was a cousin of the diarist.

diminutive body is animated by a bold spirit. Notwithstanding all this, however, people do not respect or trust the Kanes.

MAY 19, 1861 | Morris Hallowell[22] has failed & Henry says that all Market St. is bankrupt because of the debts due from the South, which southern merchants refuse to pay, writing the most insulting letters. Indeed, these debts have been confiscated by some of the southern states. They amount to many millions of dollars. Bad as all this is, we have as yet scarcely seen the commencement of this war. There has been no fighting. When blood has been shed the terrible nature of the conflict will be felt.

MAY 20, 1861 | My article, "Maryland," was published in the *North American* this morning as an editorial.

MAY 22, 1861 | In the evening Dickinson Logan & his wife here. Like Dickinson much, a fine, manly, good fellow. He has been a great sportsman and was in the habit of going every year into the wilderness of the West, Iowa &c. to shoot, camping out for months, far from the settlements. He shot grouse on the prairies & moose on the Canada frontier, going into the depths of the forest accompanied only by two or three Indians to carry luggage.

MAY 24, 1861 | The aggressive movement of our troops commenced last night. Alexandria and Arlington heights that command Washington and a point on some railroad near that city were occupied successfully. There was scarcely any resistance, the Virginia force in Alexandria dispersing immediately. A painful event, however, occurred. Col. Ellsworth, commander of the New York Zouaves, went up to pull down the secession flag on the tavern in Alexandria where the company was quartered. As he came down stairs with the flag in his hand, he was shot dead by the keeper of the tavern, named Jackson, who fired from some place of concealment. Jackson was instantly

22. Morris L. Hallowell (1809-80) was the senior partner in a large dry goods house, importer of "silk and fancy goods."

killed by one of the Zouaves.[23] Ten thousand U. S. troops have marched into Virginia and now the war has begun in earnest.

MAY 28, 1861 | This is our wedding day. Ten years ago we were married and came out here. It seems like a dream these ten years, but a dream of happiness, unclouded by a painful recollection connected with my dear wife, an unkind look, word or thought. What happy days, what delightful emotions, what deep feelings of peace & joy & content, what priceless affections, what intellectual and moral growth do I owe to her. These ten years at any rate are beyond the reach of evil fortune. During all that time my love, respect, and admiration for my sweet companion have increased as I have better known the strength & tenderness of her nature, her truth & nobleness, & her bright & clear intelligence. During all that time, I have rejoiced more & more every day over the blessing that God has given me in her. It would be presumptuous to expect ten years more of such happiness, but I do not much dread any evil that does not affect her or separate me from her, and I cherish the hope that when the inevitable separation does occur, it will be temporary and that hereafter, in some way that I cannot imagine, we may live with & for each other forever, as we do now.

MAY 29, 1861 | An event happened in Baltimore a day or two ago that may prove important. Mr. Jno. Merryman, president of the Md. Agric. Socty., and a gentleman of high respectability & good estate, was arrested by Genl. Cadwalader, in command of the U. S. force at Baltimore, for treason.[24] He had enlisted a troop for the secession cause. A writ of habeas corpus was issued by Taney,[25] Ch. Just. of the U. S. To

---

23. Elmer Ephraim Ellsworth (1837-61), a friend of President Lincoln's, had recruited a regiment from the New York volunteer firemen and had uniformed them like French Zouaves. He was killed at the Marshall House, in Alexandria, by its proprietor James W. Jackson on May 24, 1861.

24. John Merryman (1824-81), of the Maryland state militia, was arrested for "various acts of treason" by the order of Gen. George Cadwalader.

25. Roger B. Taney (1777-1864), of Maryland, was chief justice of the United States, appointed by President Andrew Jackson in 1835 and confirmed in 1836. Taney

this Cadwalader *sent* a reply, stating the cause of the arrest and refusing obedience to the writ on the ground that the habeas corpus was suspended by order of the President. The judge immediately issued an attachment against Cadwalader. The officer on going to the camp to serve it was refused admission. Here then is a conflict between civil & military authority that may become very serious. I have no doubt of the authority of the President to suspend the writ under the circumstances. The Constitution declares that it *may be* suspended, when the public safety requires it, in case of *rebellion* or foreign invasion, and surely the dangerous and uncertain condition of Baltimore at this time would justify such a step. It is nevertheless likely to create much excitement & cavil.

MAY 31, 1861 | Went to McMichael's. He told me that it was much desired that Meredith should accept the office of attorney general of the state, which had been offered to him by the governor. I told him I thought it would be a great thing to get Meredith's knowledge & intellect at such a time as this in an influential position, but that I feared his state of health was an insuperable objection. McMichael replied that it would be arranged that the active service, the work, would be performed by subordinates, that consultation & advice only would be expected from him, and asked me to speak to him on the subject & urge him to accept. I went to his office & had a long talk with him on various affairs, among them this offer. He said he had positively rejected it four times, that his health made it impossible to perform the duties. I told him that all the duties would be to talk as he talked with me, as the *work* would be done by others. That Phila: and Penna: were sadly deficient in men who could think & who had any knowledge of constitutional law & the principles of government. That for want of this knowledge in such a crisis as the present, blunders were likely to be made from zeal & passion & wrong views which might produce most serious consequences. That as the legal adviser

was sitting in his capacity as a judge of the U.S. Circuit Court for the District of Maryland.

of the government he could be of essential service, if only by preventing false steps and rash actions upon erroneous ideas. That there was no one in the city fit for the place and that if he would take it I felt sure he could not only do important service but would inspire confidence in the public mind. I got him at length to say that he would reconsider the matter.

JUNE 4, 1861 | Meredith has accepted the attorney generalship.

JUNE 5, 1861 | We have had civil war now for more than two months and yet active operations have scarcely commenced. The country had enjoyed the blessings of peace so long that the use of arms was almost forgotten and when the occasion arose which demanded them, tho men enough to form armies were forthcoming, everything else was deficient—discipline, clothing, weapons, & ammunition. All these had to be provided on short notice, and that they have been furnished so soon is proof not only of the intelligence and energy of the people, but of the enthusiasm by which they are animated. A large force has been assembled, equipped and posted at the strategic points. The interest at the present moment centres in Virginia, which is expected every day to be the scene of the first conflict. The army has already commenced an advancing movement from Washington. The troops of the enemy are concentrating to oppose it, in what strength is not certainly known. They are commanded by good officers, most of them southern men in our army who have resigned their places & joined the South, and their supply of arms is abundant. It is probable they can make a stout resistance at first, that the U. S. forces may meet with checks & reverses, but the ultimate result is certain, for the South is too weak in wealth and numbers to resist the North.

JUNE 7, 1861 | Fanny Butler was at Wakefield[26] this morning. She said that she had got a letter from young Hartman Kuhn, who is in the

---

26. Wakefield was built about 1798 by the diarist's grandfather, Thomas Fisher, and was subsequently the residence of the diarist's uncle, William Logan Fisher. It was inherited by the Fox family who ultimately sold it to the city. Wakefield stood near Lindley Avenue and Ogontz Avenue, what is now Wakefield Park, until 1985, when it was torn down.

First City Troop, giving an account of the hardships of camp life, which must be severe enough to young men like him, accustomed to luxury. This troop has always been and is now composed of gentlemen, many of them rich and of the best families. It has always been prompt and efficient when needed to suppress riot and disorder at home. It is equipped with arms and horses at the expense of its members and volunteered eagerly for this war. It left town a few days ago and the start was quite a scene. A crowd of ladies was present with bouquets, garlands, waving handkerchiefs, tears, and affectionate farewells. It has gone to Chambersburg and is likely soon to see service. Tom James is the captain, two of the Kuhns,[27] Harvey Ashhurst, young Camac,[28] & many others of the "curled darlings" of the city are members. Pat Kane is also in it, much to Lilly's grief.

JUNE 10, 1861 | The city quiet, except that companies of soldiers are constantly met in the streets. We have suddenly become a military people and are likely to remain so. It has been discovered that laisser aller won't do in politics at any rate, and that society must be armed for self-defense. A military career will be permanently added to the occupations and ambition of life in this country. A standing army will henceforth be a necessity—Union or no Union. The only news is of military operations in Virginia preparatory to a conflict, which is looked forward to with some apprehension. The enemy has certainly a large force, variously reported from 70 to 140,000. It is commanded also by generals of experience & scientific ability, Davis, Beauregard and Johnston.[29] The latter is the husband of my old friend Lydia

---

27. The other Kuhn was James Hamilton Kuhn, elected to the First Troop Philadelphia City Cavalry in 1858 and killed in battle on June 30, 1862.

28. William Camac, second lieutenant of the Troop.

29. Pierre Gustave Toutant Beauregard (1818-93), of Louisiana, was a graduate of West Point in 1838 and a veteran of the Mexican War. In February 1861 he resigned his commission in the U.S. Army and was appointed a brigadier general in the Confederate Army. Joseph E. Johnston (1807-91), of Virginia, graduated from West Point in 1829, was a veteran of the Mexican and Seminole Wars, and was appointed quartermaster general of the U.S. Army in 1860. In 1861 he also resigned his commission to join the Virginia militia and later the Confederate forces.

McLane, a very intelligent and beautiful girl when I knew her. I saw her last autumn in the cars at Wilmington on my way to Mount Harmon and she retained her good looks and graceful, animated manner. Johnston was a distinguished officer in our army, but resigned a short time ago & entered the service of the "Confederate States," under the influence of that powerful sympathy that binds southern men together and which so many of the officers of our army & navy have been unable to resist. They give up good pay & all hopes to fight for a cause which cannot succeed, in which they have to endure every privation and hardship. They have the merit therefore of disinterestedness. They say they cannot fight against their native states and against their *social class*, for they consider this a war against slavery, & slave owners constitute a *caste* in the South.

JUNE 12, 1861 | Met Captn. Coppee[30] in the street. He is a southern man by birth, was educated at West Point, served with distinction in the Mexican War, and is now a professor in the University of Penna. He is a friend of Wm. Palmer, and E. H. Butler publishes some works which he edits or writes for schoolbooks. Thru Butler, I made his acquaintance a year or two ago & have met him occasionally since. He is gentlemanlike and well educated, and I doubt not accomplished in his profession. Butler says that Genl. Scott has great confidence in his ability. It has more than once occurred to me that at a time when military knowledge, especially in Penna:, was greatly needed, such a man should be employed not in the university but in the army. I said as much to him this morning. He replied that the state has not asked for his services, that if it did they would be rendered provided he had an appropriate rank offered to him. I went to McMichael & spoke to him. He said he knew Coppee well, that his services would be very valuable, that he had been thought of & suggested, but that his being a southern man was an objection as perhaps Penna: troops would not

---

30. Henry Coppee (1821-95), a Georgian, graduated from West Point in 1845, and resigned from the army in 1855, when he became a professor of history and literature at the University of Pennsylvania. Following the Civil War he was president of Lehigh University.

like that, and that all sorts of intrigues were going on and all sorts of influence brought to bear on the military appointment, which, many of them, were very bad. He said that the appointment of two brigadier generals was now under consideration by the governor, Charles J. Biddle being spoken of as one and Richd. Rush[31] as the other. I said that there could be no doubt as to Biddle's capacity and as little that Coppee was far superior to Rush. He agreed with me and advised me to speak to Meredith, who as attorney general would have controlling influence. I went to Meredith and stated my views. He listened to all I said, but did not choose to commit himself, tho I could see that he thought as I do about Rush. I went to Butler, told him what I had done & asked who else I could see that knew Coppee & could exert influence.

JUNE 13, 1861 | Heard today that Ch. Biddle will probably be selected as one of the brigadier generals, and that if the governor selects one from the eastern he must take one from the western part of the state. Such are the petty maxims that rule our politics. Suppose there are two in the east fit for the place & none in the west, what then? Take an incompetent person from the west, of course. Under this rule Coppee has no chance.

JUNE 16, 1861 | A "Confederate" privateer out of Charleston has been captured and brought into New York. How will her crew be treated by our government, as prisoners of war or as pirates?[32] Under the theory that the Union is unbroken, they are by act of Congress pirates. On the other hand, this rebellion is of such large proportions that it is in fact a sectional war. Will the government treat it as a mere insurrection or accord to the South the rights of war? If so, privateers cannot be regarded as pirates. The question is not free from difficulty in

---

31. Richard Henry Rush, a graduate of West Point in 1846, resigned from the army in 1854. He was later to command the 6th Pennsylvania Cavalry, known as Rush's Lancers.

32. The privateer was the *Savannah*, captured by the *Perry*, a naval brig. The Philadelphia newspapers assumed that the *Savannah's* crew of thirty would be hanged as pirates.

principle or in policy. If these men are punished as pirates, measures of retaliation of a desperate character may be expected on the other side, passions would become more and more exasperated and a frightful character of ferocity may be given to a contest which is deplorable at best.

JUNE 17, 1861 | Some time ago McMichael asked me to write an article on the necessity at the present crisis of selecting men of education and ability for public stations. Began one this morning.

JUNE 19, 1861 | Copied the article in the morning—14 pages. It is entitled "The right men in the right places." Got a letter from Severson.[33] He says the sweet potatoes are dying, that they have the black rot. If I lose the crop it will be a disappointment as I calculated to make $1000 by it. Went to town at 1½. Took the article to McMichael & told him he might either print it as an editorial or a communication.[34]

JUNE 24, 1861 | There is soon to be an election for a member of Congress in Phila: to supply the vacancy left by the appointment of E. Joy Morris as minister to Turkey. It was hoped that someone fit for the place in such a crisis as the present would be nominated without distinction of party. But it seems our people cannot be taught even by civil war that knowledge & ability are necessary in public life. The Republicans, by strict party action and the ordinary party means, have nominated one Chas. O'Neill, late a member of the state legislature & a small, hack politician of no mark or reputation. The Democrats have nominated Chas. J. Biddle, a man of high character & ability, but, as I know, very southern in his sympathies, opposed to this war &, tho now serving in the army, very far from sympathizing with the purposes of the government.[35] It is very unfortunate, for Biddle is likely

33. Thomas Severson was Fisher's farmer at Mount Harmon from 1853 to 1867, when Fisher, suspecting that Severson had cheated him out of the farm's profits year after year, discharged him.

34. It was published on June 24, 1861, as an editorial.

35. Col. Biddle's point of view was that of a large number of prominent Philadelphians who, although loyal (Biddle himself took the field three times during the war

to be elected & the power of the city given to the Democrats, whose leaders are all unsound & disloyal. Anything that now tends to divide the North is most dangerous.

JUNE 28, 1861 | In the evening went with Bet to pay a visit to the Wm. Wisters. His son Langhorne is in the army and William is in a state of faddish and extreme excitement about the war, denounces all who are opposed to it in terms of absurd violence and advocates lynch law & mob rule to restrain opinion, the very things which now desolate & disgrace the South. His language was very intemperate &, considering that Bet's family are sympathizers with secession, very ill bred.

JULY 3, 1861 | Charles Biddle was elected yesterday. Only half the usual vote was brought out, the Democrats voting and the others being indifferent. Had the Republicans selected a suitable candidate Biddle would have been defeated by a large majority. But many would not vote at all. He was elected only by 200 majority, which with such an opponent as O'Neill would have been much larger, but he is suspected of a leaning towards the South and justly suspected. But that he is now in the army, which by many is regarded as proof of his loyalty, he would have been defeated even by O'Neill. The folly of the Republicans has been suicidal. They chose a candidate of no mark or reputation & chose him by the narrowest partizan means at a time when public opinion demanded a man of the highest ability & they were justly punished by defeat.

JULY 4, 1861 | Francis Bolivar, who is still at Somerville,[36] came over in the afternoon. He brought an invitation for us to go there in the evening as Dickinson was to have the Rising Sun Home Guard & an

---

despite ill health), deplored many of the measures used to prosecute the war and were repelled by abolitionist sentiment in the Republican party.

36. Somerville, on the west side of Germantown Avenue, opposite the Fair Hill Burying Ground and extending to Broad Street, was erected early in the nineteenth century by Albanus Charles Logan, and was later occupied by Dr. J. Dickinson Logan.

exhibition of fireworks.[37] I determined to go and drove Francis over at 7½. The Guard came at 8, marching with flag & drum. Dickinson is their captain and drilled them on the lawn. He is a fine, manly fellow and very popular with them. He told me that they insisted on his being their captain and as he had been born and bred in the neighborhood he could not refuse. That he should go on until he got them uniformed & armed and then give it up. There were tables for refreshments under the trees, & a bountiful supply and a beautiful display of fireworks. Besides the Guard, there were many villagers present & many women & children, I suppose altogether three hundred people. They seemed to enjoy themselves and I thought the scene rather pleasant, but, as I was suffering all the time from gout, somewhat fatiguing. I left the crowd & came home by 10 o'clock.

JULY 6, 1861 | The President's message in the paper this morning. Read it with great satisfaction. In sentiment, thought and style it is similar to the inaugural speech. It is simple, clear, positive & is marked throughout by evident sincerity & truth. It is wholly free from egotism or desire to produce an effect, but is earnest & candid. It shows, moreover, remarkable power of thought & argument. The reflections are eminently just and the right of secession is treated in a manner at once clear, comprehensive and original. It contains the following happy definition of a sovereign state, "a political community without a political superior," which is so terse & complete, that it deserves a place in the science of politics. The style is not polished or graceful, but nervous, compact & clear, the utterance of strong convictions seeking expression. The whole production is pervaded by good feeling and loyal catholic spirit.[38] In this hour of its trial, the country seems to have found in Mr. Lincoln a great man. I should judge that he has a clear head, a good heart, a strong will and high

---

37. Francis Bolivar, ill-fated natural son of Fernando Bolivar, nephew of Simon Bolivar. Francis had been brought to Philadelphia by his father in 1857 to attend Germantown Academy.

38. Fisher was so pleased with Lincoln's message that he wrote an article about it which appeared as an editorial in the *North American* on July 10, 1861.

moral sentiment. Should he prove equal to the promise given by his speech, his message and his conduct thus far, he will be an unspeakable blessing to the nation. He was got, however, by accident, by the chance of a caucus nomination. His selection was a surprise to himself and to the people. By far the most prominent candidate was Mr. Seward, who had been intriguing for the place for years. Next to him was Simon Cameron of this state.[39] Had either been chosen, we would have been ruined. The ability and character Mr. Lincoln displays opens, beyond the gloom of the present, a happy future for the country. He calls for at least 400,000 men and 400 millions of dollars to make the war short & decisive. Congress will grant them without hesitation. He may be trusted with this power and will carry the country with him.

JULY 18, 1861 | The news this morning is that [General Irvin] McDowell, with 55,000 troops, had advanced into Virginia and taken Fairfax Court House without resistance, the enemy retreating towards Manassas Junction. It is said the rebel force in Virginia is now 60,000 at the Junction, 10,000 at Richmond, 15,000 at Yorktown, 20,000 at Norfolk—in all 105,000. It is supposed that Genl. Scott wished the advance movement delayed a fortnight, but yielded to the impatience of the army and of the public. A battle is now expected every hour.

JULY 22, 1861 | The news in the morning paper was that yesterday there was a severe battle, at Bull's Run, which lasted for 9 hours, with great loss on both sides and that the enemy was driven from their batteries and our army following towards Manassas Gap. Mrs. Logan & her son Sidney, with Francis Bolivar, came at 10½. When they left, Bet & I drove to the station at 7th St. & went to town. Found the city in a ferment at news received by telegraph since the morning

---

39. Simon Cameron (1799-1889) was a U.S. senator from Pennsylvania, serving as a Democrat from 1845 to 1849, and as a Republican from 1857 to 1861 and again from 1867 to 1877. Cameron was Lincoln's first secretary of war and also minister to Russia in 1862. In 1863 he unsuccessfully attempted to bribe enough Pennsylvania legislators to elect him to the Senate.

papers were out. The intelligence was that our army had been completely routed and put to flight, 10,000 men killed, 8 rifled cannon and two batteries of light artillery taken by the enemy, and that our troops were in rapid flight towards Washington. Making allowance for the usual exaggeration on such occasions, there seems little room to doubt that we have met with a signal defeat. It appears, so far as I can make it out, that our force was attacked on its march to Manassas & repulsed by Genl. Johnston, who had just arrived in time from Winchester. This result is due to want of military knowledge on our side and the possession of it by the enemy. Genl. Patterson ought to have prevented Johnston from going to Manassas.

JULY 23, 1861 | I went to McMichael's office and saw there an intelligent man, who is the chaplain to the Minnesota Regiment, and who was in the battle on Sunday from first to last. I listened to his account of what he saw with great interest, as it was a vivid picture of the scenes of war. He marched with his regiment until it went into action and was on the battlefield until the retreat. He saw nothing of the panic & flight, which happened at a distance from his position. He said they crossed the Run early in the morning & entered a wood. Soon they found wounded & dying men along the road. After a time they met a carriage in which was seated an officer in rich military dress, badly wounded, with bloody bandages around his neck, who bowed & smiled and faintly cheered them as they passed. This was Col. Slocum of a Rhode Island Regiment, who died the same day.[40]

As the duty of the chaplain was not fighting when his regiment was engaged, he employed himself in getting the wounded into an ambulance. He collected eleven & took them to the hospital. He was frequently exposed to fire, the balls whistling above his head. Of his company only 200 returned to their quarters. He marched with them in their retreat & was 30 hours on his feet with scarcely anything to eat. His narrative was very simple and circumstantial & free from egotism or ostentation. Gov. Sprague, the commander of the Rhode

40. Col. John S. Slocum, a veteran of the Mexican War and colonel of the 2nd Rhode Island Infantry, was killed on July 21, 1861, at Bull Run.

Island Regiment, a young man worth 6 millions of dollars, was in the battle & had his clothes torn with bullets and his horse shot under him. He lost the fine battery of the regiment, which, however, he spiked, but could not bring away as the horses were killed. Russell, the correspondent of the London *Times* was a spectator of the whole affair on horseback from a hill, and said that he never saw better fighting even in the Crimea.[41] There is a much better feeling in town today now that the truth is known, but everyone is impressed with the conviction that the war is a very stern and serious reality.

JULY 30, 1861 | Saw at Henry's office a brother of Harrison Smith,[42] a lieutenant of a regiment in Genl. Patterson's division, who has just returned with his company from the neighborhood of Harper's Ferry. He is a handsome, intelligent, gentlemanlike young man and gave us some interesting details of the war. He was in skirmishes and under fire several times. He says that the life of soldier is very pleasant. That one soon gets accustomed to hard fare, and fond of the excitement of new scenes and adventures every day. . . . That the soldiers are well fed & tho the first uniforms, hastily supplied, soon wore out & clothing was deficient for a time, new clothing has been furnished of good quality. The men enjoy good health, are in high spirits and all resolute & eager in the cause. In marching thro Virginia he had an opportunity of judging the sentiments of the people. Their hatred of the North is violent. The women hissed at the troops and reviled them as they passed thro villages; the men were all in the Confederate army. It happened often, however, that the soldiers were kindly received. They paid for everything they got, even for the privilege of camping in open fields, and no outrage of any kind was permitted. The people were not prepared for this, for they had been led to believe that the "northern hordes" came to ravage the country, plunder & destroy &

---

41. William Howard Russell, ace Crimean War correspondent of the London *Times*, came to America in 1861 to report the Civil War.

42. Charles Ross Smith (1829–97), brother and business partner of Harrison Smith, having completed the three months' campaign of 1861 as an infantry lieutenant, was about to join the 6th Pennsylvania Cavalry as a captain. He was to see much service during the war and rise to the rank of colonel.

set the Negroes free. On one occasion, some runaway Negroes joined the troops. They were immediately sent back to their masters. In the town where this occurred, there was, the next day, an election at which the Union ticket was carried in consequence of this act.

He was at Charlestown, one of the best villages in Virginia & surrounded by large farms of wealthy gentlemen. He said that they were constantly receiving information that arms were concealed in these houses, which, tho almost always false, made it necessary as a precaution to search them. That he was frequently detailed for this duty and visited many handsome residences in performance of it. In almost every case, nothing was found but fowling pieces, such as country gentlemen always keep, and uniformly none but the ladies of the family were at home, the men being in the army. His practice was to place a file of men at the door & make known in courteous language his errand to the mistress of the house, stating that he was obliged to perform his duty, but if she would send a servant with him he would give as little annoyance as possible. He was received with very cold politeness and some remonstrance at first, but his visit always ended in a friendly manner, often he was asked to dine and sometimes the house was offered as quarters for the officers, who were, indeed, a protection. Surprise was generally manifested at the orderly conduct of our troops, who committed no depredations, whereas the secession soldiers took without pay and without ceremony whatever they wanted, and they wanted whatever a farm could supply—horses, mules, cattle & provisions of all kinds. On one occasion, Mr. Smith made a search at the house of the wealthiest man near Charlestown. It was a handsome establishment. No one was at home but the lady of it and her daughter, a beautiful girl. The lady had a son, the daughter a lover in the Confederate army. When his duty was performed, Mr. Smith was invited to dine, which he did. The daughter, however, would not speak to him, and her mother apologized for her by saying that she had made a vow never to speak to a northern man. In the course of talk it appeared that they had many mutual acquaintances at the North, whom they & Mr. Smith, too, had met at Saratoga & other watering places. He spoke of one young lady, who was an intimate friend of the daughter, and the latter forgot her vow and began to make eager inquiries about her friend. She then laughed & said that as the vow was broken she would forget it in the present case and they parted very good friends.

AUGUST 1, 1861 | Met Genl. Patterson in the street. It seems to me that he has been unjustly censured by the press and I told him I thought so. He spoke in the highest terms of the ability of Beauregard & Johnston, both of whom he knows well. He thinks Washington in no danger, that no attack will be made or, if made, repulsed. He says there will be no battle now for some time. That the policy will be to drive the enemy if possible further South by making each successive position he takes untenable, thus avoiding the animosity produced by shedding blood, our object being to conquer and, at the same time, conciliate.

AUGUST 9, 1861 | There is an article today in the *New York Times*, recommending the emancipation of the slaves in the South as a war measure that would be speedy & effectual. Why not? says the writer. Slavery caused the war and it is waged for the sake of slavery. Destroy slavery then, which always has been and always will be the source of strife, and thus at one blow get rid of the cause of present and future mischief. It is by no means improbable that his advice will be followed.

AUGUST 12, 1861 | Called at McMichael's. Found several gentlemen there, Henry, Tom Turner, Capt. du Pont of the navy, & others. They were listening to an account by du Pont of things he had heard in Washington, whence he had just returned. He says the government will be obliged to declare martial law there as the place is full of secessionists, men & women, ladies & gentlemen in society, who communicate intelligence to the enemy and openly sympathize with the South. The ladies send delicacies to the prisoners of war—wine, cake, morning gowns & embroidered slippers. [Henri] Mercier, the French minister, is a secessionist; so is Lord Lyons[43] & others of the diplomatic circle. There is quite a clique of them who dine together every

---

43. Richard B. P. Lyons (1817–87), First Earl Lyons, was British minister in Washington from 1858 to 1865.

week. du Pont dined at Mr. Seward's with the Prince.[44] In his suite are some men of distinction and rank.

AUGUST 16, 1861 | Dined with Bet & Sidney at Brookwood. The place looks very well as the trees now make a fine show. From what Henry told me, he is likely to be able to keep it. He says that people in town are much discouraged about the war. Volunteers do not come forward as freely as they did and the feeling exhibited some weeks or months ago seems on the wane. The Democrats are organizing a peace party, in order to divide public opinion and weaken the efforts of the government. Such a party is really in alliance with the rebels of the South and playing into their hands.

AUGUST 17, 1861 | When I am without some employment which tasks my faculties, I am dissatisfied and feel that I am living to no purpose, which in such stirring times, or indeed in any times, no one ought to do. I cannot go to the wars, I am not in public life and do not wish to be, I see nothing that I can do unless it be to write articles for the newspapers & thus try to influence opinion. If McMichael's paper had a higher tone & standing, I would do this oftener.

AUGUST 20, 1861 | The only news of interest this morning was that yesterday Pierce Butler was arrested on a charge of treason and sent off to Fort Hamilton at New York. It is said that he had been in correspondence with the secessionists in the South, which I do not believe, unless about private business. He has expressed, however, since his return the strongest opinions in favor of the southern cause and wishes for its success in earnest language, as he did here the other day, and in such times as these that alone is sufficient to justify his arrest. I am sorry for him and for his daughters & sisters, and yet think it was right to commit him. Perhaps also it is a good thing for

---

44. Prince Napoleon Joseph Charles Paul Bonaparte, second son of Napoleon's brother Jerome, was traveling incognito with his wife, the eldest daughter of the King of Spain. Two weeks after this diary entry, three more French princes embarked for America to witness the war.

him, as it will keep him quiet and out of harm's way. I suppose he will be comfortable at the Fort and he will meet there a number of gentlemen from Baltimore, prisoners like himself & congenial companions. At 1 drove with Bet & Sidney up to Alverthorpe. Fisher in town. Saw only Mrs. F. and Lilly. We walked in the woods and enjoyed the beauty of the scene. The place is the handsomest by far in this neighborhood or in Penna: and displays good taste throughout. Mrs. F. soon got on the absorbing topic. She was very indignant at Butler's arrest and is in a state of painful agitation and excitement about the war and its consequences. She read us a letter she had received from Mrs. Allen Izard, full of bitterness against the North and declaring that the southern people will be exterminated rather than submit. She sees in the war only invasion and an attempt to subjugate the South. She cannot see that the South made war on the government, which is now only asserting its rightful authority. But every one in South Carolina has long since been beyond the reach of reason. Notwithstanding our discussion, nothing in the least unpleasant was said on either side.

AUGUST 21, 1861 | Went to McMichael's. Told him that I thought I would write an article on the writ of habeas corpus as I had some views of the subject that would show clearly the propriety of the conduct of the President, and which were new, so far as I was informed. McMichael said when I explained them, that they were new and important and begged me to write the article, as it was much needed at the present moment. Mr. Boker, Gibbons &c came in. They were discussing a plan to bring social opinion to bear upon those who expressed sentiments hostile to the government and the war. I disapproved them as they looked too much like mob law. This is the great danger at the North. Several newspapers have been suppressed by mobs, one in West Chester within the last few days, and in New Hampshire an editor was tarred and feathered and ridden on a rail. The people are in earnest and excited by the war and do not brook opposition. They feel outraged by the open expression of opinions which favor the enemy and look upon those who utter them as no better than the enemy. The people are right in their feelings but wrong in their violent action.

AUGUST 24, 1861 | In the evening drove with Bet up to Mr. J. R. Ingersoll's. He was alone, Miss Wilcocks being with her sister, Mrs. McCall, at Trenton. Mr. and Mrs. John Borie, who have a cottage adjoining Mr. I's, came in. She is an agreeable and handsome woman. Mr. I. showed us a long letter he had received from Frank Markoe, who for 28 years held a clerkship in the State Department at Washington. Not long after Mr. Lincoln came into office, Markoe was turned out because he was known to sympathize with the South. Soon after, he was arrested on a charge of treason, but was released when it was found that nothing definite could be proved against him. Since then it has been discovered that he actually applied to Jeff. Davis for an office in the Confederate government. He has a son in the Confederate army. In this letter, he abuses the government, denounces the war, expresses the strongest sympathy for the secession cause and has the extraordinary impudence to complain of unjust treatment. He is by birth a northern man and married Miss Maxey of Maryland,[45] with whom he got a considerable landed estate. In the letter, he gives an extract from a letter to him from Mr. Geo. W. Hughes, who married another Miss Maxey, who was of obscure parentage in New York, was educated at West Point, and as an army officer and the holder of other places owes most of his support & position to the government. He also is violent in his denunciation of the government & the war and zealous in support of the South, declaring that the northern people are no longer his countrymen, that "he repudiates them."

AUGUST 27, 1861 | Met Fisher in the street. He talks in the most absurd manner, professes to be for the Union, but denounces the war and Mr. Lincoln and the government in bitter & violent terms. I told him that he had better be careful or he would be arrested. That as Mr. Davis could ask nothing better for his cause than a party at the North who expressed such sentiments & thereby weakened the efforts of the

---

45. Francis Markoe (1801–71) married Mary Galloway Maxey in 1834.

government, all who did express them were in fact his allies & friends. Fisher, I am sorry to say, has lost character since the war began, not only by his partial sympathy with the South, but by the weakness he has shown in lamenting the possible loss of property on all occasions and to everybody, as if anyone at such a time cared for *his* property. One would think that he supposes the preservation of his estate was a national concern. At a time when everyone else is animated by patriotic and disinterested feeling, or professes to be, he shows that he is thinking only about himself & his money and absurdly expects others to think about either. He cares overmuch for his property. The ridiculous part of it is that his property is in no danger. He is free from debt, his investments are of the best description and he can lose nothing but income and not enough of that to interfere in the slightest degree with any of his luxuries, for he does not spend half his income. Other people, as much accustomed to comfort and entitled to it as he, have lost everything or are subjected to severe privation and yet are ashamed to make a complaint. A crisis like the present reveals character, shams are exposed, littleness, selfishness, meanness, cowardice and imbecility are displayed, when danger and trial make the opposite qualities necessary and true men are made evident.

AUGUST 29, 1861 | My article on the writ of habeas corpus in the *North American* this morning.[46]

Met Dr. Meigs. He said that he had just received a letter from his son Montgomery, who has an important command in Washington, giving very hopeful accounts of the state of affairs.[47] Saw Henry. He said that the marshal, with himself, and Genl. Cadwalader this morning examined Pierce Butler's papers & found nothing to compromise him.

SEPTEMBER 2, 1861 | Went to town. Stopped at McMichael's. A number were discussing the nominations for judges at the next election, &

---

46. "The Writ of Habeas Corpus," signed by Cecil, occupied two and a half columns on the front page of the *North American*.

47. Dr. Charles D. Meigs was the father of Gen. Montgomery C. Meigs (1816–92), quartermaster general of the U.S. Army from 1861 to 1882.

chiefly the nomination of Sharswood[48] for re-election in the District Court. He is an able lawyer, of unquestioned integrity & long experienced in a place for which he is well fitted by talents and knowledge, but he is a Democrat and on all party questions most intolerant & bigotted. He is supposed to be unsound on the subject of the war and no doubt has fully sympathized with the South. Nevertheless, I urged his renomination, because of his ability & character, because of the difficulty of supplying his place & because in his official capacity he is very unlikely to have an opportunity of exhibiting his political bias & if he had would be restrained by Stroud and Hare.[49]

SEPTEMBER 3, 1861 | On my way [to town], passed Severson going out. Luckily he saw me and got into the car. He came up in the boat. He gave good accounts of affairs at the farm. There will be some more peaches and a moderate crop of sweet potatoes and cabbages. The former were greatly injured by the black rot. On the whole, tho "trucking" has not been very profitable to us this year, but for accidental causes it would have been, & he thinks with me that it will pay much better than grain. He went with me to various places that I had to visit on business, & I then proposed to show him some of the better parts of the city which he had never seen. Took him to the City Library,[50] Independence Hall, and then got into a Walnut St. car & went up to Rittenhouse Square to see it & the fine houses near it. We then came down Chesnut St. and stopped at the Continental Hotel, where we went up to the 6th story in the hoisting machine just introduced. It must be a great convenience & save a great deal of running

---

48. Judge George Sharswood (1810-83) served on the District Court of Philadelphia from 1845 to 1868, and on the Supreme Court of Pennsylvania from 1868 to 1882, being chief justice from 1879 until his retirement.

49. The other two members of the District Court were Judges George McD. Stroud and John Innes Clark Hare (1816-1905). Hare, a Whig and later Republican, was elected to the court in 1851. In 1867 he became president judge of the court, and after the reorganization of the Pennsylvania court system in 1874 he was a president judge of the Court of Common Pleas in Philadelphia until his retirement in 1896. During the war he was also a founding member of the Union League.

50. The Library Company of Philadelphia on the northeast corner of Fifth and Library Streets.

up and down stairs. You enter a nicely furnished little room ten feet square. A man pulls a string and the room ascends with an easy motion. You can stop and get out at any story.

SEPTEMBER 5, 1861 | Met a company of soldiers in Chesnut St., remarkably well dressed and well looking. Could not imagine who they were till I saw Clark Hare in the ranks. They were part of the City Home Guard.

SEPTEMBER 7, 1861 | We drove to town at 9, stopped at Logan Square on the way, where I got out & took Sidney to look at the deer in the Square, some 35 head. Beautiful & graceful animals they are, a fitting ornament to a park. They were reclining in a group on the grass. I wonder people of fortune in the country do not add such an elegant embellishment to their places. Henry has a few, but they are in a small paddock.

SEPTEMBER 12, 1861 | Saw Henry. He asked me if I would go to Congress should the nomination be offered me. I told him I did not wish to go, but would think about it when the offer was made. He said that C. J. Biddle would probably remain in the army, in which case another must be elected to fill his place in Congress and that some influential persons thought of proposing me. There are many considerations pro and con, on such a matter. This is a critical time, and I might be of use. It is likely to be a period of great events and it is agreeable to connect one's name with such. I have some confidence in my ability to do good in such a sphere. If I did, it would be something for Sidney. On the other hand, it would be a new and untried scene, would involve the abandonment of agreeable habits and pursuits, would engage my thoughts in an inferior line of study to that which is my taste, and, worse than all, would separate me during long periods from Bet and Sidney—from happiness![51]

51. Because of poor health, Col. Biddle declined a promotion to brigadier general to accept the election.

SEPTEMBER 16, 1861 | Tomorrow, being the anniversary of the signing of the Constitution, it is to be celebrated by a parade of the Home Guard, by a public meeting and speech. The City Councils invited Mr. Geo. M. Dallas to make the speech. They could not have done a more foolish thing and the party here are doing so many foolish things that they will end by throwing the city into the hands of the Democrats. Mr. Dallas is a demagogue, his past history shows, a most unscrupulous & reckless one. His name has no influence & his character inspires no respect either for his moral or intellectual qualities. This is no time for public meetings or speeches. It is a time for prompt and energetic action only. The Federal Capital is in danger, this city is in danger from a formidable army of rebels. Who wants to hear an old hack politician, whom everybody despises, twaddle about the Constitution which he cannot understand and has all his life disregarded. The imbecility, the childish folly, the ignorance, the miserable helplessness of Philad are things amazing to behold. There are no leading men here, no one to inspire confidence or guide public sentiment. This brilliant idea of a public meeting and a speech from Mr. Dallas originated, it seems, in Ben. Rush, and is worthy of him. I saw him today. He is evidently proud of it and thinks it was a compliment due to Mr. Dallas on his return from Europe.

SEPTEMBER 17, 1861 | Bet would go to town to take Sidney to see the parade. So at 10$^{1}/_{2}$ we started with Bridget & drove to the passenger car at 4th St. They went to Mr. Ingersoll's, which, being opposite Independence Square, in which the speech was to be delivered, afforded a good view of the show. I went up to Joshua Fisher's, which is next to Mr. Dallas' house.[52] Found no one there but Fisher's son, Geo. Harrison, who is at home on a holiday from his school in New England. I arrived just as the head of the procession came in sight. After two or three regiments passed, came a barouche and four grey horses, into which Mr. Dallas and three others got. Several regiments followed. The show was not very grand as a military display. I suppose that all of the Home Guard did not appear, the First Troop was

---

52. J. Francis Fisher's address was 909 Walnut Street, George M. Dallas's, 925.

not on the ground. When the whole had passed, Fisher came in. We had some conversation about the war, in which he spoke with so much extravagance that I told him he was morbidly excited on the subject, that he was doing himself serious injury by the way in which he talked and begged him, if he could not take a more sane view of the subject, at least to restrain the expression of his sentiments.

At Henry's office saw Major [Hartman] Bache, who told me that Jas. Wadsworth was in the army near Washington as a brigadier general.[53] He was an aid to Genl. McDowell at the battle of Manassas and distinguished himself very much by his gallantry and ability. Am glad of it. Bache has a son in the army who was also in that battle.[54] He is said to be a lover of Fisher's daughter, Sophia, favored by her & by her mother, but not by Fisher. He has no property, is idle & careless, tho, it is said, amiable & gentlemanlike. When he comes home, however, with the laurels of war, Fisher will find it difficult to resist. What with his property, the war and his daughters, Fisher has a hard life. He says he wishes he was dead.

SEPTEMBER 18, 1861 | Mr. Dallas' speech of yesterday in the paper. I must do him the justice to say that it is a good one. He paints in strong colors the guilt and folly of those who are attempting to overthrow the Constitution and destroy a government which has produced so much prosperity & happiness and he sustains fully the war, appealing to the people to be united in their efforts to prosecute it with success. As Mr. Dallas is a leading Democrat, his speech will have a good influence throughout the country. It was free from partizan spirit, altho he is a partizan, and from the insidious arts of a demagogue, altho he is one or has been all his life. With all his faults, & they are

---

53. James S. Wadsworth (1807-64), a Free Soil Democrat who joined the Republican Party in the 1850s, was commissioned a brigadier general in 1861 and was the military governor of the District of Columbia in 1862. In 1862 he was the unsuccessful Republican candidate for governor of New York, losing to Horatio Seymour. Two years later he was killed at the Wilderness in May 1864.

54. Francis Markoe Bache served throughout the war, retiring as a lieutenant colonel.

grave ones, Mr. Dallas is liked because of his amiability in domestic and social life and his gracious and gentlemanlike manners.

SEPTEMBER 23, 1861 | Saw Henry. He went to Washington on Saturday & returned last night. He went for the purpose of obtaining Pierce Butler's release and succeeded. I think he was wrong to make the application & the government to grant it. It is true that no overt acts of treason were committed by Butler, nor was he committed for punishment or for trial, but as a precaution & because his general conversation was seditious & tended to strengthen the influence of the rebellion in this part of the country. He refused to take an oath of allegiance and is morally as much a traitor as any man in the Confederate army. His arrest had a very good effect here and his release will have a bad effect. It will be ascribed to the influence of his position and of rich friends. I hope when he gets out he will either go to Georgia & stay there or go to Europe and am sorry that Henry has connected himself with the affair at all.

OCTOBER 9, 1861 | Saw Fisher. He is the most unhappy man I know. This engagement of Sophy to young Bache is a sore distress to him. He cannot speak of it with any composure. He said that he could not prevent it, that he cannot control anything in his own family. I really feel anxious about him for he is in a very dangerous state of mind.

OCTOBER 13, 1861 | The result of the election in Penna. cannot be accurately known till November, because of some provision in a recent law.[55] It is known, however, that the vote of the Democrats was very large, that they have elected many of their candidates & have probably carried the city, perhaps the state. How this can be explained, I do not know. It does not, however, show that the people are opposed to the war. On the contrary, all parties profess equal zeal

---

55. A reference to the counting of soldier vote. In fact, the Pennsylvania law permitting soldiers to vote dated from 1839, and the state had allowed soldiers to vote as far back as 1813.

on that point. The war is popular, the passions of the masses are enlisted in it, and the party leaders, finding that they could not resist the current, immediately determined to swim with it, if possible into power. They are endeavoring to get the control of the movement and, should the opportunity offer, will display their real sentiments, which are thorough sympathy with the South. Their object now is, whilst affecting enthusiasm for the war, to denounce the administration for the way in which it is carried on, to magnify all mistakes & reverses, to impeach motives, to deny merit, to disparage & vilify Mr. Lincoln & his advisers in every possible way, so that if possible the operations of the government may be thwarted and embarrassed.

At 1 we drove with Sidney to Mr. J. R. Ingersoll's. Charles Ingersoll came whilst we were there. He is wild & rabid about secession & the South, and if his notions should prevail we would have civil war all over the North or else become here the tame & submissive servants of Jeff Davis & the cotton planters.

OCTOBER 15, 1861 | At 3½ drove with Bet & Sidney up to Brookwood to dinner. The place looks very well as the trees now make a goodly show, tho the "keeping" of the grounds is far less elaborate than it used to be, as Henry has very much reduced his force of men. He keeps only two horses himself, a saddle and driving horse, instead of eight. Mrs. Atherton,[56] however, has her carriage, which answers all necessary purposes. Henry goes to town in the cars and misses the enjoyment of his daily drive in and out. The misfortune about the place is that the house is so large. Its size creates unnecessary expense and the grounds are laid out on a corresponding scale. No one will buy it, for very few even in prosperous times can afford to live at such a place & those who can prefer building. It cannot be rented for the same reason. The only thing is to live at it and to do that, without ruinous expense in Henry's present position, the place cannot be properly kept up.

56. Sarah Atherton was the widow of Humphrey Atherton (1784-1849), a Philadelphia lawyer.

OCTOBER 30, 1861 | Today a flag was presented to Col. Rush's troop by Mrs. Geo. Blight for the ladies of Germantown.[57] Her brother, Robert Milligan, is one of the captains. The ceremony came off at 2 o'clock & I walked over with Bet and Sidney. The road in front of the camp was crowded with carriages and omnibuses and a large multitude was assembled of all classes. There was space enough, however, in the ample field and there was no disorder. We got places near the stand & soon found many acquaintances, ladies & gentlemen, many of whom had relatives in the troop. We saw Mrs. Geo. Thompson, Mrs. McKean, Mrs. McAllister, Mrs. John Sergeant & her daughters, Mrs. Logan, Mrs. Blight, Miss Milligan, Mrs. [John Jones] Milligan, &c. McMichael was there, [James] Murray Rush, Clem. Barclay, Henry on horseback, &c.[58] The troop was drawn up in line before the stand, the officers in advance and Col. Rush mounted on a very fine horse in the centre. He looked well and rides admirably. Wm. Rotch Wister made the speech[59] and Rush replied. I was near enough to hear what he said & thought it appropriate and well expressed. The little flags were then presented and borne aloft by the troopers whilst the regiment performed various evolutions in good style. It was to me an impressive spectacle. These men are soon going into active service, real war. Many of them will never return. Most of them are animated by a high sense of duty & by noble sentiments. The mothers, sisters, wives of many of them were present. It was an occasion when true feeling was brought out by stern reality. It was no holiday parade, no playing soldiers, but what we saw was the preparation for actual war and the men before us were, we knew, in a few days to be marched

---

57. Actually, a stand of colors and a set of guidons. Rush's 6th Pennsylvania Cavalry were encamped at Camp Meigs, on Second Street above Nicetown Lane on the Logan estate.

58. James Murray Rush, a Philadelphia lawyer who died February 7, 1862, at the age of forty-nine, was a brother of Col. Richard Henry Rush. Clement C. Barclay had taken a great interest in the formation of the regiment and raised much money for it. Henry Fisher had also lent his energies to this cause.

59. William Rotch Wister (1827-1911), a Philadelphia lawyer, politician and businessman, was the grandson of the diarist's uncle, William Logan Fisher; he delivered the speech on behalf of the ladies of Germantown.

away to a distant region, there to encounter danger and death. There is a satisfaction in knowing that they enjoy the life, as many of them have told me. They like the adventure & novelty, the manly exercises & the companionship and soon get used to the privations & hardships of the camp & the march. A good result of the war will be the formation of a taste for active & athletic pursuits, in which our young men are deficient, and the development of courage, temperance & the spirit of submission to just authority and of self-sacrifice.

OCTOBER 31, 1861 | Went to town at 9½ with Bet & Sidney to attend the marriage of Joshua Fisher's daughter Lilly to Patterson Kane. The ceremony came off at 11 o'clock at St. Peter's Church. We were invited last week. A large number of persons were assembled, some that I was surprised to see, as I could not think why they were asked. Henry's children went with Geo. Smith. The bridesmaids were Sophy & Helen, her sisters, Betty Ingersoll and Miss Mable Bayard. They were in full dress & looked very well. After the ceremony a certain number were invited to the house to a collation. After attending to some business, I went there & found Bet & Sidney. Saw & talked to a good many. Sophy introduced me to her lover, Markoe Bache, a handsome fellow with good manner. He is in the army & was at the battle of Bull Run. Like all others with whom I have spoken, he says that he likes the life of a soldier. Today I went to see Mr. Rodney Fisher, an officer of the Bank of Commerce, and asked if I could have a loan of $1500. He introduced me to the president, Mr. Ziegler,[60] and the matter was soon arranged satisfactorily. They lend me the money for a year or longer if I want it. The failure of the crops of sweet potatoes & sugar corn made a difference between my receipts & calculations this year of $2000, and I find that I must have $1500 to carry me thro till next harvest. It is unpleasant to be obliged to borrow, but that is better than to put off paying bills. My peach crop next year ought to more than pay the debt. Altho my expenditure exceeds my income, I feel confident that my affairs are improving.

60. G. K. Ziegler was president and Rodney Fisher vice-president of the Bank of Commerce.

NOVEMBER 9, 1861 | My diary has become little else than a record of the events of the war, which occupies all thoughts and conversation. Fortunately, I have not, so far, any private troubles to relate. The evils of the war have not as yet affected me or those intimately connected with me, for tho Henry has lost a great deal he will, from all that I can learn of his affairs, come out of his difficulties with quite as large a fortune as is necessary for his comfort and respectability; indeed, the chances are that he will still be a rich man. His failure, therefore, or rather suspension, for he has put up ample security for every dollar he owes, may, I hope, prove a great blessing to him by breaking up his course of business, which was chiefly speculation, not one favorable in its influences to mind, morals or reputation. If his active mind and powerful energies can be led now into better & higher spheres of usefulness, his loss of money will be a great gain to himself and his family. My own affairs are, I think, prospering, for tho my books show an increase of debt, the increased value & productiveness of my farm far overbalance that. I intend to make it a fruit & vegetable farm to a great extent and unless some unforeseen event prevents the execution of my plans, I think I shall soon have an income sufficient to live comfortably & begin to pay off my debt to Henry, which is the burden of my life, for altho he has frequently & repeatedly declared that he does not consider it a debt, I consider it one & have done so always, but now that he has lost so much property, more than ever. In all other respects, at no period of my life have I been more happy than at this. Bet & Sidney, literature, the enjoyment of the country & of the society of my friends fill my mind and time and I am content with my lot.

NOVEMBER 10, 1861 | No news in the Sunday paper. It contained an account of a Democratic meeting in town on Friday night, at which Chas. Ingersoll presided.[61] The professed object of the meeting was to denounce certain fraudulent proceedings in making false returns of

---

61. This mass meeting was held in Independence Square to obtain an expression of sentiment relative to the "intended frauds" in the return of the vote cast by the army.

the vote of the soldiers in camp at the last election. The frauds were very gross, but all parties were guilty. The meeting, however, only noticed those against the Democratic Party. The absurdity of the Democratic Party displaying virtuous indignation at an election fraud is so flagrant that no one can be deceived by such professions. The party lives by such practices and has always lived by them. The real object of the meeting was to keep up the organization of the party and embarrass the administration.

NOVEMBER 11, 1861 | Called at McMichael's where several were assembled. Signor Blitz, the celebrated ventriloquist & juggler, among them.[62] He performed some tricks which filled me with amazement. How he did them is wholly beyond my powers of conception. They prove that small reliance can be placed on the evidence of our senses and he must have some faculties not possessed by ordinary men. Every one in high spirits about the affair at Beaufort,[63] except the Democrats and they conceal their chagrin as well as they can. Saw Fisher. He hardly knows whether to rejoice or not. He said that the Middleton estate is less than 20 miles from Beaufort. Lilly has returned and is at the house in town where she will spend the winter, the rest of the family remaining at Alverthorpe. Was introduced at McMichael's to Mr. T. Buchanan Read.[64] He is an artist and has written several volumes of poetry of much merit. His appearance & manner are very pleasing.

NOVEMBER 21, 1861 | At 1½ drove Bet & Sidney to the Fairmount Park, which I never saw before. It is the only approach to a park that we possess, unless the 40 acres on the York road may be called such. Fairmount Park contains, I believe, about 90 acres, & comprises Lemon Hill and part or the whole of Sedgley, on the east bank of the

---

62. Antonio Blitz (1810-77) delighted Philadelphia audiences for many years. He was later to write *Fifty Years in the Magic Circle* (Hartford, 1871).

63. An expedition under Capt. Samuel F. du Pont had achieved a landing at Port Royal Harbor and had taken Beaufort, S.C., thereby acquiring a naval base to strengthen the blockade of southern ports.

64. Thomas Buchanan Read (1822-72), painter and poet.

Schuylkill above Fairmount. The former was owned by Henry Pratt & the latter by Jas. C. Fisher.[65] It is a rolling piece of ground, commanding fine views of the river, but unfortunately has but little timber, that having been cut down some years ago by Isaac Loyd, a speculator who bought one or both these estates. Before that act of vandalism, it was beautifully wooded. I never saw it before today since the park was made, tho in former years, & from childhood indeed, the whole ground was very familiar to me in rides & walks. The neighborhood is so much altered by streets, factories & buildings of all sorts that I could scarcely recognize it. Not much work appears to have been done at the park, except to make some winding drives. A few clumps of trees, most of them evergreens, have been planted, but seem neglected. No work is going on there now, the city finances not being very flourishing during war.

NOVEMBER 23, 1861 | The Mason & Slidel question[66] and the combination of England, France, & Spain to send a fleet to Mexico are ominous of trouble. A large foreign force stationed in the Gulf will be a new influence brought to bear on our affairs. The Monroe doctrine was always absurd & can only be maintained by superior strength.[67] What right have we to claim exclusive control over all the rich regions around the Gulf of Mexico? European nations have already possessions on this side of the Atlantic. On what grounds can we declare that they shall not but that we may acquire more territory here? Mexico,

---

65. Henry Pratt (1761–1838) was an eminent shipping merchant whose former estate, Lemon Hill, was acquired by the city in 1844. James Cowles Fisher, another wealthy merchant, purchased Sedgley in 1812. This property was sold to Isaac S. Loyd in 1836 and was purchased by the city in 1857.

66. This question involved the Confederate diplomats James Murray Mason and John Slidell, who ran the blockade to Cuba and there took passage on the *Trent*, a British ship, for London. On November 8, 1861, the *Trent* was stopped by an American vessel and the two commissioners were taken off under arrest.

67. The Monroe Doctrine, part of President James Monroe's annual message to Congress on December 2, 1823, declared that the United States would protect the Americas from further European colonization while pledging not to interfere in European political affairs.

1861 123

Venezuela, Central America under the control of the superior and civilized races might become prosperous & powerful nations. It is unreasonable for us to say to them & to the world that they shall remain poor & weak for our safety.

NOVEMBER 25, 1861 | Went to McClees' shop[68] this morning & got two impressions, ordered two weeks ago, of the photograph taken of Bet last winter. They are by no means as good as the first, which is colored & touched also by an artist & therefore has more expression. These represent the complexion as coarse, which all photographs do, & which is not so in the colored one or in the original. The likeness, however, is, tho not agreeable, still a likeness. So I paste it on the next page.

NOVEMBER 26, 1861 | Got an invitation from Jno. Field[69] to meet Mr. [George W.] Curtis of Boston at dinner on Thursday. Accepted it. Curtis is a man of considerable literary reputation in New England and is the same person who delivered a lecture here two years ago & had to be protected from the mob by the mayor because he was alleged to be an abolitionist. Times change. He would require no protection now.

NOVEMBER 28, 1861 | At 4½ went to Field's, who has rented Rebecca Smith's[70] furnished house at the corner of Chesnut & 20th Sts. Mr. Curtis had not arrived. He had missed the train, a telegram announced, & could not come till 6 o'clk. So we dined without him. . . . In the dining room was a very old-fashioned sideboard, in perfect order, said to have belonged to Joseph Bonaparte,[71] which Field

68. James E. McClees, photographer, kept his shop at 910 Chestnut Street.
69. John W. Field, a friend of the diarist, was a man who courted literary lions and was also associated in business with Thomas A. Newhall & Sons, sugar refiners at 409 Race Street.
70. Rebecca Smith (1814–86) was an eccentric cousin of the diarist, notorious for her love affairs. Much to her family's relief, she was living in Europe.
71. Joseph Bonaparte, elder brother of Napoleon, was born in Corsica in 1768 and died in Florence in 1844. He was King of Naples from 1806 to 1808, and King of Spain from 1808 to 1813. Except for the years 1832 to 1837, which he spent in Europe, he lived in Philadelphia and on his estate near Bordentown, N.J., from 1815 to 1841, using the name Comte de Survilliers.

picked up in an old furniture store in Market St. for $25. The form is light & graceful, it is full of conveniences & is of mahogany inlaid with satin wood. I really envied him, as I also did the possession of several pieces of silver of very graceful, antique pattern, which he bought in London at a shop where such things were collected. These were of the time of George 1st. Mrs. Field said the shop was very interesting and very tempting, being full of articles of all sorts, some of them very ancient. . . .

Mr. Curtis and his friend Mr. Sturgis of Boston came at 6½, handsome, gentlemanlike in manners & appearance, both of them. Good specimens of the New England man. They were hearty, cheery, cordial and I soon felt on familiar footing with them. Curtis lives on Staten Island. He inherited or made a fortune, but managed to lose it. His rich father-in-law offered him an income, which he refused & went to work to support himself by literature and lecturing, in which he succeeded so well that Field says he makes $8000 a year. He is the author of several books, novels, I believe, but I never read them & am ashamed to say have forgotten their names. They have gained him, however, a reputation. He delivers his lectures whenever and wherever invited, and travels a great deal in the winter for the purpose. He is paid handsomely for each. He lectured this evening at Concert Hall at 8 o'clock, so we had not much time for talk. We all went. The large room was crammed with a well-dressed, respectable-looking audience, among which, however, I did not see a face that I knew. We had standing places on the platform. A member of the society in introducing him alluded to the fact that a year ago Mr. Curtis was threatened by a mob in the same place, and congratulated the audience that freedom of speech was restored to Phila. His remarks were well expressed & were received with loud applause.

DECEMBER 5, 1861 | There are two parties in Congress & the country in relation to the management of slavery, one advocating the extreme & violent measure of general emancipation & arming the Negroes; the other, the confiscation & setting free of the slaves of actual rebels only. Mr. Lincoln favors the latter, not only on the score of humanity, but of duty & policy. Of duty, because slavery is protected by the Constitution and it is his purpose to restore the Constitution; of policy, because the plan of universal emancipation, to say nothing of stimulated insurrection, would embitter the rebellion and decide the wavering in the South and even Union men to join it. It thus appears that even now, the southern people are really living under the protection of the government they are attempting to destroy and that Mr. Lincoln, whom they vilify so grossly, is their best friend. I have had faith in him ever since I read his inaugural speech & his first message. They contain clear proof to my mind of great natural ability, of a wisdom that is above learning, and of an honest, sincere & loving nature. He is certainly in my judgment the best *man* we have had for President since Jno. Q. Adams,[72] he is the man for this crisis, worth, in the strength of his mind and character & purity of purpose all the rest of the cabinet put together, and if he lives to complete his term of office, I believe the nation will think so, too.

DECEMBER 8, 1861 | Walked about the lawn with Bet enjoying the sight of Sidney in his little goat cart. The goat has been a great enjoyment to him for a year & is a very pretty animal. His grandfather gave him a set of harness for her some weeks ago & Bridget is training her to go in a little wagon, in which he sits & drives with great delight. The three made a pleasant group, a picture of the fleeting present that I would be glad to preserve if I could. Took a ride on Harry and stopped at Brookwood. Henry says business people are anxious about the course England may take in reference to the Mason & Slidel affair and dread a war.

DECEMBER 16, 1861 | Important intelligence has arrived from England by a steamer just in. The arrest of Mason & Slidel has caused a ferment in England. It has been regarded as an insult to the flag, for which the press & the public demand instant reparation. This reparation is to be the restoration of Mason & Slidel & an apology. As no one supposes that such terms will be granted, all the papers speak of

---

72. John Quincy Adams (1767-1848), of Massachusetts, was the sixth president of the United States.

war as inevitable & boast that our commerce will be swept from the ocean, our navy destroyed, our northern ports blockaded, the blockade of the southern ports raised and the southern Confederacy immediately recognized. These denunciations and threats of the press contain the positive assertion that several cabinet meetings have been held, at which it was resolved to send the magnificent iron-plated steamer *Warrior* to Annapolis, with despatches, demanding the release of the prisoners on her deck and satisfaction for the alleged outrage; that orders had been issued prohibiting the exportation of saltpetre, lead, powder, &c., that more troops were to be forwarded to Canada and that increased activity was displayed in the dockyards. This looks as if the government was in earnest and as our government will certainly make no concession, there may be war.

DECEMBER 19, 1861 | The spirit moved me this morning and I began an article about the position of England in relation to the South. Worked at it till 3 o'clock, when I refreshed myself by a pleasant ride on Harry. Worked at the article also in the evening.

DECEMBER 20, 1861 | Finished the article "England & the South" by 12 o'clck. Went to town & took it to McMichael who said it should appear tomorrow if possible, tho that was doubtful.

DECEMBER 22, 1861 | Another steamer has arrived at Halifax and brings news of a continuance of the excitement in England and active preparations for war. The pride of the nation seems to have been roused by an act which they acknowledge to have been legal, which they would unquestionably have done themselves, but which they resent when committed against them. Such is human nature; it always makes a great difference whether it was your bull that gored my ox, or my bull that gored your ox. . . .

At 2 rode Harry up to Brookwood & sat an hour with Henry who says orders have come from England to sell large amounts of American stocks, which depresses the market and may make it necessary that the Banks suspend specie payments to prevent the shipment of coin.

DECEMBER 24, 1861 | The article, "England and the South," was in the paper this morning. Another steamer is in. The excitement in England & the warlike preparations were unabated. The public mind is in a flame at the supposed insult. The reason is the people were previously disposed to favor the South.

DECEMBER 25, 1861 | Christmas day. . . . Our boasted 19th century, which has brought so many material & external advantages, has not brought with it the reign of peace & knowledge or Christian love. All the world seems going to war, as of old, & the cause of it is the very wealth which commerce & intelligent industry have created. It is the age of gold & is likely to become the age of iron.

DECEMBER 28, 1861 | Went to McMichael's office. He said that he had [heard] a great many speak in high terms of my article and that it had been generally read & approved. He said it was now known that Mason & Slidel would be given up. This also was the news in the street and is received for the most part with acquiescence and grim satisfaction. It is felt to be a humiliating concession, but necessary in the present crisis of our affairs. The Democrats, it is said, are preparing to make political capital out of it and to denounce it as disgraceful to the country.

As I passed Dr. James Rush's house, determined to go in and pay him a visit, which I have not done since Mrs. Rush's death, tho I have often met and exchanged kind greetings with him. He lives alone in that large & splendid establishment, which she built & furnished at great cost, where she exercised a very liberal hospitality, but which she did not enjoy long.[73] I rang more than once before a servant came & then it was a woman. I was ushered into the hall & waited there for some time before the Doctor made his appearance. The furniture was all covered up & the carpets, with drugget. The last time I was in it was at a ball, & it was filled with a gay crowd & gleaming with light. When the Doctor came he opened a door into one of the large drawing rooms. They are, no doubt, in the same state they were

73. Dr. James Rush lived at 1914 Chestnut Street.

when Mrs. Rush died in the summer at Saratoga. The floors were covered with mats & the furniture, mirrors, &c., with white muslin. We went into a verandah, enclosed with glass. The Doctor was looking well & was very animated, talking with eagerness about politics, medicine, literature, philosophy, &c. He accused me of being a transcendentalist and a Platonist, to which I willingly plead guilty. He himself confesses that he is a materialist, believes only in matter and the body, not at all in spirit or the soul. A strange thing for a man of undoubted intelligence. I asked him if he ever felt such emotions as reverence, admiration, respect, love, &c., and whether these were bodily sensations, but he could not give a satisfactory answer. He expressed himself very glad to see me & would hardly let me go away. He lives alone, entertains no company, occupies some rooms upstairs only, has an immense income, and professes, no doubt with truth, to be very happy, being occupied in writing a book on some subject that fills his mind, as he told me some years ago and intimated today. Mrs. Rush at her death requested him to continue to live in that house & left him, absolutely, I believe, her whole estate, a million. I doubt whether he spends $3000 a year.

DECEMBER 29, 1861 | The *Sunday Despatch* this morning had the news of the settlement of the Slidel & Mason affair and the correspondence between Lord Russell, Lord Lyons, & Mr. Seward on the subject.... The reply of Mr. Seward is a very clear, statesmanlike and well-written paper. The general principles involved are discussed with ability. On all points our right to make the arrest is clearly maintained. The only question was as to the manner in which it was made. The regular course would have been to have brought the vessel itself to port so that the question whether the prisoners were contraband or not could be decided by a court of admiralty. The prisoners and England too, under whose protection they were, were entitled to have this question argued before a proper tribunal. Captn. [Charles] Wilkes *voluntarily* permitted the vessel to proceed & took out the prisoners.... For this reason, Mr. Seward says the prisoners will be "cheerfully liberated." It is most fortunate for us that there was an irregularity in our proceedings grave enough to justify our government in making such a concession without loss of honor.

~1862~

JANUARY 3, 1862 | The Spanish expedition has landed in Mexico and taken possession of Vera Cruz, without resistance. It will speedily be joined by the French & English fleets.[1] This is an important event, indicative of the future. It foreshadows the power which Europe is henceforth to exert on this side [of] the Atlantic. It shows that we are here no longer supreme but are to have formidable rivals. It is a sign already, in the estimation of Europe, we have lost caste & influence. Our "Monroe Doctrine," somewhat arrogantly heretofore announced to the world, is disregarded and we cannot assert it now. The next step may too probably be the establishment of an English "protectorate" over our southern states. An extract from a London letter is in the morning paper. It says that whether there be war now or not, one of the first measures of Parliament, to meet in January, will be to recognize the South and to raise the blockade. It is dated Dec. 18. Went to town at 1. Attended to business. Saw McMichael. He agreed with me that our situation is now more critical than ever, that war with England is very probable and what the consequences would be, no one can predict.

JANUARY 8, 1862 | Went to Mount Harmon on Saturday. Weather clear and cold. Th. 20 to 24. At Middletown I stopped at the bank there to

---

1. Spain had sent twenty-six warships and transports to Vera Cruz and had landed 6,000 troops. Seven hundred British marines were already there, with one battleship and two frigates. France was to send ships and troops about equal to the Spanish

inquire whether I could borrow some money. I want it to pay bills & expenses till next harvest, most of my income being received after harvest. I have heretofore applied to Henry for this purpose and also been unable to repay him, and have thus incurred a heavy debt, as I regard it, tho he has released me from it. I must now, fortunately for me, depend on myself, and whether I shall be able to maintain my present mode of living, without going to work, depends on the success of my farming plans.

In the afternoon [Sidney] went, under the care of Bridget, to a children's party at Dr. Owen Wister's, where he was much delighted at his first glimpse of the outside world. It was a twelfth night party, a large number of children were present & they had various games, a magic lantern and other amusements.

JANUARY 13, 1862 | Went to McMichael's. Found several there. Among others Mr. Verree, a member of Congress from this District.[2] He says Congress is very impatient at the inactivity of military operations and can get no information as to the cause, as a committee appointed to inquire into it was treated almost with contempt by Genl. McClellan[3] who intimated that now the army was supreme. In answer to my question why Congress itself was so inactive in reference to adequate provisions by taxation to sustain the credit of the government, he said that he thought some plan would now speedily be matured. He did not speak hopefully of affairs and declared that unless some important steps were taken successfully within a few weeks, the country would be irretrievably ruined in every sense. Saw at Henry's office Mr. Heckscher of New York, an intelligent gentleman, connected with the high

expedition. The diplomatic explanation these powers gave was that they had joined hands to collect money due from Mexico.

2. John Paul Verree (1817-89), a Republican, was a U.S. congressman from Pennsylvania from 1859 to 1863.

3. George B. McClellan (1826-85) was a graduate of the U.S. Military Academy in 1846 and a career officer and army engineer. Promoted to major general in 1861, McClellan was given or removed from command several times before he finally relinquished command in November 1862. In 1864 he was the unsuccessful Democratic candidate for president.

financial circles of that city.[4] He says the financial prospects of the government are frightful, and of businessmen also, because of the corruptions and inefficiency at Washington and the inactivity of the army.

JANUARY 15, 1862 | Mr. Cameron has resigned and been made minister to Russia. The truth, I suppose, is that the President wished him to resign and intimated to him as much. His character for integrity is far from high and the frauds that have been discovered in all departments of the office connected with army supplies were so flagrant that some change became necessary to satisfy public opinion. The mission to Russia is intended partly to cover his fall, partly perhaps to send him away, for he is considered a vindictive, unscrupulous, and able man. Independent of other reasons, his difference in opinion with the President in relation to slavery would probably have led to his dismissal. Mr. Cameron favors the plan of general emancipation and even of arming the Negroes, whilst the views of the President are moderate and conciliatory to the South. The policy of Mr. Cameron is advocated by a strong party in Congress, which threatens to become an opposition party. It is composed of the abolitionists among the Republicans. They declare that as slavery caused the war, so it will forever prevent harmony and peace between the sections should the Union be restored. That therefore slavery should be destroyed by right of war, since now we have the power. Mr. Lincoln, on the other hand, contends that we have offered to the South protection in all their rights if they will return to their allegiance, and therefore to destroy slavery would be a breach of faith. It would also be inexpedient, as it would unite all southern men in a determination to resist the government to the last extremity. The person selected to succeed Cameron is a Mr. Stanton of Pittsburgh. I never heard of him before, but the papers say he is a man of ability & good character. He is a conservative

4. Charles A. Heckscher shared Henry Fisher's interest in Pennsylvania coal and railroads.

Democrat, that is, he is a Union man and approves the war.[5] It is a significant fact that he should have been chosen at this time. It shows an antagonism between the extreme Republicans and the administration. I heard some weeks ago that Mr. Lincoln had said that he would be obliged to depend on the conservative portion of the Democratic Party for support.

JANUARY 25, 1862 | Mr. and Mrs. Joshua Fisher here. They have recent letters from Charleston giving favorable accts. of their friends, but of course no political or military intelligence or opinions, as the letters are sent unsealed to Fortress Monroe, & then read by our army officers appointed for the purpose. In this way communication is permitted between families & friends, North & South. Fisher brought me a pamphlet just written by Wm. B. Reed.[6] Mr. Stanton, the new Secretary of War, has appointed John Tucker one of the under-secretaries. It would be a good appointment if Tucker's moral character was good, for he has just the sort of ability requisite for the place in a very high degree, as he proved by his long & masterly management of the vast & complicated affairs, financial and mechanical, of the Reading Railroad, of which he was president for many years. But Tucker is thoroughly corrupt. He has no moral sense or self-respect whatever. He has not the slightest regard for truth & is ready to bribe or be bribed. He has long been a reckless gambler in stocks and has made & lost half a dozen fortunes, always lives with lavish expense, is overwhelmed with debt and is a most unprincipled adventurer. Because of all this, the Reading Railroad Co. was obliged by force of public opinion to turn him out of the management, tho, because of his rare ability, it has also been obliged to retain him at a salary of $7,000 as unofficial adviser. Altho no one respects Tucker in the least, everybody likes him. He is handsome, gentlemanlike in his manners, easy & fluent in

---

5. Edwin M. Stanton (1814–69), an antebellum Democrat, had been attorney general in the last days of Buchanan's administration. He was Lincoln's second secretary of war and continued to serve in that capacity under Andrew Johnson.

6. Reed was opposed to the war and was considered to be a strong sympathizer of the South. His pamphlet was titled *Paper Containing a Statement and Vindication of Certain Political Opinions* (Philadelphia, 1862).

conversation and generous and kind in his feelings, always ready to serve a friend or, indeed, anyone in need. When this place was offered him he refused it. The salary is only $3,000, a small object for Tucker. Stanton insisted on his serving, however, so earnestly that he consented.

FEBRUARY 6, 1862 | Had some talk with Henry. He dined a day or two ago at Geo. Cadwalader's with Cameron, late Secretary of War. He, Cameron, does not seem to have a very high opinion of McClellan & prefers Halleck[7] as a general. He thinks there has been a lack of energy & boldness in prosecuting the war.

FEBRUARY 8, 1862 | At 1 drove up to Alverthorpe. Saw Fisher, Sophy, & Mrs. F. We had the usual discussion about the war & the rights & wrongs of the South, Mrs. F., of course, taking the secession side very warmly, in which she is excusable. Dr. [Samuel H.] Dickson came out to dine. He is a So. Carolinian & a professor in the Jefferson Medical College of Phila. He also, it was evident, sympathizes strongly with the South. Fisher is wavering & cannot decide between his feelings & his convictions. The place looked very beautiful in its winter garb and the house is replete with luxurious comfort & elegance.

FEBRUARY 18, 1862 | Every branch & twig of the trees was this morning encased in ice, producing a beautiful effect of silver arabesque. They glittered in the sun like so many gigantic chandeliers of cut glass. The news is that Fort Donelson is ours.[8] It is a most important position and was defended with great obstinacy. The courage displayed in the attack, however, was greater than in the defence, as the enemy fought behind entrenchments, whilst our troops marched up hill to armed batteries, exposed to a deadly fire from an unseen foe, and this too after exposure without tents to rain & storms.

7. Henry Wager Halleck (1815-72), a graduate of the U.S. Military Academy in 1839, was a lawyer and career army officer who served as general-in-chief of the Union armies from 1862 to 1864.
8. Fort Donelson, in Tennessee, with its garrison of 14,000 was captured by Gen. U.S. Grant on February 16, 1862.

Mrs. Kemble came in. She was as usual exuberant & animated, a little theatrical, very clever & somewhat dictatorial, tho in a good-natured way. She is very enthusiastic about the war & predicts from it the destruction of slavery. She expressed profound regret at the hostile opinions exhibited by England, but said that we have much more to dread from France & that her English letters informed her that, but for the remonstrances & advice of the English government, the Emperor would ere this have recognized the South & opened the blockade.

FEBRUARY 25, 1862 | Went to McMichael's. He has just come from Washington. His paper has been one of those which have disparaged Genl. McClellan for his inactivity in the conduct of the war, attributing this to want of energy & military ability or something worse. I asked him if he was not now convinced of his mistake and if it was not apparent that the skill of McClellan's combinations was demonstrated by our late victories, which were the result of the plan of the campaign made by Genl. Scott and steadily pursued by McClellan, whose inactivity on the Potomac had gained for us successes on the southern coast & in Tennessee, by holding fast at Manassas the flower of [the] enemy's army. He said no, that if more energy had been shown these successes would have been gained at an earlier day, that much time had been lost as well as much money by delay and that the late victories were due, not to McClellan, but to the talents & energy of du Pont & Burnside, of Halleck, Buel, Thomas, & Grant.[9] He then said that during his recent visit to Washington he had conversed with some prominent members of Congress who told him that McClellan was suspected of a design to become the candidate of the Democratic Party for the next presidency; that the well-known design of that party was to favor the South, which they exhibited by doing all that they dared now do to embarrass the government in its military operations; that this party did not wish to see the South weakened, but were waiting

9. Capt. Samuel F. du Pont and Gen. Ambrose E. Burnside had been engaged in amphibious operations on the Carolina coast. Gen. Don Carlos Buell and Gen. George H. Thomas were with the western forces cooperating with Gen. Ulysses S. Grant.

a favorable moment to restore the Union by an offer to the South of all its old pretensions & claims as the price of its return, expecting to form another alliance with it & thus govern the country as before in the interests of slavery. All this I believe so far as a portion of the Democratic Party is concerned, tho I doubt it very much as to McClellan's conduct, tho McMichael says that Bayard,[10] Biddle, Vallandigham,[11] & other secessionists in Congress all support & defend McClellan.[12] He may have aspirations to the presidency, for these are the bane of our politics, but that as a soldier he should not desire victory, and that even as a politician or demagogue, if he be either, he should not be able to see that victory is the surest way to create popular enthusiasm in his favor is incredible.

Got an invitation to dine at Jno. Field's tomorrow to meet Mr. Anthony Trollope, the author of *Barchester Towers, Dr. Throne,* &c., which I have recently read with much interest.[13] He has written many others & certainly ranks with the eminent literary men of the day.

FEBRUARY 26, 1862 | Went to Field's at 5. Was introduced to Miss Carey of Cambridge & Mr. Wild of Boston who are staying with the Fields, the former a sister-in-law of Agassiz,[14] both of them intelligent & well informed. After a while Mr. Trollope came in. He is

---

10. James A. Bayard Jr. (1799-1880), was a U.S. senator from Delaware from 1851 until he resigned in 1864 to protest newly adopted Senate rules that required senators to take the "ironclad test oath." Bayard again served in the Senate after the war, from 1867 to 1869.

11. Clement L. Vallandigham (1820-71), a Democrat, was a U.S. congressman from Ohio from 1858 to 1863. In May 1863 Vallandigham was arrested by the military for treasonable speech and banished to the Confederacy. After making his way to Canada he became the unsuccessful Democratic candidate for governor of Ohio, in 1863.

12. Fisher, like many Republicans, was prone to use the term "secessionist" somewhat liberally to include those who disapproved of certain government policies but who were emphatically not in favor of disunion.

13. Anthony Trollope (1815-82), English novelist, was visiting the United States on a nine-month furlough from his post-office career.

14. The second wife of Professor Jean L. R. Agassiz was Elizabeth Cabot Cary of Boston.

short & well made, his head bald, has moustaches & long bushy beard, irregular features, florid complexion, and a quick, brusque, self-possessed, but not elegant or graceful manner. There is nothing intellectual or noble in his face, which expresses merely intelligence & hearty good nature. The conversation throughout was eager & animated and chiefly between him & me, I anxious to give him the lion's share, which he did not seem disposed to appropriate. He was very genial & earnest and a tone of familiarity & good-fellowship was immediately adopted. Social pleasures & those of the table also are evidently habitual to him & enjoyed with zest, tho the latter in moderation. He drank wine with judgment & smoked cigars also. At first we talked of literature & living literary men, authors in this country & England, most of whom he knows well, as Emerson, Hawthorne, Carlyle, Disraeli, Thackeray, Read, Tennyson, Longfellow, Ruskin, &c. He was very enthusiastic in his praise and, tho I agreed with him for the most part, some of his judgments surprised me. For example, he prefers the poetry of Longfellow to that of Tennyson and of Mrs. Barrett Browning to either and says that is the general opinion in England. I should think not, however, among the judicious. I asked him if he knew the author of *Adam Bede,* and he spoke with much feeling of her as an intimate friend. Her name is Miss Evans, but he said he never would allow anyone to speak of her to him except as Mrs. Lewes. She lives with Mr. Lewes as his wife, which she is not, as he has a wife living.[15] From this wife he is separated & he & the other, for the sake of living with & for each other, have accepted all the evil, the loss of caste & character which such an act brings with it. She has no beauty, but has genius and no doubt a high & pure moral nature &, in reality, her marriage is the true one.

There was much other talk and I was much pleased with Mr. Trollope. He converses with ease, there is not the slightest assumption about him or apparent consciousness of being an eminent man, but he is cordial & friendly, easy, earnest, & enthusiastic. He is, however,

---

15. Mary Ann (or Marian) Evans (1819-80), who wrote under the pseudonym of George Eliot, entered into a union with the philosopher George Henry Lewes, who could not marry her because his wife would not divorce him.

not up to the appreciation of the higher order of men or books, he is not spiritual or philosophical, and, in truth, I felt surprised that he could have written his own works & created the men & women who interested me so much in his novels. His mind must have latent powers not revealed by his countenance or conversation.

FEBRUARY 28, 1862 | Bet brought news that a dreadful battle is going on & has been all day at Leesburgh. McClellan has attacked the enemy's lines. The town was full of all sorts of rumors but nothing was considered reliable except the fact of a battle.

The night is cold, there is a fierce wind. I can think of nothing but the wounded now lying exposed to the weather on the battlefield. What a scene of suffering & horror it must be, yet in spite of it all, who does not love war & its glory? Such is our mysterious nature that under the excitement of danger and a struggle we court what else we shrink from instinctively, pain & death.

MARCH 1, 1862 | The news of a battle yesterday turns out to be a hoax, got up by speculators in stock. All was "quiet on the Potomac" as usual.

MARCH 6, 1862 | A gap in my diary has been caused by the severe illness of Henry. About 9 o'clock on Sunday morning a servant came to ask me to go up to Brookwood as Henry was very sick. I went up immediately on horseback. Geo. Smith was there & soon after Wister came. Henry had a headache on Friday & staid out of town all day. On Saturday morning, whilst talking with Wister as usual, to the great surprise of the latter, he suddenly had a convulsion. This was succeeded by others thro the day and Saturday night Wister staid with him all night. On Sunday morning after I arrived he had another, the seventh & last. I saw him as the fit was going off and a painful sight it was, the breathing hard & stertorous, the teeth set, the eyes fixed & without expression, his hands fumbling nervously with the bedclothes, & his voice muttered sounds which were not words. Through Sunday he did not know any of us & his mind was flighty. The hope was that the affection of the brain was functional, not organic, tho

Gerhard, who was sent for, told me on Sunday night that he thought him in great danger. Geo. Smith, who is not a bad physician and a capital nurse, sat up with him all Sunday night and I was up till 1 o'clock. In the night, about 12, he spoke in his natural voice, & when he saw & recognized George & me at once concluded that he must be very ill and was much puzzled to account for the interval of Saturday & Sunday, during which he had been unconscious of outside things.

The attack was brought on by overexcitement and overwork, long continued. Last winter, he went thro a severe trial, expecting utter ruin every day and striving to avert it. When the blow came it was far less severe than he expected; his failure turned out to be merely a suspension with a fair prospect of being able to settle his debts & get thro all difficulties with a very handsome fortune left. Unfortunately, some months ago the controversy about the affairs of the Little Sch. Co. arose in which he was deeply interested. This excited him as much as his own previous troubles, not because of his pecuniary stake in the company, but because his motives and conduct in its management as a director were assailed. All these things have proved too much for his brain, which gave way under them. Happily, he has escaped with his life and without paralysis or danger, so the doctors think, of permanent mental injury. But it will be necessary for him to avoid the causes which brought on this attack & therein lies the difficulty. His own affairs are not settled tho in a prosperous condition, and the bill in equity, filed against him & others, directors of the Little Schuylkill Co., will go on thro a long course of litigation, most probably, for a year or more.[16]

MARCH 10, 1862 | At 3 o'clock this morning I saw my brother *die*.

---

16. The Little Schuylkill Navigation, Railroad, and Coal Company, which owned 5,000 acres of coal land in Schuylkill county and some forty miles of railroad running between Port Clinton and Catawissa, had been largely under the domination of Henry Fisher. Following some years in which dividends had not been paid, its affairs were investigated by a committee of stockholders. Their findings tended to cast discredit on Fisher's financial manipulations.

MARCH 14, 1862 | I wish to make now merely a simple record of the facts of this the greatest calamity that has yet befallen me. On Thursday evening, as before mentioned, Henry was so much better that the doctors thought there was no reason whatever why anyone should remain with him all night. As I had been away three nights, I therefore came home. On Friday morning, I found that I had taken cold from my long drive to Frankford the previous day and, the weather being still damp & raw, I feared to increase it by going up morning & evening to Brookwood and, feeling no anxiety about Henry, I remained at home till three o'clock. On my way up I met Harry Ingersoll in Green Lane, who told me that Henry was much worse & had had a bad night. When I reached the house, I was informed that during the night the fits had returned with great violence, that he had been quite out of his mind, had got out of bed, tried to jump out of the window, & could only be controlled by the coachman, the only man in the house. In the morning, he had a few hours sleep, the effect of opiates. George Smith & I sat up with him, Wister & Gerhard there in the evening. He continued to grow worse thro Saturday & Sunday and at 10 minutes past 3 on Monday morning he died.

It seems like a horrible dream. I cannot describe the scenes of those dreadful days & nights, the shocking contortions of his face, the ravings, the stream of words, of inarticulate sounds which were not words, poured forth in torrents by the hour, with such terrible expression of voice & countenance that it seemed to me a wonderful exhibition of the power of both. A new view of human nature was opened to me, impressive, solemn, fearful, never to be forgotten. Grief at times was overcome by amazement not unmixed with admiration at the spectacle, whose various horrors were governed by an order and harmony of their own, which passed in rapid succession &, when over, left on the mind, like a storm, the impression of sublime power & terrible beauty. George Smith & Stewardson were with him nearly all the time, Wister came twice a day & staid all Sunday night, Gerhard staid two nights. All that skill could do was tried in vain. The disease was meningitis or inflammation of the brain, which caused the convulsions & the astonishing effects of countenance & voice, and his great vital power made the struggle long & severe. At 12 o'clock on

Sunday, Wister announced to Liedy that he was sinking. The convulsions, the ravings, the distortions had ceased & he laid panting but quiet. We all assembled around the bed, Liedy, Ellen, Jim, Mrs. Atherton, Mrs. Purviance & myself, and there we all remained until three o'clock on Monday morning, *15 hours*, during which he was dying.[17] Liedy had been in constant attendance on him night & day, ever since he was attacked, with rare intervals of sleep, the others were more or less exhausted. Human nature could endure no more. Before he died they were all asleep. Half an hour before he died, the loud hoarse panting subsided into a soft, gentle, regular moan, which grew fainter until at length the last breath was expired and he *was gone*. We got the ladies & children to their rooms & soon after went to bed ourselves.

Today I went to town. Went to Henry's office. Read his will. It is very short. His two clerks, [Peter C.] Hollis & Henry Muirheid, are his executors and also the trustees of his estate during the minority of his children. The property is to be divided into 4 equal parts, for each of the children, as soon as possible after Liedy is of age. My debt to him is directed to be cancelled. Hollis showed me the books. After all liabilities are paid, the estate at present prices is worth a million. Hollis is a very worthy man, has been with Henry for many years, was extremely attached to him & wholly trusted by him. He & I understand each other. As I am & must be the natural protector & guardian of the children, it is proper that I should be made acquainted with the disposition & management of their estate.

MARCH 16, 1862 | In the morning looked over some law books in reference to points likely to arise under Henry's will. My habits of life will be much changed. New duties and responsibilities have been suddenly imposed upon me. I cannot, if I would, shrink from them and I would not if I could. I am the natural guardian and protector of a family of orphans.

17. Eliza "Liedy" George Fisher (1841-1916), Ellen Fisher (1845-1903), and James Logan "Jim" Fisher (1849-1925), were children of Charles Henry Fisher, and nephew and nieces of the diarist.

MARCH 18, 1862 | Got a letter from Severson informing me that old Stephen is dead. He died on Friday. He was very old. He belonged to my grandfather & was set free by my mother. When I began the management of Mount Harmon in 1834 he came there as a hand & has remained ever since. He considered himself as belonging to me & always called me master. He has been past work for several years & I gave him a cottage and a patch of ground & supplied all his wants.

MARCH 26, 1862 | Came out at 4 ½ on the N. P. road. Sally Ingersoll & Mr. Hunt in the car. A little while ago I used to meet Henry there also. Never again in this world shall I see him. Bet & Sidney dined in town. I alone with *his* portrait before me on the wall, taken 29 years ago, a joyous youthful face, with an expression of sweetness & frankness, like him to the last, tho years & care had greatly altered him. It was painted by Sully, who at the same time painted one of me, now at Brookwood, and one of my brother James, from description & made a good likeness tho he never saw him. This last I have.

MARCH 28, 1862 | Truly, this is a world of the dying. We are all indeed dying with greater or less speed and belong to the transient, fleeting things which are never for a moment the same, and which Plato calls the "becoming" and the nonexistent, for what sort of existence has that which is always changing? Life rides upon the present moment, which is inconceivably small & swift. The past is not, the future is not, the present in the act of conceiving it becomes the past. What then are we? Spirits taking form for a time & becoming visible, soon to become spirits again & invisible, & still to live? Or manifestations of the great oversoul & thus phenomenal, without independent life? Or outgrowths from the tree of humanity, the archetypal man, like leaves on an oak, grown in the successive crops which perish tho the tree lives, man surviving tho men die? Or immortal souls with separate & individual life, growing here & strengthened by toil and suffering, aspiring ever to good we cannot reach because of the obstructions of the flesh and released by death from earthy bonds, so that death is really a birth into a new sphere of higher & purer living? All these possibilities we can think, but who can know what really & soberly to believe. What I do know is that a little while ago Henry was to me what seemed a living reality, his clear, kind, manly voice sounded in my ears, his expressive face, his spirited, decisive, energetic manner & movement I could see, and now they are recollections only, ideas fading away from my mind. I cannot get nearer to him than that ever again in this world. Every moment bears him farther from me, the things which we call realities, which affect the senses, wife, child, farm, nature, books, thronging in & pushing him out, in spite of my efforts to prevent it. And so he is gone and so the present, by a law of my nature that I cannot resist, usurps his place and I have lost him forever, unless we may meet again after I too have passed the valley of the dark shadow. Ah, if that shall only prove to be the case, how gladly shall I meet him and others whom I loved in the spirit land & explain things we did not understand in each other here and exchange forgiveness & assurances of true & faithful affection. With this faith there would be no sting in death or victory in the grave.

APRIL 1, 1862 | This is Henry's birthday. Had he lived he would have been 48 today. He was born April 1, 1814, at Ellwood, a place on the lane next south of this. I perfectly remember being taken the next morning by Mrs. Cavender, our housekeeper, into my mother's chamber to see him. She died at her house in Arch St., south side, above 10th, next above the Presbyterian Church in 1821. We afterwards lived together with our excellent aunt, Ann Worrell, who was a second mother to us. Henry went to school in Philad: and then to Princeton College where he graduated. Soon after that, he went to Havre, to the house of Courant & Co., to fit himself for mercantile pursuits. At Havre, he was under the kind care of Mr. Jeremiah Winslow, a friend of Uncle William's, an eminent merchant and a very worthy man, who was extremely kind to Henry, who indeed acquired the confidence of Courant & Co. and was well received and on friendly & familiar terms with all the principal families of the place. He went to Havre in 1832. James went to Europe in the spring of 1833 & died in Paris in October, 1833. Henry after that event came home for a few months & then resumed his place at Havre. Having stayed the usual time in the countinghouse, he travelled on the Continent & in England & returned to this country in 1835. In 1837 he was married. He did not engage in any regular business, but soon displayed in the management of his property such talents for affairs as acquired for him the confidence of leading men of business. He made money. He connected himself with banks & railroads. He went in [1843] to England to negotiate a loan for the Balti. & Wilmington Railroad Co. He succeeded far beyond the expectations of the company & his own. Part of the money was obtained from the Morrisons, who were so well pleased with the ability he displayed that they made him their agent in this country, at first with limited, afterwards with discretionary, power over their vast investments here amounting to about ten millions. This, of course, gave to Henry great influence in business circles and great opportunities for making money. He had the talents to use both with effect and did so use them as to acquire the position of the leading man of business in this city and to accumulate a large fortune.

For some years after his marriage he lived with his father-in-law, Mr. Atherton, in Girard Row, north side of Chesnut St., above 11th. As his means soon justified him, he moved to a house in Walnut St., south side, 3rd house above 10. Soon after, he bought & altered & enlarged the house at the s.west corner of Walnut & 10th. During this time in the summer, he either went to a watering place or rented country houses, Magarge's on the York Road, Cowperthwaite's on the Delaware, &c. His establishment was lavish, he entertained a great deal of company, keeping numerous servants, horses & equipages, & spending a great deal of money, 40 to 50,000 a year. His hospitality & generosity were unbounded. His prosperity seemed equally so. His business operations were immense and uniform success seemed to be his peculiar attribute. Unfortunately, in this tide of fortune & in this extravagant expenditure were planted the seeds of future trouble and of the only faults that marred his noble & amiable character. He was caught by the snares of the world; the excitement of business & of large & dangerous business operations became necessary to him because he wanted the resources that mental culture supplies. His faults were on the surface and did not reach the solid basis of moral worth on which his nature rested. They gave me many painful reflections during his life, but never injured or weakened my genuine respect or warm affection for him and now that he is gone, as they were the offspring of worldly things, they have vanished as the world has to him vanished, they seem to me unreal and I shall neither remember nor record them. In 1849, he purchased the land and then built the house at Brookwood and in 1855 he sold his house in town and lived wholly at Brookwood. Henry's first great affliction was the death of his daughter Emily in 1848. Next came the malady that made Ellen a cripple, I fear for life. In 1858, his wife died & from this blow he never recovered. All these events I have described in former diaries. In the spring of last year came his business embarrassments and suspension of payment, greatly aggravated by a most painful controversy with the Morrisons, last winter arose the contest with the Little Schuylkill Coal Co., and all these successive causes, acting upon a sensitive nature, prepared the way for the disease that terminated his life on the 10th of last month.

APRIL 4, 1862 | At 10 drove up to Brookwood. Geo. Smith, Hollis, & the appraisers there. They got thro two wine rooms, the china, glass, & silver. The stock of wines is immense & very choice, several hundred demijohns of rare & fine sherry & Madeira. The china & glass are of the most elegant & costly character, one set of Sevres having cost $1500. There is a large quantity of plate, a dinner service, pitchers, tankards, wine coolers, tea service, &c. It was a melancholy thing to see all these articles, the instruments of Henry's lavish hospitality arranged for such a purpose. How many scenes of festive & domestic enjoyment they recalled. They remain, more durable than the pleasures of which they are the symbols and the persons who used them. The men are to go out again to examine the wine cellar which contains the hock & claret, the plated ware, & the attics, &c.

APRIL 26, 1862 | Saw Chas Ingersoll in town. He gave me a pamphlet he has just published about public questions involved in the war.[18]

18. Charles Ingersoll, *A Letter to a Friend in a Slave State: By a Citizen of Pennsylvania* (Philadelphia, 1862).

APRIL 27, 1862 | In the evening read Chas. Ingersoll's pamphlet. It is a strange mixture of extravagant ideas & good sense and displays a very narrow partizan spirit. It cannot be called an argument. He thinks the Union must be restored or the country doomed to ruin & constant war for many years. That the southern people can never be conquered. Therefore the only thing to be done is to conciliate the South. This will never be done he says by the party now in power, but would be done by the Democratic Party, which of course alone can save the country. The Democratic Party is sure to triumph he thinks at the next election, in Dec. 1863—& will restore union, Peace & Prosperity if the South can hold out that long. By conciliating the South he means treating with armed rebels & yielding to all their demands. When the Democrats return to power, he declares that their former alliance with the South will be renewed & the nation be saved, unless meanwhile, the Republican Party carry out its plan of abolishing slavery, in which case reunion would become impossible. It is the dread of this very union of the South & democracy which induced many to advocate sweeping measures of abolition, that the cause of the war may not become again active.

APRIL 30, 1862 | Bet . . . brought out a pamphlet by Edward Ingersoll, about the war, the writ of habeas corpus &c &c.[19] Looked over it. It seems a confused jumble of misunderstood facts & principles, written in a bad style & worse spirit, evidently dictated by the narrowest partizan feeling, which seems in some minds strong enough to overcome love of country & love of truth. All the family, except Uncle Joe & of course Bet, sympathize with the rebellion.

MAY 5, 1862 | Yorktown has been evacuated. The rebel generals became convinced that McClellan's attack could not be resisted & so determined to abandon the place. They did this with skill, keeping up a fire & show of resistance whilst they were employed for some days

---

19. Edward Ingersoll, *Personal Liberty and Martial Law: A Review of Some Pamphlets of the Day* (Philadelphia, 1862).

in sending away their sick & wounded and what they could of artillery & stores. Much of both, however, were found by our people on entering the town, which was entirely deserted by its inhabitants. The rebels here also displayed their barbarous disregard of the usages of civilized war by concealing torpedoes at wells, springs, in streets & roads, at the telegraph office, &c., by the explosion of which some of our men were killed & many wounded.

MAY 11, 1862 | Geo. Smith came in at 10 ½ o'clock. Had much conversation with him about Henry's affairs & family of a painful character. He first spoke of things relating to the estate & some pending difficulties. About these however I was already informed & told him my views, which coincided with his own. He next said that it was necessary that a guardian should be appointed for the children & he wished to speak to me about that. I told him that I had thought much of the subject, that I was the nearest male relation of the children, that I felt all possible interest in them and was desirous of performing my duty toward them in the fullest manner. That of course I was the proper person to be their guardian, but that I had as yet said nothing on the subject, because from certain things that I had noticed I feared that an offer of the sort from me would be rejected. That the children, tho I did not suppose they disliked me, certainly had no affection for me, or, if they had, would resist anything like an attempt on my part to control them or interfere in their concerns. . . . That Liedy possessed a strong will & concentrated character which it was impossible to influence. What she determined to do, she would do, that was evident, and she ruled all the others absolutely, including Mrs. Atherton. . . . I told him also that my belief was that Liedy would prefer him for the guardian. He replied that he thought I had better not be guardian, but advised *me* to propose Mrs. Atherton for the place. I asked his reasons. He declined giving them. I told him I thought he had no right to refuse & with some reluctance I gathered that he considered the view I had taken of the case correct. That Liedy would resist my appointment. . . . I shall take time to reflect on the line of conduct I shall pursue. I have only one desire & that is to do my duty to the children, which I fear will be rather a difficult duty.

MAY 13, 1862 | Saw Hollis. He told me that a number of Henry's friends are to meet at the office tomorrow morning to consult on important business relating to the estate & wished me to come. He had already written me a note to that effect. Went to Mr. Ingersoll's at 3. Went up to the parlor & saw Mrs. Chas. Ingersoll who told me that he was sinking. After some talk with her went up to his chamber. Bet was there & Charles sitting by his side. He was evidently dying, breathing hard with a low moan, scarcely conscious, and without suffering.

MAY 14, 1862 | Drove to town at 9. Went to Mr. Ingersoll's. He died this morning at 2 o'clock with great tranquillity, or rather apparent unconsciousness. Last Wednesday he was out here in his usual health, which during the last winter had been very good. He was 79. He had a remarkable constitution & retained his powers of mind & body in great vigor to the last. His illness was short & without much suffering & his death easy. He was fortunate. The last four or five years of his life were clouded by the condition of Mrs. Ingersoll, but there were many alleviations to even that trouble. He was easy in his fortune, was surrounded by children & grandchildren so that he was rarely alone, had good health & animal spirits that could scarcely be much depressed, found occupation in books & writing & the sole cause of distress that he had, Mrs. Ingersoll's condition, was of a sort which by being habitual becomes bearable. He bore it very well & exhibited uniform kindness & patience under very trying circumstances. The great question is now what is to be done with her. Bet I know will wish to bring her here & the result would be the destruction of the happiness of our home.[20] Saw Bet, Charles & Edward.

20. Fisher's wife brought her mother to Forest Hill on May 23, and, although her arrival was not promising—"It was long before she could be induced to get out of the carriage"—her actual presence in the Fisher home did not prove distracting, for she was quiet, kept to her room, and was tended by a nurse.

Went then to Henry's office. Found there Mr. Jno. A. Brown,[21] Mr. Mercer, pres. of the Farmers & Mechanics' Bank, Frederick Fraley,[22] Mr. Fell,[23] Adolph Borie,[24] Geo. Smith, & Ben Gerhard. Mr. Hollis stated the case. A suit is threatened against the estate by the Morrisons for some of Henry's transactions with them connected with investments made by him for them in stock & bonds of the Little Schuylkill Railroad Co. The bill in equity filed against the trustees of that company in the beginning of last winter, in which Henry was the chief party aimed at, is still going on. These two claims amount to about $500,000, & if recovered would bankrupt the estate. Counsel say they most probably cannot be recovered, but that possibly they might be. The transactions on which they are founded are of a nature capable of very painful construction and open to much remark, which, as Henry is not here to explain them, would be of a most unpleasant & injurious character. These suits can now be settled by the payment of $100,000. All agreed that the money ought to be paid. But the doubt was about the legal power of Hollis to pay it. In case the estate should prove insolvent, creditors might make Hollis liable for the amt such payment exceeded the pro rata of all the creditors. The gentlemen then present agreed that they would indemnify Hollis in case an event so improbable should occur, some saying they would be responsible for $10,000, some for $5000. I said I would go $10,000. I considered it my duty to do this. I could not bear to see strangers, tho rich, becoming responsible for money in order to benefit my brother's children & do nothing myself, poor as I am, when he had by his will released a debt due from me to the amount of $20,000. The risk is very slight. . . . Hollis said he hoped to make the estate turn out

21. John A. Brown (1788-1872), a successful merchant banker who established a branch of his family's Baltimore house (Alexander Brown & Sons) in Philadelphia in 1818, but retired when the panic of 1837 impaired his health. He devoted the rest of his life to philanthropies and church work.

22. Fraley, president of the Schuylkill Navigation Company, had been closely associated with Henry Fisher in business.

23. John G. Fell, wealthy coal merchant and intimate associate of Henry Fisher.

24. Adolphe E. Borie (1809-80) had achieved success in the trade with China.

$400,000. Had much painful talk with him about Henry's career & he told me some things most deplorable, showing how just have been the dismal impressions, the reluctant judgments & prophetic fears that filled my mind for so many years.

MAY 17, 1862 | At 8 o'clk went to town to attend Mr. Ingersoll's funeral. It was private. None were asked except near relations and it was made known that none were expected unless invited. There were not more than twenty persons present. These were conveyed in Charles', Edward's, Harry's, Mr. J. R. Ingersoll's, & Mr. McKean's carriages. We started at 9 & went to the Woodlands cemetery, which has filled up very rapidly since I last saw it. The bier was carried by Charles, Edward, Harry, & Jno. Meigs. I went out in the carriage with Mr. J. R. Ingersoll, Alexander Wilcocks,[25] & Mr. [John M.] Thomas. Everything went off with great propriety. When I returned, sat for an hour or two with Bet who feels the loss of her father very sensibly. As his age affected neither his health nor his mind nor his spirits, he was a burden to no one and as much an object of interest and affection to his children to the last as ever.

He was in many respects a remarkable person and during a long life held a conspicuous position as a public man, having been twice in Congress and for many years district attorney in this city when the place was far more respectable than it has since become. He was a partizan and a Democrat and his speeches and writings are imbued not only with the opinions but the passions of a partizan. He was not learned as a lawyer or a scholar, tho his mind was cultivated by reading. His intellect was not of a high order, but he wrote & spoke with ease, animation, and earnestness & was witty at times, generally sarcastic, clever, pointed, odd, never eloquent or profound. His reasoning faculty was limited, he had faint perceptions of abstract truth, none of natural beauty. His talents were of a kind that lead to worldly success but not to durable fame. He wrote a history of the war of 1812, which is amusing rather than instructive, contains some lively sketches of

---

25. Dr. Alexander Wilcocks was a nephew of the deceased's wife.

men & scenes connected with his public life, but wants method, clearness, & thought, and is deformed by his eccentric style.[26] His best literary performance is a little work published in his youth, the Inchiquin letters.[27] He made many mistakes as a public man; among them was his monstrous attack on Mr. Webster which failed utterly & caused his disappointment in the great object of his ambition, the French mission, which he otherwise would have got as he was nominated to the Senate & rejected.[28] Mr. Ingersoll possessed many social accomplishments & talents that always made him a marked man. His face & figure were striking, expressive & graceful, his manners easy & gentlemanlike, his conversation flowing, animated, sprightly & intelligent, abounding in interesting anecdotes accumulated during a long life spent in public business and among eminent men. He was very temperate & simple in his habits, caring nothing for luxury or show, priding himself, indeed, on his contempt for appearance, but tho frugal he was liberal & particularly so to his children. He was easy & amiable in his domestic relations, sometimes passionate but never austere, exacting or reserved, generally kind, seldom impulsive or affectionate. His gentleness, patience, & forebearance under the severe trial of his wife's condition for the last four years were admirable. This and the insanity of his son Alexander, now in the hospital, were the great afflictions of his life. His children were much attached to him and treated him with uniform respect and attention. He outlived most of his friends & contemporaries & for many years before his death was secluded from the world & occupied himself chiefly in literary labors, which, if not of the highest order, afforded him occupation and a resource.[29] Several notices of his death have appeared in the papers,

26. *Historical Sketch of the Second War between the United States of America and Great Britain*, 2 vols. (Philadelphia, 1845-49).

27. *Inchiquin, The Jesuit's Letters, during a Late Residence in the United States of America: Being a Fragment of a Private Correspondence, Accidentally Discovered in Europe* (New York, 1810).

28. While in Congress, Ingersoll engaged in an acrimonious controversy with Daniel Webster concerning the latter's handling of public funds.

29. His final literary effort was a projected two-volume work entitled *Recollections, Historical, Political, Biographical, and Social*, the first volume of which was printed by J. B. Lippincott in 1861, but withheld by the author because of the Civil War. It was

all of them laudatory that I have seen. Like most of us, he had his good qualities & his faults & weaknesses. I do not wish to record the latter. In my intercourse with him there was a little that was agreeable that I am glad to recall & much more that was painful that I would be glad to forget.[30] It is a good maxim that one should say nothing but good of the dead.

MAY 21, 1862 | At 3 ½ rode Delly up to Brookwood. . . . Saw only Mrs. Atherton. Spoke to her about the guardianship. I said it was necessary that a guardian be appointed and asked her if she had thought of the subject. She said she had & that Liedy & Ellen wished her to be the guardian & that she was willing. . . . So the matter ended. I do not feel satisfied with myself at giving the thing up so easily yet do not see what other course I can pursue with advantage to the children. Were I to insist on assuming any control over them I am sure I would be resisted by the whole family. . . .

JUNE 12, 1862 | There has been a good deal of severe skirmishing in Virginia between the forces of Banks & Fremont & the Confederates under Jackson, on the whole ending favorably to our side.[31] I cannot pretend to keep the run of these military operations. I think the war virtually over, tho how soon we may have peace is doubtful. All interest now centres at Richmond, where the rebels say a great battle is to be fought. I doubt it. McClellan is making his approaches scientifically & as soon as it becomes evident that he can certainly take the place, I think it will be abandoned, for why sacrifice life uselessly in attempting to defend it.

JUNE 20, 1862 | Stewardson is intimate with the author Oliver Wendell Holmes of Boston. Some months ago I asked Stewardson to send

finally released in 1886. The second volume was never published since not enough of it had been completed before Ingersoll's death.

30. None of the Ingersolls liked Fisher, whose opinions and way of life irritated them intensely. They tolerated him because of his wife.

31. Fisher to the contrary, the operations of Gen. Nathaniel P. Banks in the Shenandoah and of Gen. John C. Fremont in western Virginia were not at all successful against Gen. "Stonewall" Jackson.

him copies of *Rustic Rhymes* & the *Winter Studies*, & ask his candid opinion of them. Today I inquired whether he had done so & what was the reply. He read me a letter he had received from Holmes, very reluctantly. It was by no means flattering. He gives me credit for some merits, but thinks that poetry is evidently not my vocation. I fear he is right.

JUNE 26, 1862 | The President has just made a hurried visit to Genl. Scott at West Point. He was closeted with the old hero for several hours & then went home as fast as steam could carry him, making the journey from New York to Washington in 7 hours & 20 minutes, the fastest time on record in this country. It is thought that some new difficulties have appeared in the war & that Genl. Scott will be recalled and resume his place as commander in chief.

JUNE 28, 1862 | As I walked up Chesnut St. this morning saw workmen pulling down Mr. Edward Burd's fine old house at the corner of 9th & Chesnut.[32] The rooms could be seen thru the broken walls. They recalled many long-past scenes & persons. It was a very hospitable house in Mr. Burd's time and I have been there at many a ball & party. I was first introduced to my dear wife at a brilliant ball at that house, a fortunate event for me. I well remember her look & manner & the impression they produced on me, never afterwards to be effaced, but constantly renewed & strengthened up to the present hour. This happened I think in 1833 or 1832. The society of Philad: was very good at that time, well marked in its outlines and rather exclusive. The principal families had large and handsome establishments and entertained habitually. How many with whom I was intimate and had daily intercourse have passed away.

JUNE 30, 1862 | People much excited by news of a very severe battle at Richmond, which began on Friday & had not ceased at the last

---

32. Edward Shippen Burd built this mansion in 1810 and it was long considered to be one of the showplaces in the city. He died in 1848 and his widow lived in the house until her death in 1860. According to Burd's will, the property was to be maintained for one year after Mrs. Burd's death and then to be demolished and replaced by stores.

accounts on Sunday. The result was not known, but the general opinion seemed to be that we had the best of it. As McCall's division[33] was attacked, many Philadelphians were in the fight & of course much anxiety was felt by their friends. What a scene Richmond must be now, what terror & what distress as the wounded are brought in, how many tragedies & houses of mourning. The war is getting to be a fearful thing and there is less confidence expressed as to its fortunate termination. The southern people seem inflamed by the most bitter hatred of the North. How then can the Union be restored? On the other hand, the spirit of the North is roused and the people are determined to conquer & to keep the country undivided if they hold the South in absolute subjection. What then will become of the Constitution and free government?

JULY 3, 1862 | No special news in the morning paper. There are no official accounts of the battle, all is rumor and conjecture. The opinion seems to be that McClellan has made good his position on the James River, withdrawing his force according to a preconceived plan in good order, tho pursued constantly by a greatly superior force. I suppose the truth is that he saw that because of the strength of the enemy he could not maintain his position & that his movement was in reality a retreat to seek the protection of the gunboats on the James River.

Went to McMichael's office. Found a group there with very gloomy faces. News had come by telegraph that McClellan had met with a disastrous defeat yesterday in a very severe and bloody battle & that several Philadelphians were killed—Genl. McCall, Harry Biddle, Hamilton Kuhn, & young Watmough.[34] Geo. Meade,[35] a brigadier general,

33. Gen. George A. McCall (1802-68), of Philadelphia, commanded the Pennsylvania Reserves.

34. Gen. McCall was not killed, but was captured and sent into Richmond for two months before his exchange. Henry J. Biddle, McCall's assistant adjutant general, was killed, as was Lt. James Hamilton Kuhn, but William Nicklin Watmough, one of Meade's staff officers, was merely wounded.

35. George Gordon Meade (1815-72), born to American parents in Spain, graduated from the U.S. Military Academy in 1835 and was a veteran of the Mexican War. Meade was promoted to brigadier general of volunteers in 1861 and brigadier general in the

was severely wounded and on his way home. He married a daughter of John Sergeant & served with distinction in the Mexican War. All this is sad enough. Was very sorry to hear the news about Hamilton Kuhn, tho I have not known him since he was a baby. He was the youngest, very amiable & a sort of pet in his family, about 24 years old with a handsome fortune. He was on Geo. Meade's staff. The town was in a state of excitement and 3rd St. filled with people, crowds surrounding the newspaper offices. Left McMichael's & went to bank. On my way back saw a throng clustering around the *Inquirer* office and heard a shout. Went to McMichael's. Official news had come from the War Department containing a dispatch from McClellan up to 5 o'clock yesterday. There had been a terrible battle all the morning, but he had made good his position and repulsed the enemy. This was hailed as a victory. Nevertheless, he is now 17 miles from Richmond instead of 4 & is obliged to rely on gunboats for protection.

JULY 6, 1862 | At 3 o'clock drove Monkey up to Wakefield. Uncle William has rallied again & is much better. Went up to his room & sat with him nearly an hour. He was calm & cheerful and talked in his usual manner. He said that when I saw him last he expected to die today or tomorrow, but now he felt as if he should live a few days longer. He asked me what I considered the best arguments in favor of the immortality of the soul. I told him that one was that we could think of it, desire it, hope for it, & have a lively foresense here of another life, in which our love of truth would find gratification & virtue its reward & that it was inconsistent with our ideas of the Deity to suppose that we could be deceived in these wishes & expectations & that our thoughts were without substance. That another argument was, that our minds were capable of perceiving eternal truths, that truth was divine & therefore we had communion with God and that what was able to participate in eternal things must be itself eternal. I told him also that we knew nothing really of death, what it is or

---

Regular Army in 1863. He commanded the Army of the Potomac during the Gettysburg campaign, leading the Union troops to victory in July 1863.

whether it is, that Plato's reasoning on the subject appeared conclusive to my mind, which is that death, so far as our consciousness is concerned, has no existence. So long as we live it is not, and when we die, if we enter on another state of being, that is not death but life; if we really die, or if consciousness and memory cease, then death has no existence for us. So we talked, cheerfully, mingling other topics, and such are the things we call realities.

Sarah Wister was in the room. Her father near his end, he & she speaking of it in pleasant mood. He said his life had been prosperous, that he was now old, had nothing more to do or enjoy in the world & was quite ready to go. He said he should leave an estate of $400,000 to his family, which I was very glad to hear, as with what they have already it will make them well off.

JULY 13, 1862 | Started at 2 and drove up to Alverthorpe where I had not been for a long while. Found them just finishing dinner. Markoe Bache, Mr. Kane, & Lilly there. The two last are spending the summer there. We soon went to the drawing room & soon began to talk about the war, the slavery question, the rights & wrongs of the South, and the errors and wickedness of the government. Mrs. Fisher was excited—her feelings are strong, her reasoning weak. Fisher wavers and has not yet made up his mind on which side he is, but abuses the administration for its antislavery measures because they "will irritate the South." His notion seems to be that in this war the chief duty of the government is to protect slavery & put down northern abolitionists. Kane was petty, foolish, sarcastic, abused the government & the army, and showed the cloven foot of the small demagogue & partizan. Nothing approaching an argument, a liberal view of the situation of the country or the rights and duty of the government, not a patriotic or noble sentiment was expressed by any of the party. Everything they said was narrow & ignorant, evidently dictated by selfish feeling arising from the position of each; Mrs. Fisher, a southern woman, with her friends & family & So. Carolina exposed to every sort of danger & calamity; Fisher, sympathizing with her, feeling for her friends who are also his friends, dreading & hating war because of its effects on his property, & in his heart willing that peace should be made on any terms, however humiliating and disgraceful to the country; Kane, a Democrat, wholly a partizan, ambitious of political success, with the talents of an attorney & unable to understand an abstract principle or to feel enthusiasm for a just cause. Was not pleased.

JULY 26, 1862 | There is more gloom & anxiety now than at any period of the war since the battle of Bull Run. The currency panic increases and it is difficult to get silver for change. Gold has disappeared. Post office stamps & railroad tickets are used for currency.

JULY 27, 1862 | They say Mrs. Jno. Butler speaks of the South as ruined. She was in Richmond during the late battles. Saw wounded men die in the street. The whole town was a hospital. She stayed at the hotel frequented by the officers of the rebel army & heard their comments on the events of each day. They fully expected to "bag the federals," & were greatly disappointed at the result. They expressed high respect for the ability of McClellan. Langhorne Wister has returned & is recruiting soldiers.[36]

AUGUST 1, 1862 | Chas. Ingersoll came in. He and Mr. I. [Joseph R. Ingersoll] were speaking of a case, just decided by Judge Hare, in which the question was whether a party who had expressly contracted to pay a debt in gold and silver could nevertheless pay it in notes made a legal tender by the late act of Congress. Charles contended that the act of Congress was unconstitutional because no express power was given for such a purpose. I replied that it clearly came within the implied powers, according to all the authorities, that it was essential to the power of making war as it was impossible to carry on a war without a resort to paper money. "But we don't want the government to carry on this war," he replied, a speech that means a great deal. It shows a reckless disregard of principle, for the question is one of law, wholly independent of the nature or purpose of the war. If Charles approved the war, he would, no doubt, say the government had the

---

36. Langhorne Wister (1834–91), of Germantown, was brevetted brigadier general after the battle of Gettysburg.

power. The Democrats will, I suppose, from other remarks he made, endeavor to obtain a decision by the courts declaring that Congress had no power to make paper a legal tender. Should they do this, the currency would be discredited and a fatal blow might be struck at the power of the government to carry on the war.

AUGUST 2, 1862 | Porter's mortar fleet has gone to the James River, which, it is thought, will insure the safety of McClellan's army.[37] Very serious doubts are entertained of his skill & ability, which, it is said, are shared by the President who has therefore placed Halleck in chief command.[38] Unfortunately, party feeling is enlisted in the question, which excludes truth from its discussion. McClellan is opposed to the plans of the abolitionists. He is therefore denounced by them, & would be were he a Napoleon, & is lauded by the Democrats, & would be were he an idiot.

AUGUST 8, 1862 | A war meeting has been held at Washington at which some very strong resolutions were passed declaring that the Union must be restored tho the South should be depopulated and made a desert. Mr. Lincoln went to it & made a short, pithy, humourous speech in which he expressed confidence in McClellan, said there was no truth in the rumours of disagreement between him & Stanton, that the latter had sent McClellan all the reinforcements he could and that, if any one was to blame, it was himself, Mr. Lincoln. Genl. Wadsworth, provost marshal of Washington, has just been to Harrisburg, where he caused the editors of two newspapers to be arrested for expressing disloyal and seditious opinions. At a large town meeting recently held in Baltimore, a resolution was passed recommending Genl. Wool[39] to cause the oath of allegiance to be administered to all suspected of disloyalty & that those who refused to take it should

---

37. David D. Porter (1813-91), a member of the U.S. Navy since 1829, commanded the Mississippi River squadron in 1862-63 and the North Atlantic blockading squadron in 1864.

38. Gen. Halleck was appointed military advisor to the president on July 11, 1862, with the title of general in chief.

39. Gen. John Ellis Wool (1784-1869), a veteran of the War of 1812 and the Mexican War, commanded the Middle Military Department.

be sent South. Most of the rich & prominent men in Baltimore are notoriously secessionists. Many of them, it is said, have already left the place for Canada & other foreign parts to escape this test. These are strong measures, but not too strong for the emergency, for the war has become really a matter of life or death, not to the Union only, but to the government. We must conquer to maintain the authority & dignity of the government of the northern states, whether we can retain the South or not. They are safe measures, provided the government is sustained by the northern people, which appears to be the case as yet, notwithstanding the machinations of the Democratic Party.

AUGUST 15, 1862 | Went to town, driving Bet, Sidney, & Bridget in the big wagon with Delly. As we were going along Broad St. we met a Dummy engine lately put on that road.[40] The mare was very much frightened, shied first to one side & then to the other, & if they had not stopped the engine & the conductor had not come to my assistance, we would have been upset. When I saw the probability of this & thought of Bet & Sidney, my feelings are not to be described, nor my relief & thankfulness when the danger was over. These Dummy cars always frighten horses. They move without any apparent motive power, tho why that should have the effect I cannot imagine, unless horses are capable of being astonished at an effect of which they cannot see the cause. It is an outrage to permit the use of such engines in the streets, but the passenger railroad companies seem to have seized on the highways of the city as their property. They control councils & the legislature.

AUGUST 18, 1862 | Fisher mentioned a circumstance which he said he had directly from one of the parties, and which exemplifies the devastating moral influences of slavery. His informant, a lady, was visiting at the house of another lady in Virginia, where she saw a

---

40. Streetcars propelled by small vertical steam engines were called "dummies" by Philadelphians.

remarkably beautiful mulatto girl, 12 or 13 years old, a slave. What can you do with such a pretty creature as that, said the visitor. "Oh," replied the other, "we intend her for our son. We shall give her to him, when she is old enough, to keep him out of low dissipation." Civilization cannot exist under such influences. This is Turkish, not American.

AUGUST 22, 1862 | Edward Ingersoll here in the afternoon. He brought me a paper to sign addressed to the grand jury, remonstrating against the outrage of the Dummy on Broad St. Mr. McKean's[41] horses have been frightened and his also by it. I told him I would write an article on the subject for McMichael's paper and he said he had written one for the *Ledger*.

In the evening wrote the article.[42] Perhaps something may come of these efforts, but it is doubtful. This Dummy company got its charter by sheer bribery and cannot be defeated by fair means. Even the grand jury I fear cannot reach it.

AUGUST 25, 1862 | On Saturday evening the Democrats had a town meeting to express their opinions about the war. It had been announced for some days & great efforts were made to render it successful. It is represented in the paper this morning as a failure. The numbers at it were few & there was no enthusiasm, many of the wards refusing to turn out at all. Peter McCall[43] presided. The resolutions professed loyalty, but denounced abolition & the course of the government, tho they were not extravagant in their tone and neither were the speeches, except that of Chas. Ingersoll. He was extremely violent, far beyond the general feeling of the assembly. He declared that the Democratic Party had a majority and at the next election would hurl the administration from power, with much more wild talk of the same

---

41. Henry Pratt McKean (1810-94) built the mansion "Fern Hill" in Germantown.

42. "The Dummy Engine on Broad St.," signed "S," appeared in the *North American* on August 25, 1862.

43. Peter McCall (1809-80) was a prominent Democratic lawyer in Philadelphia during the Civil War; he had previously been mayor of the city, elected as a Whig.

sort. Young Terry, who comes every day to copy the essay for me, was at the meeting.[44] He said the applause was confined to a few around the stand, that Charles' speech was "rabid," and did not meet with approbation. That he heard many denounce it as going too far. Terry is a Democrat and, as the son of an old servant of the Ingersolls, is disposed to receive with favor anything that Charles does. I can easily understand what sort of a speech he made from what I have heard him say on the subject. He is very excitable & impulsive, even passionate, and wholly incapable of thinking or speaking calmly about the war or anything connected with it.

Came home by Dewey's Lane. Met there Mr. [Alexander] Bacon, who had just got out of the cars at the station. I asked him what was the news. He said nothing from the army, adding, "I suppose you have heard that Charles Ingersoll was arrested this morning." I asked the reason & he said because of his speech at the Democratic meeting on Saturday. As I was near William Wister's gate, I went in to hear more. William could tell me nothing, but that he had heard of the arrest. I told both him & Bacon that I thought it an impolitic step. That the meeting was a failure, that the Union Party was strong enough to despise such efforts and that severe measures would only tend to make side issues, to excite passion and to give consequence to men, who, let alone, would become insignificant. They agreed with me. When I got home told what I had heard to Bet, who was much distressed, tho not much surprised, for we had often talked of the probability of such an event. Edward Ingersoll here after dinner. He confirmed the news. He said that Charles was arrested by [William H. Kern] the *provost marshal,* for it seems one has been appointed for this city, who took a bond for his appearance next Wednesday. Edward said that Charles & his family laughed at the whole affair and treated it very lightly. I hope they may find it a laughing matter.

---

44. Terry Mahoney, son of a former employee at Forest Hill, was employed by Fisher on several occasions to make clean copies of his manuscripts for the printer. At this time, he was copying Fisher's latest work, *The Trial of the Constitution.*

AUGUST 26, 1862 | At 2 went to town, chiefly to hear about Charles. Met him in 4th St. near McCall's office and McCall & a Mr. Bullitt,[45] a member of the bar, soon joined. Before they came, Charles had told me that he was arrested by the provost marshal and had given a bond to deliver himself up to him tomorrow at 12 o'clock. I asked him what course he intended to take. He said he would take out a writ of habeas corpus. I told [him] I thought it would be very unwise to do so. That the writ was suspended. That to appeal to it would be regarded as an act of contumacy & defiance & make his position far worse. That the best plan would be for some one of his friends who knew Mr. Seward to write to him and state the case, suggesting that it did not justify an arrest as there was nothing treasonable in the affidavit on which the arrest was founded. He said that he could not take such a course as it would be derogatory to him. That he would not succumb to the government. That the writ was not legally suspended & he intended to try the question of legality. He was going to McCall's to consult him & when he & Bullitt came they invited me in. We had a regular discussion in the office. I urged the same views already mentioned. I said that whether the writ was legally suspended or not, the fact of its suspension was a reality not to be resisted. That if the court should issue the writ & order his discharge, the order would be, of course, disregarded and that his imprisonment for an indefinite period would follow as a matter of course. McCall thought I was right. What Mr. Bullitt said was not very wise or worth repeating. Charles, however, had made up his mind. He thought the arrest an outrage, that his rights were invaded, that the course of the government was unjust, tyrannical, & unconstitutional, and he felt it due to himself to appeal to the law. He had hopes, however, that the provost marshal, who had gone to Washington, would bring back an order for his release. After leaving them I met Pierce Butler & spoke of the matter to him. He approved of Charles' course & said that an appeal to Mr. Seward would certainly fail. He spoke of the arrests and what he considers

---

45. John C. Bullitt (1824-1902), originally from Kentucky, was of the law and collection office of Bullitt & Fairthorne.

the tyrannical conduct of the government with great bitterness, and said that Charles could not be taken without bloodshed in the streets, that he *knew* that an attempt to carry him to prison would be forcibly resisted. Butler, however, is very wild in his notions, and, having been arrested himself, resentment is added to the passions by which he is moved as a secessionist and a southern man, as he considers himself, tho he was born & bred in the North.

AUGUST 28, 1862 | Went to Charles' house. Another charge, it seems, had been made against him, on which he was still in the custody of the marshal, who had an officer in the house keeping a nominal watch over him. He was treated throughout with courtesy & every consideration, the officer was sitting in the office. I went up to the drawing room, where the family was assembled, gay as usual. Charles had taken out a writ of habeas corpus which was heard today at 12 o'clock. He was unmoved in his determination to try the case & seemed to contemplate with unconcern the possibility of a contest should the judge order his discharge and the marshal refuse to give him up. The writ was issued by John Cadwalader,[46] the district U.S. judge, and Charles feels quite sure of a favorable decision from him, why I do not know, unless because Cadwalader is a Democrat & known to have sympathies with the South. Wrongheaded & violent as Charles is & absurd in his notions, he shows spirit & pluck. Edward was there & looked worn and anxious. Left them at 9 & came home. When I went upstairs found Mrs. Ingersoll evidently dying. Sent Daniel up to Medary[47] in the wagon . . . to inform Harry. Sat with Bet by her dying mother for an hour. She was sinking slowly & quietly, wholly without consciousness or strength, panting more & more feebly. At 11 ½ Harry came and at ¼ to 1 o'clock this morning the poor old lady was calmly released from this mysterious state which we call life, but which was

46. John Cadwalader (1805-79), a former Democratic congressman, was the U.S. District Judge for the Eastern District of Pennsylvania, appointed by President James Buchanan in 1858.

47. Medary was built by the Harry Ingersolls in 1847 on Green Lane near Fern Rock Station and next to Brookwood. C. Morton Smith inherited the property in 1892 and sold it about 1910.

hardly life to her, since mind & memory had departed long before the body gave way. Harry, Elizabeth, & I sat by her till all was over and Harry closed her eyes, and there she lay in the stillness of death, the worn, attenuated remains of what was once a beautiful & charming woman, the mother of many children. A few months ago her husband preceded her to the unknown realms, whither we are all going so rapidly. They married early & lived together 57 years.

When all was over, Harry & I came down to the library and talked over Charles' affair. We differed entirely in our notions about the rights of the government and the duties of the citizen & the legality of Charles' arrest. We agreed, however, in the desire to get him released, and, as I thought the arrest at this time impolitic, I was willing to do anything I considered right to get him released. Harry suggested that perhaps if the government knew of his mother's death it would have an effect & said he thought I was the proper person to make the statement to the marshal or the district attorney. I said I would do it with pleasure. Went to town at 8 o'clock. Saw Milevan, the marshal.[48] He was very civil & sent a telegram to Washington at once. When Charles' case came up in the morning, the hearing was postponed till Monday on account of his mother's death. Went to Wroth's.[49] Saw Eli there.[50] He says he expects to return to Mount Harmon after the 1st of September. Edward & Jno. Meigs here this afternoon. The funeral will take place on Sunday. Bet is sad but tranquil. The case is not one for deep grief, but the death of a mother must always be a distressing thing. Going to town I read in the cars this morning the last affidavit against Charles, containing extracts from the *phonographic* report of his speech.[51] It is much stronger & more violent in language and sentiment than that in the *Ledger*. He declares that the whole object of the war is to abolish slavery and that no government in the world is so

---

48. William Millward, marshal of the United States for the Eastern District of Pennsylvania, not to be confused with the provost marshal.

49. Fisher sold the produce of his Mount Harmon farm through James W. Wroth, produce dealer at the Delaware Avenue Market.

50. Eli Welles, one of Fisher's farm hands.

51. Not phonographic in the modern sense, but a verbatim report taken down in shorthand.

corrupt & tyrannical as this.[52] If he is sent to Fort Warren,[53] I must say he will meet merited retribution. This is no time to denounce the government & to tell the people that it is not worth supporting or defending. I omitted to say that when I went to town this morning I first called at his house & communicated to him the death of his mother. He received the intelligence with becoming emotion.

AUGUST 31, 1862 | Langhorne Wister paid me a visit. He has permission to raise a regiment, of which, if he succeeds, he is to be the colonel. Such are the urgent demands of the government, however, that he will be obliged to take what he has got to Washington on Tuesday with his former rank of captain. He is a handsome, intelligent, gallant fellow, much developed and improved by army life. He was at the battle of Malvern Hill & all the others that occurred during McClellan's change of position from the Chickahominy to the James River, & participated actively and usefully in some of the hardest fighting. He said that after the first round in an action all fear vanishes. That the painful & anxious moments are those which immediately precede a conflict, and that it is a great relief to be under fire. He said that after the experience of one battle the horrible sights of the wounded & dying strewing the field are viewed with perfect indifference. Habit & circumstances then develop qualities of our nature otherwise unsuspected. But for this, war would be impossible. I said it seemed to me that the most terrible thing in a battle must be a charge of bayonets, that a confused melee of furious men armed with such weapons, stabbing each other & fighting hand to hand in a mass of hundreds, was something shocking even to think of. He said it was so shocking that it very rarely happened that bayonets are crossed, one side or the other almost always giving way before meeting. That he had seen many charges, but had never seen bayonets crossed.

52. The *North American* for August 26, 1862, reported Ingersoll as having said: "The despotisms of the old world can furnish no parallel to the corruptions of the administration of Abraham Lincoln."

53. Fort Warren was in Boston Harbor. It was there that the Confederate vice president Alexander H. Stephens was imprisoned after the war.

september 1, 1862 | Charles Ingersoll has been released by order of the Secretary of War. Came out at 5 o'clock. Edwd. Ingersoll here. He said that the government had "backed down" from its position in releasing Charles. These Democrats never give anybody credit for good intentions who is not of their own party. The truth is that the arrest was made by the provost marshal without orders, except general orders from the government, and as soon as the facts were known to the department a discharge was ordered.

september 4, 1862 | Went to McMichael's office. Mr. Wm. D. Kelley, member of Congress from this city, there.[54] They thought our situation could not be much worse than it is and ascribed it to the want of ability in McClellan. Others said that everything would now go well, because McClellan is again in command. There is a party for and another against him. By one he is praised, by the other abused in unmeasured terms. Stocks went up because he now is at the head of the army. I do not pretend to form a judgment about him other than this, that he is not a great general nor a humbug, as some think him. McMichael read a letter just received from Washington which said that Lincoln is panic-stricken. Absurd.

september 6, 1862 | Harry Ingersoll here in the morning. He talked more absolute nonsense about the Constitution, etc., than I supposed possible for any sane man to utter. He had now become the *personal* enemy of the government because it had arrested his brother! Mr.

---

54. William D. Kelley (1814–90), a Republican, was a lawyer and judge in Philadelphia before serving as a U.S. congressman from 1861 to 1890. In 1866 Fisher wrote that he "never liked or approved him as his manners are vulgar & his appearance far from attractive." A year later Fisher recorded in his diary that Kelley "said that I had 'published in 1862 a most remarkable book entitled the *Trial of the Constitution* & he who will read that work will find incorporated in it the philosophy that pervaded the 39th Congress. In that work is embodied in elegant style all the theories that enabled Congress to grapple all the subjects and bring the country thro safe.' Kelley is a self-made man of very considerable ability," Fisher concluded. "I have never been an admirer of his, but after such a compliment I can never again say anything in his disparagement." Diary entries, March 15, 1866, and March 28, 1867.

Lincoln was a mountebank. He had violated the Constitution & *therefore* was not legally President & might be resisted. Mr. Binney's essay on the habeas corpus was *prattle*, etc.[55] The worst of it is others talk in the same way and meetings of the people express similar absurdities in their resolutions.

SEPTEMBER 8, 1862 | The news this morning is not very agreeable to a landowner in Maryland. The enemy has no doubt invaded the state with a large force, crossing at three places near the point of rocks and has occupied Fredericktown. Union men were flying to the North, secessionists supplying the rebels with food & clothes, of which they appear to be very destitute, one reason, no doubt, why they invade the North, as Virginia is exhausted. Something decisive must now happen very soon. Letters from Washington say the government is vigilant and active. Halleck has been made Secretary of War, McClellan, commander in chief, Pope[56] is sent to the West, there, I suppose, to commit more blunders. Worked at the essay all the morning. Mrs. Barton[57] & afterwards Elizabeth Fisher here. In the evening went up to Wakefield to hear the last news. The afternoon paper says that the enemy have entered Maryland with 60,000 men and that McClellan is in pursuit of them. So closes another volume. What may not the next disclose.

SEPTEMBER 9, 1862 | My last volume closed with an account of the invasion of Maryland by the rebels. The news today is that they have entered Pennsylvania at Hanover in York County. It is supposed they intend to march to Harrisburg. The governor has issued orders for collecting and arming troops to resist them, the Home Guard of the

55. Horace Binney, *The Privilege of the Writ of Habeas Corpus under the Constitution* (Philadelphia, 1862).

56. John Pope (1822–92), a graduate of the U.S. Military Academy in 1842 and a veteran of the Mexican War, was promoted to brigadier general in 1861 and major general in 1862. Pope showed promise as a military commander in the western theater early in the war but was disastrously defeated at Second Bull Run in August 1862.

57. Mrs. Barton was Susan Ridgway, who was first married to Thomas Rotch of Rhode Island, and later married John Rhea Barton.

city is prepared to take the field, & recruiting goes on with greatly increased activity.

The aspect of the city is greatly changed. Fewer people in the streets, recruiting stations with flag flying & drum beating in all directions, wounded soldiers walking about, tents pitched in Independence Square—these are novel sights in America.

SEPTEMBER 10, 1862 | So far as is known, the news amounts to this: the rebels have not entered Penna., they have not gone further in Maryland than Fredericktown, they are supposed to be there in large force, variously estimated at from 70,000 to 120,000. What their intention is is a matter of conjecture. The most reasonable idea, I think, is that they intend to make an effort to take Washington. McClellan has marched with 80,000 of his best troops to intercept them.

SEPTEMBER 16, 1862 | The enthusiasm for enlisting was never so great. Troops are pouring into Harrisburg for the defence of the state by daily thousands. All the young men of good family have gone. All of William Wister's sons but one have gone, that is to say, five of them. John is obliged to remain at Duncannon to attend to the business.[58] Had a pleasant dinner at George's. Went to Brookwood. Saw Dr. Wister there. He is very desirous to enlist & tried to find someone to attend to his practice in his absence, but without success, so he cannot go.

SEPTEMBER 18, 1862 | The news is that a terrible battle raged all of yesterday with great loss on both sides & that an armistice was agreed on to bury the dead. Reports say that our side has the advantage, but there are no official accounts.

SEPTEMBER 19, 1862 | On the way back [from Brookwood] met Alexander Smith who had an evening paper. The enemy abandoned his

58. William Wister (1803-81), who married Sarah Fisher in 1826, had six sons: William Rotch Wister, born in 1827; John Wister, born 1829; Langhorne Wister, born 1834; Jones Wister, born 1839; Francis Wister, born 1841; and Rodman Wister, born 1844.

position at Sharpsburgh last night & retreated. McClellan pursued & the retreat became a flight. The news is official from McClellan, who by this achievement has regained his former position & more, tho probably Halleck is entitled to the credit of planning the movements that led to the result.

SEPTEMBER 24, 1862 | At 9 o'clock got a note from Elizabeth Fisher saying that Uncle William was gone. He died this morning at 6 o'clock.

SEPTEMBER 29, 1862 | At 11 this morning drove up to Wakefield in the big wagon and Delly, taking Daniel. Went to Uncle William's room up stairs where the near relations were assembled and some more intimate friends. According to Quaker custom, there was preaching, first by Lucretia Mott and then by Deborah Wharton.[59] There was nothing original or striking in what they said, but it was appropriate and impressive. A large number of persons were assembled and many private carriages. I counted 15 and I think there were more. At about 12 1/2 o'clock the cortege started and proceeded to Laurel Hill, where Uncle William had a lot. Many women were present for whom benches were provided. We all remained until the grave was filled.

OCTOBER 6, 1862 | Drove with Bet & Sidney in the light wagon to Roberts' Mill to order flour,[60] thence out the Schoolhouse Lane and along the road by [Ellis] Yarnall's place to the Wissahickon, & home by the township line. Enjoyed the weather, the beautiful countryseats on Schoolhouse Lane & the wild scenery of the Wissahickon very much. Mr. [Samuel] Welsh, who has one of the best places on Schoolhouse Lane, was here this afternoon to inquire the character of a servant, and mentioned an incident significant of the times. A neighbor of his some days ago discharged an Irish servant and in his place

---

59. Lucretia Coffin Mott (1793-1880), a Quaker minister, abolitionist, and advocate of women's rights, lived near Philadelphia in Montgomery county. Deborah Fisher Wharton (1795-1888), a Quaker and a founder of Swarthmore College.

60. Roberts' Mill was the first gristmill in the vicinity of Germantown and was situated on the northern side of Church Lane, one mile northeast of Market Square.

employed a Negro. Shortly after, his garden was trespassed on, plants & shrubbery destroyed and a paper stuck on one of the trees, threatening further injury if he did not send away the Negro. The Irish hate the Negroes, not merely because they compete with them in labor, but because they are near to them in social rank. Therefore, the Irish favor slavery in the South, and for the same reason the laboring class of whites support it—it gratifies their pride by the existence of a class below them. The Democrats have industriously represented that the Republicans intend to emancipate the Negroes & make them the equals of the whites; also, that when the slaves are free, there will be a great emigration of them to the North to the injury of the white workingmen. The Irish are all Democrats and implicitly believe & obey their leaders. There have been heretofore riots in this city caused by the jealously & hatred of the Irish to the Negroes, & more trouble is anticipated now.

OCTOBER 11, 1862 | Startling news in the morning paper. The rebels have made a dash into Pennsylvania with 3000 cavalry and 6 pieces of artillery. They crossed the Potomac, turned McClellan's flank, took Mercersburg and Chambersburg. They offered no violence to anyone, but helped themselves to what they wanted. This happened yesterday. It is probably a mere foraging raid to furnish themselves with needed supplies. The paper intimates that they have another object. The election comes off next Tuesday. A much larger proportion of Republicans or Union men have gone to the war than of Democrats, which greatly increases the chances of the latter. An invasion of the state at this time would withdraw still greater numbers of Union men. The Democrats, being opposed to the war, would stay at home to vote. The rebels are well informed of our affairs, indeed, it is hinted, may have received intelligence of this very predicament from Democrats here, & so timed their incursion to aid the cause of the party which is their ally.

OCTOBER 12, 1862 | Went from Wakefield to Mr. J. R. Ingersoll's. He told me that Charles had challenged Judge Kelley for calling him a traitor in his speech at the Union meeting a few days ago. Kelley classed him with Reed & other Democrats here as traitors because they sympathize with the rebellion, and in my opinion very justly. Charles made a speech announcing his sentiments & thus laid himself open to such remark & Kelley had a right to say what he did. To challenge him was absurd. Mr. Ingersoll says that Kelley in reply said that he did not know or did not remember that he had mentioned names, a poor evasion of responsibility. He ought either to have accepted the challenge or refused it on proper grounds. Kelley was a member of the last Congress and is again a candidate. He is an abolitionist. He was formerly a Democrat. He is a man of obscure birth & vulgar manners, but has ability, is a fluent speaker not without a coarse popular eloquence, and, tho a good deal of a demagogue, is, I believe, generally considered an honest man. I should think he does not belong to the class that fight duels. It was a most foolish thing in Charles to challenge him. If he does the same thing to everyone who calls him a traitor, he will have fighting enough. His passions are as extravagant as his opinions.

OCTOBER 19, 1862 | I am leading an ideal sort of life, just such as I like. I have leisure, comfort, domestic happiness, literary occupation, & the country. I wonder how long it will last. Happiness inspires fear, it hangs by such a frail & uncertain tenure.

NOVEMBER 5, 1862 | Saw Clark Hare. He thinks the restoration of the Union hopeless. That the Northwest will separate & so will the New England states and that an effort will be made to join Pennsylvania to the South. He talked rather wildly. Went to McMichael's. Several persons were there listening to some statements from Mr. Hickman, a member of Congress from Chester Co.[61] He is a weak & vulgar man. With such people to rule the country what can we expect. McMichael thinks the victories of the Democrats mean dissatisfaction with the manner in which the war is conducted, the inactivity, delay, want of ability, extravagant expenditure, & corruption, not with the war itself.

61. John Hickman (1810–75), a U.S. congressman from Pennsylvania, served as a Democrat from 1855 to 1859, as an Anti-Lecompton Democrat from 1859 to 1861, and as a Republican from 1861 to 1863. In 1862 he decided not to seek another term.

NOVEMBER 6, 1862 | At 1 started with Bet to go to the Insane Asylum to see her brother Alexander, for many years an inmate of the institution. We went out Nicetown Lane to the Falls Bridge, & then by the old Monument Road in the rear of Belmont to the Lancaster Turnpike, over a beautiful, richly cultivated & wooded country, glowing in autumn colors, and very familiar to me many years ago in daily rides. It recalled many of the scenes & feelings of youth. We drove first to the house of Dr. Kirkbride, the superintendent, whom I know very well.[62] He is highly respectable and has managed this admirable institution for more than 20 years with signal ability & success, so that it is a model establishment, probably the best in America. The buildings & grounds are extensive & kept in perfect order. He received us very kindly & gave us a note to the superintendent of the new asylum in the same enclosure & under his care also, where Alexander lives. He was brought down to us in the reception room. I had not seen him for, I suppose, thirty-five years & have a faint recollection of him as a very handsome young man, as he was, and very promising. He has been hopelessly insane for almost the whole of that time. He is now nearly idiotic, did not seem to know Bet, and uttered only a few monosyllables. Dr. [John Y.] Clarke, the superintendent, showed me over the building, which is very large, with ample halls & corridors, perfectly ventilated, heated by steam, furnished with baths, water closets, & every possible convenience & as clean & orderly as possible. Nothing that can contribute to the comfort & amusement of the patients is wanting. Books, billiard tables, parlors for conversation, nice bedrooms, a lecture room, music, &c., indoors, and gardens, lawns & park without. Such are the results of wealth and civilization. We got home after a drive that was pleasant in spite of the cold, damp weather and enjoyed a warm house and a good dinner all the more for it.

NOVEMBER 11, 1862 | On the way to Wilmington [*en route to Mount Harmon*] fell into conversation with a young soldier who was wounded

62. Dr. Thomas S. Kirkbride (1809-83) was elected superintendent of the Insane Department of the Pennsylvania Hospital in 1840, and held the post until his death. His hospital for the mentally ill, located at 44th and Market Streets, received its first patients in 1841. Prior to that time, they had been housed at the Pennsylvania Hospital.

at the battle of Antietam in the foot. He was an intelligent, manly fellow, full of enthusiasm for the war. He gave me an account of the battle & of the dreadful scenes that accompanied it, by which he seemed much impressed. He saw 1,100 men buried at once, in a long trench, but so hastily was the work done that hands, feet, & heads stuck out above ground. Another man joined in the conversation, who said he was a farmer in Maryland & lived not far from the battlefield, which he visited immediately after the fight. He could not find words to describe the frightful sufferings he witnessed. He saw many of the rebel prisoners. He said they were a horrible-looking set of men, ferocious, filthy, in rags, many without shoes or hats, & with trousers made of old guano bags.

NOVEMBER 13, 1862 | There has been a Democratic meeting in New York at which John Van Buren made a speech, recommending the calling of a convention to settle the dispute between North & South, to alter the Constitution, to extend the presidential term to six years, to depose Mr. Lincoln & put Gen'l McClellan in his place. Van Buren is a clever, reckless and thoroughly unprincipled demagogue, ready to cause anarchy if he can to further his own schemes. Unhappily, in such times such men have much power for mischief. The city of New York has given a large majority for the Democratic Party. The population is largely composed of foreigners. The vote of the city outweighed that of the state.[63]

NOVEMBER 19, 1862 | Having got a note yesterday from Betty [Fisher] asking me to go with her to Duncannon tomorrow, called to see her this morning. Agreed to go on Friday or Saturday.

NOVEMBER 26, 1862 | Attended to some business and at 11 $\frac{1}{4}$ went to the station of the Penna. Railroad at 11th & Market. Found Betty there. We started at 11 $\frac{1}{2}$ and got to Duncannon at 4 $\frac{1}{2}$. Enjoyed the journey.

---

63. John Van Buren (1810-66), a Democrat, was a son of President Martin Van Buren and a New York politician. Fisher here refers to the election of Horatio Seymour, a Democrat, as governor of New York on November 4, 1862.

The cars are very comfortable, the track smooth, the pace rapid, all the arrangements admirable on this great work which traverses our noble state, does an enormous business, and is managed with great ability. The cars, the station houses, the bridges, all indicate wealth & liberality. The road passes thro the finest agricultural & mineral regions and the most beautiful scenery in the country. Rich farms, mills, factories, towns, coal & iron, every mark of prosperity, industry & wealth, meet the eye in all directions. At the same time it must be said that there is a deficiency of taste and embellishment everywhere. Large barns, well-cultivated fields, fat cattle, but houses bare, unadorned, without trees or shrubbery or any evidence of mental cultivation or of a desire above mere material life.

Soon after leaving Harrisburg the road winds along the banks of the Susquehanna, the winding river is enclosed by mountains & dotted with islands and presents a constant succession of views which combine the grandeur of mountains & the beauty of a river. Between the two in many places there is a space of varying width of rich land, well cultivated. On one of these spaces Duncannon is situated. The house is of good size, but old & not in good repair. It stands close to the railroad & is surrounded by furnaces & mills. It has no lawn, trees or shrubbery, no attempt at embellishment, but commands a superb view of the river enclosed by mountains. It is a place of business, not a home. The property contains several thousand acres, much of it mountain land, & is an iron factory. One half of it belongs to Uncle William's estate, the other half to Mr. Charles Morgan of New Bedford. It is managed by John, Jones & Langhorne Wister, the latter being now in the army. The mills were planned & built by Uncle William & the concern is now doing a large business with good prospects of making money, after many reverses and mishaps. We dined at $5 \frac{1}{2}$ & spent the evening in pleasant talk. At 9 I went with John into the rolling mill, which is a striking scene at night. The glowing furnaces, the red-hot pieces of iron, contrasting with the darkness of the vast building, the dusky forms of the men brought out by the concentrated light & the constant clang of the machinery, made a picturesque & novel display. The labor is very severe. On Tuesday morning went with John over the whole establishment and was interested by the wonderful machinery & the order & system everywhere apparent. Then took a walk with Betty along the river shore, delighted with the glorious views which varied at every step. The Susquehanna is far superior to the Hudson. We walked to Langhorne's farm, a good one of about 300 acres on the river, which he is improving and which pays him a good income. At 2 we dined and at 4 I took the train to Harrisburg in order to pay a visit to Meredith. After a delightful run along the river, got to Harrisburg at 5. Went to Coverly's, now Jones', excellent hotel,[64] where I secured a comfortable room &, after ablutions & supper, walked to Mrs. [James] Espy's on the river where Meredith is living. He seemed glad to see me, is in much better health than he was before he went to Harrisburg & better spirits; we had a long talk, about public affairs chiefly. He thinks everything is now going on well. Left Harrisburg this morning at 9 & got to town at 1 o'clock after a very satisfactory trip, during which I was more impressed than ever with the wealth, resources, and beauty of Pennsylvania. Tokens of redundant prosperity & rapid improvement are visible everywhere, and, but for the soldiers to be seen in all directions, no one would imagine that the country is in the midst of a gigantic war. The war indeed has revealed to us & to the world the immense power & unbounded resources of the nation.

NOVEMBER 28, 1862 | Went to McMichael's. I left for him yesterday the mss. of my note on the President's proclamation. It will appear tomorrow.

NOVEMBER 29, 1862 | My note in the paper. It is longer than I expected, occupying 5 1/2 columns. It is preceded by an announcement that it is a note appended to a volume entitled *The Trial of the Constitution*, by Sidney G. Fisher, soon to be published by J. B. Lippincott & Co.[65] This is the first time I ever published anything, except

---

64. Wells Coverly's hotel, by now the Jones House, was situated at the corner of Second Street and Market Square.

65. "The President's Proclamation of September 22," which referred to the Preliminary Emancipation Proclamation, appeared on the front page of the *North American* on November 29, 1862.

speeches, &c., with my name, altho it has always been mentioned in newspaper notices of other works. I have now left the shelter of privacy & come before the public as an author & of a book that contains many opinions on important & exciting topics likely to provoke attack & unfriendly criticism. I must take the consequences, some of which may be unpleasant. I believe the principles I have advanced to be true & have expressed them because I am convinced of their truth & from no selfish motives.

DECEMBER 9, 1862 | If I may judge from what many have said to me, the note published on the 29th in the *North American* has been very generally read and approved. I think it will help the sale of the book, a matter about which I am anxious because, owing to the advance in the price of paper, the cost of printing it will be very high, not much less than $1,000. I shall print only 1,000 copies and if they sell at $2. per copy, of which I get $1, the cost will be covered. Lippincott, if he will *try*, can easily insure a sale of 1,000 copies, or more, but will he try? His business is so large that a small affair like this, in which he has no money at stake, will hardly be worth much effort.

Meredith has been in town. I have seen him several times. He speaks hopefully about the success of my book. He is not an admirer of Mr. Lincoln, thinks him honest but deficient in force, knowledge, and ability, & greatly wanting in dignity of manners. He has had several interviews with him & says he is unable to appreciate & grasp the case of the country or the true nature of the war. That he is under the influence of the border state men & that it was with great difficulty he was brought up to the point of issuing his proclamation of September, which ought to have been done months ago. That he is familiar in his manners, eternally joking and jesting and fond of telling bawdy stories in gross language. If all this be true, it is very bad, considering how much is at stake just now on the wise administration of the government. The high praise I have bestowed on Mr. Lincoln in my book I fear may turn out to be exaggerated and may appear to some ridiculous. However, I do not swallow all that Meredith says, and the praise I have given to the President is chiefly for honesty & purity of purpose, which all admit that he possesses. I think also he has native sagacity & power of thought & that these are displayed in his inaugural speech & his messages. That he may be infirm of purpose, I do not doubt, tho not to the degree charged. He is uneducated, his manners are uncouth, he wants dignity & reserve befitting his station, & has a vile habit of telling dirty stories, all this is no doubt true & I have heard it from others.

DECEMBER 12, 1862 | A bill has passed Congress admitting Western Virginia as a state. It was, of course, opposed as unconstitutional, but the Constitution in this case, as it must in others, was obliged to yield to necessity, illustrating thus the principles advanced in my book. The morning paper contains no further news of the battle at Fredericksburg. Our troops had taken possession of the town and driven the enemy to their entrenchments beyond it, where a severe fight was expected. Went to town. Attended to some business. Met Joshua Fisher whose state of mind about the war gives me much anxiety. I really think he shows signs of derangement. Went to Sherman's[66] and corrected proof of the note. Brought out with me proof of the Preface & "Contents" as I had not time to finish.

In the evening corrected the last proof and so my pleasant labor ends. The book has been a source of great interest and enjoyment to me since last February, afforded me constant and delightful occupation & been a resource in grief. The capacity for intellectual occupation is a great blessing, and work which tasks & exercises the higher faculties of mind is an inexhaustible pleasure. It is also an excitement which, once indulged, becomes necessary, for nothing else can supply its place. The want of it after a time becomes a torment. I dare say that ere long I shall find myself at something else of the kind & should not wonder if I became an author.

DECEMBER 16, 1862 | News came in the course of the morning that Burnside had withdrawn his whole force across the river [*after his*

---

66. C. Sherman & Son, book, job, and lithographic printers, southwest corner of Seventh and Cherry Streets.

defeat at the Battle of Fredericksburg].[67] The reason given is that the river was swollen by rain. The truth no doubt is that he was repulsed by the enemy in his attack. . . .

DECEMBER 17, 1862 | Met Charles Ingersoll in the street. He expressed such exultation and delight at the defeat of the Union army and his language was so violent & extravagant, that I was disgusted. He is imbued with narrowest partizan passions & is wholly insensible to argument, and incapable of any but the most petty views of the situation of the country.

DECEMBER 18, 1862 | Details of the battle at Fredericksburg in the paper. The enemy was entrenched on a natural terrace in the rear of the town. Our troops were obliged to cross a plain and ascend a slope to make the attack, exposed to the fire of ranges of rifle pits and cannon which swept the ground. The slaughter was terrible. Whole ranks were mowed down. The men fought with the greatest bravery, but it was evident that success was impossible and they were withdrawn.

DECEMBER 25, 1862 | At 2 ½ drove with Bet & Sidney to Edward Ingersoll's to dinner. Mrs. Harry Ingersoll there. Had a pleasant evening. The house was built by Mr. McKean on a part of Fern Hill[68] and is very handsome & complete & is furnished with good taste.

DECEMBER 26, 1862 | Went to Lippincott's. For business reasons they will not send copies of the book to the booksellers until after the first of next month. Ordered copies sent to Meredith, McMichael, & Hetty

---

67. Ambrose E. Burnside (1824-81), a veteran of the Mexican War, began the Civil War as a colonel, rising to the rank of major general. Although an unsuccessful military commander, Burnside launched a long political career after the war, serving as the governor of Rhode Island and later as a U.S. senator from that state.

68. Fern Hill was built by Henry Pratt McKean in 1849-50 on what later became McKean Avenue, Germantown. The house was demolished in 1913.

Wistar.[69] Brought out 4 copies & sent one to Wakefield. Saw Jno. Tucker. He thinks affairs are in a bad way at Washington from divided counsels, want of energy & decision on the part of the President, etc. Gave him a copy of the book which he promised to deliver to Mr. Lincoln but did not.[70]

69. Esther "Hetty" Fisher Smith, the wife of Dr. Mifflin Wistar, was a cousin of the diarist.

70. The words "but did not" were added by Fisher at a later date.

~1863~

JANUARY 3, 1863 | Met Joshua Fisher. He is more violent than ever about the war and I really fear that his mental & bodily health will be seriously affected. He absolutely raves incoherently.

JANUARY 5, 1863 | A club, to be called the Union League, has been got up. The conditions of membership are unwavering loyalty and support of the government in all its efforts to suppress the rebellion. They are to rent Mr. Kuhn's old house in Chesnut St. above 11th. Clark [Hare] handed me the prospectus & list of names and wants me to join it, which I am by no means disposed to do for many reasons.[1]

JANUARY 8, 1863 | Gen'l Butler, who was in command at New Orleans since its capture until a few weeks ago when he was removed[2] and Gen'l [Nathaniel P.] Banks put in his place, was in town yesterday & had a reception last night at the Continental Hotel. He made a very good speech which is in this morning's paper. He is a coarse man, no doubt, & was a Democrat, but has done good service in the war. He has intelligence, administrative talents, firmness & decision. He was

---

1. Hartman Kuhn's mansion was occupied by the Union League during its first two years and was later sold to Matthias Baldwin. The building was torn down in 1901. Judge Hare was one of the founders of the League.

2. Gen. Benjamin F. Butler (1818–93) commanded the land troops in the 1862 expedition against New Orleans, and after its capture was placed in command of its military government. After a controversial tour of duty in that capacity, he was removed on December 16, 1862.

the man for the place and for the southern people, who hate him with a concentrated bitterness which is unmeasured in its language. Davis has issued a proclamation declaring that he will hang him if he can catch him.[3] He governed New Orleans no doubt with stern severity, but also with justice and with so much ability that for the first time the city was orderly & safe and also healthy.

JANUARY 10, 1863 | McMichael told me that Chas. Ingersoll had made a speech on Thursday at the opening of a Democratic club, just established, & that it was in yesterday's *Press*.[4] Went to the office of the *Press* & read it. It is even more extravagant than his former efforts. He declares that slaves are just like any other kind of property; that the northern people are pro-slavery; that the Union must be restored and as that cannot be done by war, it must be done by submission to the South; that when the Democrats come into power, they will say to the South, "Gentlemen, make your own terms." He recommends calling a national convention to settle the war, and as the governor & Senate of Penna. are Republican, whilst the House is Democratic, he thinks the House should stop the supplies to coerce the government into its measures. These sentiments, the report says, were loudly applauded. I think they are calculated to injure him and his cause, as their extravagant folly & absurdity must disgust all sensible men of his own party.

JANUARY 14, 1863 | The election for senator came off yesterday at Harrisburg and resulted in the choice of a Mr. Buckalew, a Democrat.[5]

---

3. The order read, in part: "Now therefore, I, Jefferson Davis, President of the Confederate States of America, and in their name, do pronounce and declare the said Benjamin F. Butler to be a felon, deserving of capital punishment. I do order . . . that, in the event of his capture, the officer in charge of the capturing force do cause him to be immediately executed by hanging."

4. Morton McMichael was referring to the opening of Democratic headquarters, the Central Democratic Club at 524 Walnut Street, on January 8, 1863, when Charles Ingersoll was elected president of the club. The Philadelphia *Press* was an influential Republican newspaper edited by John W. Forney.

5. Charles R. Buckalew (1821–99), formerly minister to Ecuador, served in the Senate from 1863 to 1869 and later was a U.S. congressman from 1887 to 1891.

Went to town. Saw Col. Patterson,[6] a Democrat, who told me all about it, and the whole affair was most disgraceful to all concerned, as well as significant of our condition. The Democrats had a majority of one on joint ballot & were therefore entitled to success. Simon Cameron was the Republican candidate. It was known that Cameron was prepared to pay a large sum for Democratic votes enough to elect himself. As the venality of members was well known, the Democrats sent up to Harrisburg a large body of rowdies, pledged to put to death anyone of their party who voted for a Union man. They filled the hall. Buckalew was elected and the affair went off without disturbance. Here, then, were exhibited the two characteristics of democracy, fraud & violence. The Republicans disgraced themselves in selecting Cameron, a man notoriously corrupt, and the Democrats by resorting to force proved alike the corruption of their own party & their contempt for law & order. Patterson thinks we are on the verge of anarchy, that the Democrats will be able to stop the war & grant their own terms to the South, & thinks they will insist on calling a national convention to restore the Union & alter the Constitution. Met Ch. Ingersoll. He was in a state of great exultation at what he considers the triumph of the Democratic Party & said that soon they will resort to mob law & physical force to carry out their views. I told him that would only be in accordance with democratic principles in all ages & that I did not doubt but they would willingly imitate the Jacobins in France, if they could.

JANUARY 16, 1863 | Drove with Bet & Sidney at 2 to Edward Ingersoll's.[7] Mr. John Emory of the Eastern Shore of Md. is staying there. He thoroughly sympathizes with the rebellion, yet his brother is an officer in our army. When the war broke out, he left his resignation with his brother John to be sent in should Maryland join the South. John sent it in prematurely, expecting & hoping that Maryland would

---

6. Robert Emmet Patterson (1830–1906), a son of Gen. Robert Patterson, was appointed colonel of the 115th Pennsylvania Infantry on June 25, 1862.

7. The diarist's brother-in-law Edward Ingersoll lived on what had been part of the Henry Pratt McKean Fern Hill property.

secede. She did not, however, and then his brother applied to be reinstated & had influence enough to succeed, much to the disgrace of the government.[8] We found them at dinner & did not go in. This morning read a pamphlet entitled "The way a free people make war" by Mr. C. J. Stillé, a member of our bar.[9] It has attracted much attention & is very well written. He shows that in the contest by England with Napoleon, which ended with his downfall, the English people behaved just as our northern people do now, eager & enthusiastic at first, expecting immediate success, depressed by reverses, abusing the government & the army, with a disloyal party sympathizing with the enemy. He shows also that, tho the cost of the English war was greater than ours is likely to be, it was easily borne by the people, tho the resources of England then were far less than ours are now. In fact, the prosperity of England increased greatly during the war, notwithstanding its burdens, just as the North is now prosperous. The parallel, however, is not perfect in all respects. England was not a democracy and her statesmen at that time were men of the highest ability. The democratic element in England then sympathized with the enemy, just as it now does with us, but it did not rule & had no chance of ruling.

JANUARY 17, 1863 | In the trial before a court-martial of Gen'l McDowell, now in progress,[10] a letter from the President to Gen'l McClellan was put in evidence. It is marked by the good feeling, good sense & sound principle that distinguish Mr. Lincoln. It shows also firmness and decision. He is the only man worthy of confidence in the government and has shown great qualities in a position of immense difficulty

---

8. Lt. Col. William H. Emory (1811-87) resigned May 9, 1861, and was reinstated five days later. He served throughout the war, attaining the rank of major general of volunteers.

9. Charles J. Stillé (1819-99) was president of the Historical Society of Pennsylvania from 1892 to 1899. The pamphlet is actually entitled *How a Free People Conduct a Long War*.

10. Gen. Irvin McDowell (1818-85), commander of the III Corps, was severely criticized for his conduct at the Second Battle of Bull Run, and was relieved of his command. McDowell at once applied for an inquiry and was exonerated at the proceedings to which the diarist refers.

and responsibility. He is abused with every opprobrious epithet by the Democrats, who abused Washington in the same way, but the time will come when even they will be obliged to acknowledge his virtues.

JANUARY 28, 1863 | A disgraceful scene has occurred in the Senate. Mr. [Willard] Saulsbury of Delaware, an extreme Democrat, became so violent in his denunciations of Mr. Lincoln & the government that he was called to order & at length arrested by the sergeant upon whom he drew a pistol.[11] So we go.

JANUARY 29, 1863 | No news of interest except that yesterday the office of the *Evening Journal*, the only Democratic paper here, was taken possession of by the government & its editor arrested. It had been recently very violent in its abuse of the administration and was distributed in large quantities among the Army of the Potomac, which is thought to be greatly demoralized & dissatisfied with affairs at Washington. It is a bold step to take in the face of recent Democratic triumphs & if the demagogues want a pretext for making trouble affords one. If the government was consistently and uniformly thus decided & stern in its course, a step of this sort would have a good effect, but general weakness & spasmodic energy is an unwise policy. I should not be surprised if trouble grew out of this act. Interference with the liberty of the press attacks a sensitive part of the American character & must be not only justified by necessity but accompanied by respect for the government to be quietly endured.[12]

JANUARY 30, 1863 | Judge Ludlow[13] of the Court of Quarter Sessions in this city has made a charge to the grand jury, directing them to

---

11. Willard Saulsbury Sr. (1820-92), a Democrat, was a U.S. senator from Delaware from 1859 to 1871.

12. The *Philadelphia Evening Journal*, established in 1856, ceased publication soon after this event, leaving the city without a Democratic paper until the *Age* was established a month or so later. The editor of the *Journal*, Albert D. Boileau, was held under arrest for only five days.

13. James R. Ludlow (1825-86), a Democrat, was elected an associate judge to the Court of Common Pleas in Philadelphia in 1857. In 1875 he became a president judge of the court, a position he held until his death.

inquire into the facts of the arrest of the editor of the *Evening Journal* & present them to the court, that indictments may be framed against the parties concerned. The charge is printed in this morning's paper. It is very strong in its language and denounces the course of the government as illegal and tyrannical. The argument amounts to nothing. The judge is a Democrat and his conduct is one proof among many, constantly exhibited, of the fatal consequences of an elective judiciary.

JANUARY 31, 1863 | In the paper was the presentment of the grand jury in obedience to the charge of Judge Ludlow. They find that the cause of the arrest was an article printed in the paper a few days ago, commenting in terms of high praise on the last message of Jefferson Davis to the Confederate Congress, and comparing his character, talents & policy with Mr. Lincoln's to the great disparagement of the latter. Was provoked to begin article about it & other parts of the policy of the Democratic Party, which occupied, not unpleasantly, the morning and evening.

FEBRUARY 14, 1863 | Morning & evening looked over Mr. Ingersoll's history of the late war, an odd book, sensible & extravagant, amusing and well written in parts, without method or order, illogical, passionate, on the whole interesting and a good picture of the time & events, seen from the Democratic point of view. It shows that the Federalists in that war pursued very much the same course that the Democrats are doing now. They denounced the war, opposed the administration, voted against supplies, abused Madison, & went so far in New England as to call the Hartford Convention to declare the neutrality of New England, if indeed they did not intend secession. The victory of New Orleans, however, brought all parties together in joy at the triumph of the country & consigned the Hartford Convention to popular disgrace, & such would be the effect of victory now. Took a ride in the morning.

FEBRUARY 20, 1863 | Charles Ingersoll has just published another pamphlet. Its topic is the suspension of the habeas corpus by the

President, arbitrary arrests, &c.[14] Read it this evening. It is clever, in parts well written, has glimpses of the truth, but is wholly partizan in its purpose, passion & tone, & perverted in its reasoning, both logically & morally. He takes the same ground that I did in my book in relation to English analogy, but stops short of its legitimate conclusions, stating a part only of the English law, just so much as suits his purpose.

MARCH 5, 1863 | Met Fisher, who told me he has just written & is about to publish a pamphlet with his name.[15] I dare say it will be something very extravagant & foolish; if half as absurd as his talk, it will be unreadable.

MARCH 6, 1863 | Came out in the N.P.[16] car at 4 ½ with Sally Ingersoll. She was very gay & agreeable. We had some little talk about the war & she said that Mr. Lincoln was a mountebank. "Oh," said I, "you are moderate. Joshua Fisher calls him a gorilla & Mrs. Fisher says that her brother Oliver says he is a kangaroo." "And *you* say," replied Sally, "that he is a hero & sage." Not a bad retort. I am afraid the description of his character in my book is too rose-colored.

MARCH 11, 1863 | The Union League has been successful. Others have been formed in New York & elsewhere & last night a meeting was held to form a National Union League. Speeches were made, some of them by prominent Democrats, all urging a vigorous prosecution of the war and an uncompromising determination to crush the rebellion and reduce the South to absolute submission, at any sacrifice. Domestic traitors & northern sympathizers with rebellion were denounced with great bitterness. The crowd was immense and enthusiastic. Similar meetings have been held in the West and in New York at which

---

14. Charles Ingersoll, *An Undelivered Speech on Executive Arrests* (Philadelphia, 1862).

15. J. Francis Fisher, *The Degradation of Our Representative System and its Reform* (Philadelphia, 1863).

16. The North Pennsylvania Railroad.

leading Democrats have united with Union men to sustain the government in pushing on the war until the South submits without terms or conditions to the authority of the government. The reaction against the plans of compromise and negotiation for peace & submission to southern dictation seems general & strong.

MARCH 19, 1863 | Stopped at Newhall's to see Field. He told me that Chas. Ingersoll had just made another violent & absurd speech at the Democratic Club. He proposes, should any more "arbitrary arrests" be made, that the government of Pennsylvania should seize officers of the federal government & hold *them as hostages* till the prisoners are released. Such are the extravagant, revolutionary plans of the Democrats, who profess to respect the Constitution. The best way to treat such men is to let them alone. Their monstrous ideas injure themselves & their party more than they do us. There is a strong reaction among the Democrats themselves, caused by these excesses of their leaders; resolutions denouncing them have been passed by the Army of the Potomac, & of the West, and thus we see the beginning of what may become military power.

MARCH 21, 1863 | Called at Joshua Fisher's. Helen, Sophy, and a son of Jno. Cadwalader were in the parlor.[17] Went with Fisher into his study. He immediately began to rave more violently even than usual against Lincoln, Seward, & everyone connected with the government. His language, gestures, voice, & countenance were all so wild & extravagant, & his sentiments so absurd that I only laughed at him. Reasoning or reply was out of the question, even if he had allowed me time.

MARCH 26, 1863 | Our finances are very flourishing. Gold has fallen from 1.70 to 1.38. Specie has disappeared. Even cents are very scarce. A paper currency issued by the government in sums as low as 5 cts. is the only circulating medium, and answers the purposes very well so

---

17. John Cadwalader Jr., a beau of Helen Fisher, Sophia's younger sister.

long as the government maintains its credit. The paper of the Confederate states has sunk very low.

MARCH 27, 1863 | The expression of opinion that has come from the army & the reaction of sentiment among the better sort of the Democratic Party against the extreme & revolutionary movements of its leaders have induced the latter to moderate their tone. They declare now that they are in favor of the war for the Union & tho they disapprove the "unconstitutional" measures of the administration, they never intended to carry their opposition to the point of resisting the laws or the government, &c.

MARCH 30, 1863 | Went to Athenaeum. Saw Clark Hare. He urged me to write some articles of a popular character for the Union League, which has a publication fund of $100,000 dollars and is constantly printing thousands of copies of pamphlets to spread thro the country. Told him I would. A hopeful feeling about the war prevails. Our finances are prosperous, business is active, labor well employed, supplies of all sorts abundant, and the reaction of sentiment against the insidious and treasonable schemes of the "Copperheads," as the Democrats are called, strong & universal. It is believed that in the South terrible destitution is general among the people & that their armies are suffering from want of food & clothing. The news from Vicksburg & other points is favorable & promises success.

APRIL 2, 1863 | Drove Bet up to Brookwood. It is a great satisfaction in going there to think that the estate is clear of debt & that they can keep the place. One great object of Henry's life is thus attained—his children will be well off, will, indeed, be quite rich.

APRIL 4, 1863 | Went in the passenger car up Germantown to pay my U. S. tax on plate & carriages. The war has imposed on us a heavy burden of debt, from which no nation seems exempt. Our national debt promises to be as large as that of England. *One* war has done this in *two* years.

APRIL 11, 1863 | Went up to Germantown in the passenger car & then to town to attend to some business, which I finished satisfactorily. I avoid details of money matters in my diary, except as to general results, but may as well state this affair here. Almost all of my income, as the chief part of it is from the farm, is received after the 1st of July. Consequently, I am always short of money in the first half of the year and if the farm falls short of estimates, there is a deficit on the whole year. Heretofore this has almost always been the case, thence my debt to Henry, which he generously cancelled by his will. My hope & expectation is that increased receipts from the farm by means of peaches & truck, and perhaps something from Mr. Ingersoll's estate, will enable me hereafter to make both ends meet. How it will turn out remains to be seen, but I will try what can be done by attention to the farm & by economy.

APRIL 26, 1863 | Went to town to get permit to send sweet potatoes, &c., to Mount Harmon. A new rule now requires from persons sending goods south of New Castle an oath of allegiance on which a permit is granted. There are so many traitors in Maryland & Delaware who are constantly sending supplies to Virginia to aid the enemy that this regulation is necessary.

APRIL 28, 1863 | An important event occurred in our little family today—Sidney went to school, his first step out from the shelter of home into the outside world & its manifold influences. . . . A respectable person, Miss [Mary] Stokes in Germantown, was recommended to Bet. She keeps a small school for children of Sidney's age. He was delighted at the idea of seeing the new world to be opened to him and this morning Bet & I went with him. We walked over to the Rising Sun at 9 $^1/_2$ & went up in the passenger car. Miss Stokes lives on the north or rather east side of the Main Street, a little above School House Lane, in a neat, snug little house standing back from the road & shaded by several large trees. The place is clean and comfortable & I was pleased by the appearance and manners of Miss Stokes. Sidney was most gracious to her and we left him evidently well contented.

1863

MAY 4, 1863 | Hooker's[18] army crossed the Rappahannock with entire success and he is supposed to have surprised the enemy. The rebels were withdrawing from Fredericksburg for strategic purposes. A great battle is expected. If Hooker's plan succeeds, the Confederates will be cut off from their communications with Richmond.

MAY 7, 1863 | Slow indeed is the advance of human amelioration, if indeed it does advance. Man is a very contemptible creature if we look at the masses, and, notwithstanding the lights of knowledge existing in the world, repeats at every generation the same old story. The aspect of the world is far from hopeful just now & the reign of knowledge & peace seems adjourned for our day at least. Our American life of ease, security, freedom & tranquility is gone forever. Taxation and debt, armies & war, and something to take the place of democracy are to be our portion hereafter.

MAY 8, 1863 | Damp & cloudy, just not raining. The news is as gloomy as the weather. Hooker's expedition has failed and his army has recrossed the Rappahannock with a loss of 10,000 in killed, wounded & missing. There was no battle since Sunday, but he found the force opposed to him very heavy and the rain had swelled the river so that in case of a defeat he would be cut off from his supplies & from a retreat.

This morning some offensive remarks were paraded at the door of a secession journal, *The Age*.[19] A soldier tore them down. A crowd assembled & there were indications of a riot, when the mayor appeared & quiet was restored. The feelings of the people are becoming very indignant at the men who so openly sympathize with the South & denounce the cause of the nation and the measures of the government to put down the rebellion. A disaster to our army increases this feeling. Indeed, the outrageous language & sentiments of

---

18. Joseph Hooker (1814-79) was a graduate of the U.S. Military Academy in 1837 and a veteran of the Mexican War. Gen. "Fighting Joe" Hooker commanded the Army of the Potomac from January through June 1863, suffering a disastrous defeat at Chancellorsville, Virginia, in May 1863.

19. The *Age* was established in March 1863 as a Democratic daily newspaper.

these people are hard to bear at any time, but immediately after defeat they are especially offensive & irritating.

These Democrats can see in this great war only a party contest. Every victory of the government they lament as a defeat of their party; in every success of the rebels they see a party victory & hail it with triumph. In all possible ways they oppose the administration & thus encourage the enemy to persevere. Their treasonable speeches are republished in the South. They are evidence of a divided North. Division is weakness and our weakness is strength for the enemy. We have thus to contend against the South, the Democrats, and England also, whose unconcealed good wishes as well as services induce the southern people to hope for active aid if they can hold out long enough. But for the supplies of food, clothing, weapons & ammunition furnished to the South by England, and for the hopes inspired by the speeches, newspapers and notes of northern Democrats, the rebellion would have been quelled long ere this.

MAY 9, 1863 | One would think that Fisher, with his ample fortune & fine family might contrive to be happy, but it is far otherwise and because he makes the mistake of regarding himself thus, not as a part of the whole, but as the whole, for which the nation & the government exist. I have made all arrangements, said he, "befitting my position, my establishments in town & country and an adequate surplus income to provide handsomely for my children as they got married, and now this wicked, this abominable, this abolition war has destroyed all my hopes." It never seems to occur to him that other people have hopes & fortune & children, and that whilst not a luxury or whim of his has been crossed, thousands have lost all, or that he & they and all of us depend on the operation of great principles & universal causes, before which the individual sinks to insignificance.

MAY 16, 1863 | I like this life of retirement & study. Solitude to me is not a desert, but a garden, rich with blossoms & fruits. I feel no desire to mix with the world, and there are few whose conversation interests me. I hate active life or business. Even Mount Harmon is a burden. I like the place, I like a farm, I think, indeed, that any man who does not possess a farm is unfortunate, but I detest attention to details. Such attention, however, is necessary and I force myself to give it and perhaps it is a good thing that I am obliged thus to go out of my dreamy reveries into the external from time to time. Were I sure of an adequate income, my life now would be exactly to my taste. I have seclusion, leisure, books, domestic happiness, & I live in the country. The place is too suburban, indeed, but our twenty acres give us a shady lawn, a garden, a few fields & privacy. All depends, however, on income. Therefore, I shall make what efforts I can to secure that income. But I may fail & the dread of failure depresses me at times. I am haunted also by sad memories of the past, my relations with certain persons are not satisfactory,[20] outside of my own family I have no genial companionship, and philosophy, if an interesting and absorbing study, is not cheerful; it oppresses the mind with a profound feeling of the mystery of life, of ourselves, our purpose & our fate. Life becomes more solemn, more earnest, more crowded with thought & emotion as we approach that period when it is to cease altogether on this scene. And what then?

MAY 18, 1863 | Shopkeepers say they never sold so much or at such high rates. This will continue for some time, but there must be a reaction & a collapse. There will then be bankruptcy & "hard times" for a season. Many will have made great fortunes, many will be ruined. Sudden peace would bring about an immediate revulsion because prices would at once fall. Business men therefore are not anxious for peace and peace, before the objects of the war are fully attained, is not desirable. The quarrel must be fought out until no cause of quarrel remains, or peace would be temporary and be indeed, not peace, but a cessation of active hostilities, which would be soon renewed.

---

20. The diarist was hurt that his brother Henry's orphaned children paid virtually no attention to him.

MAY 23, 1863 | Spent the day under the trees reading Schwegler[21] on the philosophy of Herbart & Schlegel.[22] In his account of the latter there was much that I could not follow. The terminology is peculiar, the thought subtle, the subject itself difficult and the principles are stated in an abstract form, with great brevity. The Germans are deep thinkers, no doubt, but it seems to me that the germ of all their systems is in Plato and that their reasoning is little more than the expansion & variation of his leading doctrines on real being and the becoming, the one & the many, the true & the phenomenal. Mind & matter, the ego & the non-ego, the finite & the infinite, the absolute & the conditioned, being & appearance, substance & attribute—these are the problems which all philosophers have attempted to solve & with the same success. It is something, however, to know these as problems, to reach the limits of science, to recognize our ignorance, to follow the track of masterly logic and to have one's mind opened to the grand & profound mystery of nature & of our own souls. I must try to get translations of Fichte, Jacobi,[23] & the other German writers whom Schwegler notices. There is nothing like going to fountain sources. I should have known nothing of Plato if, instead of reading him, I had read his commentators.

MAY 31, 1863 | The Democrats are to have a meeting tomorrow afternoon in Independence Square to express sympathy for Vallandigham & indignation at what they call the tyrannical course of the government.[24] A disturbance is feared. It is thought the meeting will be attacked.

---

21. Fisher was reading Albert Schwegler's *The History of Philosophy in Epitome*, evidently in the edition translated by Julius H. Seelye and published in New York in 1856, the year before Schwegler's death.

22. Johann Friedrich Herbart (1776-1841), and Friedrich von Schlegel (1772-1829).

23. Johann Gottlieb Fichte (1762-1814), and Friedrich H. Jacobi (1743-1819).

24. Former congressman Clement L. Vallandigham (1820-71) of Ohio, regarded as the leader of the "Copperheads" or Peace Democrats, had been arrested and banished to the Confederacy in May 1863.

JUNE 1, 1863 | The doctor [Wister] here. He says there is great danger of a riot tonight in consequence of the Democratic meeting. That people who have sons & brothers & friends in the army are indignant at the abominable clique who persistently denounce the war, abuse the soldiers & the government, attempt to create discord among the people, & to divide opinion & thus encourage the enemy.

In 1860, just before the war, Mr. Curtis came here to deliver a lecture on slavery. The Democrats threatened to attack him & his audience who were protected only by a strong police force furnished & commanded by Mayor Henry. Chas. Ingersoll was one of those who at a public meeting openly advocated mob law on that occasion. These same Democrats are now making an outcry about liberty of speech, of which, under the protection of that same Mayor, they are in the full enjoyment, and which they are using to destroy that very government by which they do enjoy this and all other rights.

JUNE 2, 1863 | Bet brought the evening paper containing an account of the meeting last night, the resolutions & speeches. They are of a superior order to others of the same party. They denounce the government for arbitrary arrests. With much false reasoning, there is a good deal of truth in some of them. The government has made a great mistake in this matter of arresting & sending off to prison men charged with treasonable language & opinions, and has thus attacked the most sensitive part of the American character. Many of these arrests were wholly unjustifiable and they have been made by military authority instead of civil, which has given them a more odious character. They are also, in my judgment, illegal, and the violation of the Constitution was entirely unnecessary.

JUNE 16, 1863 | The news is that the rebels have entered Penna: in large force & have taken Chambersburg. They are said to have 18,000 men. Went to town. Attended to business. The streets were crowded, the State House bell was tolling to call the people together to enroll for the defence of the state. Telegrams came from the governor urging strenuous efforts to send men forward to Harrisburg, which the rebels, after taking Carlisle,[25] were rapidly approaching. There was not much excitement or alarm. No one seemed to think it possible that Philada: could be in danger. Saw McMichael. He said he did not think the enemy could cross the Susquehanna, but that if they did there was nothing to prevent them from coming here.

JUNE 19, 1863 | It seems likely enough that Lee[26] will endeavor to transfer the seat of war from the exhausted region of Virginia into Maryland & Penna: where he can obtain ample supplies & inflict on us immense losses. There is a general want of confidence in Hooker who seems unequal to the work before him.

JUNE 24, 1863 | My article, entitled "Our Black Army," in the paper this morning with the signature "Kent." I do not care to be conspicuous or to seem to court notoriety just now, and if I had used my old name of Cecil I might as well have signed my real name in full. So for want of a better, I took Kent, which is the next county to Cecil & is also the name of an eminent American jurist. No reliable news, tho rumors are rife that the rebels are in the state with a large force. No news from the Army of the Potomac.

JUNE 26, 1863 | Saw several persons & heard various opinions. Mr. C. J. Stillé thought that Phila: would be taken unless Hooker could check Lee, McMichael, unless a successful stand could be made at Harrisburg so as to prevent the enemy's crossing the Susquehanna. Both are no doubt right. If Hooker can gain a victory over Lee, the latter will withdraw his forces from this state; if the advance of the rebels can be stopped at the Susquehanna, they cannot reach Philada.

25. Actually, the Confederates did not reach Carlisle until June 27, 1863.
26. Robert E. Lee (1807–70), of Virginia, was an 1829 graduate of West Point, a veteran of the Mexican War, and the captor of John Brown at Harpers Ferry in 1859. When Virginia seceded from the Union Lee resigned from the U.S. Army and accepted a commission in the Virginia military. He commanded the Confederacy's Army of Northern Virginia from 1862 to 1865.

Between Harrisburg & Phila: is a plain, open turnpike road with nothing to check the advance of an army, which cannot be opposed with success by raw recruits of ten times its number, because it will move with artillery. It seems probable, however, that Lee's real object is Washington, which, should he gain an advantage over Hooker, he would attempt to take. He cannot therefore expect to hold Phila:, but, if he can make a sudden & successful dash at it, he may be willing to plunder or even to destroy it. Its wealth would support his army for a long time. Saw at Penington's book store[27] a son of Col. [John G.] Watmough, who had just returned from Harrisburg where he took for its defences a battery of cannon. He said the country people displayed entire indifference in relation to the invasion, saying the war was a mere quarrel between abolitionists & secessionists & that they did not care which won. They were only anxious about their farms and would be glad to have peace on any terms.

JUNE 27, 1863 | No doubt exists now that the rebels have entered Penna: with a large force, for General Ewell,[28] the successor of the redoubted Stonewall Jackson, who was killed some weeks ago in Virginia, has issued a proclamation at Gettysburg, warning the people to abstain from injuries to his troops, as they may thus mitigate the rigors of war. Gen'l Dana from Boston has been appointed to the command of Phila: and its defences, & I suppose martial law will be proclaimed.[29]

JUNE 29, 1863 | The news is that Lee has invaded Penna: with his whole army, 100,000 strong, in different divisions and that his headquarters are in Chambersburg. General Geo. Meade has been appointed to the command of the Army of the Potomac in place of

27. John Penington & Son, 127 South 7th Street.
28. Lt. Gen. Richard S. Ewell (1817-72), an 1840 graduate of West Point, was formerly a division commander under "Stonewall" Jackson and had just returned to duty after losing a leg.
29. Napoleon Jackson Tecumseh Dana (1822-1905), a graduate of West Point and a veteran of the Mexican War, began the Civil War as the colonel of a Minnesota regiment and rose to the rank of major general.

Hooker. It is a good thing to get rid of the latter, but whether Meade is equal to the task before him is yet to be seen. I knew him well many years ago, as his family were very intimate with the Athertons. He married a daughter of John Sergeant. He is a manly, intelligent, honorable fellow, was educated at West Point and served with distinction in the Mexican War & in this war, having been a brigadier general in the Army of the Potomac at the time of receiving the command of it.

The streets presented a strange aspect, most of them deserted, but Chesnut Street thronged with crowds of men, chiefly of the working classes, many of them vicious & ill-looking, wandering about apparently without a purpose. Recruiting parties were marching about with drum & flag, followed only by a few ragged boys—recruiting offices empty, taverns and grog shops full. The people looked careless & indifferent. There was no excitement. The same street presented a very different scene in April 1861 when the war broke out. Then it was fluttering with flags & filled by a crowd of agitated, earnest men. War was a novelty then; it is an old story now, and the demagogues have spread abroad the opinion that the administration is corrupt & imbecile, that it is impossible to conquer the South & that we ought to have peace now on any terms.

JULY 3, 1863 | In the paper an account of the affair at Gettysburg. An advanced corps of Meade's army were attacked by a superior force of the enemy & were forced to retire after a severe contest in which our troops behaved admirably. Unfortunately, Gen'l Reynolds was killed.[30] The whole of Lee's army and of Meade's are now confronting each other and a great battle is expected to come off, probably is now going on. It will have much influence on the result of the war.

JULY 6, 1863 | The news is that Lee's army was signally defeated on Friday and on Saturday was withdrawing to the South Mountain pass,

---

30. Gen. John F. Reynolds (1820–63), of Lancaster, Pennsylvania, was an 1841 graduate of West Point and a veteran of the Mexican War. An able officer who commanded the left wing of the Union army, Reynolds was killed at Gettysburg on July 1.

pursued by Meade and also by Couch[31] from Harrisburg with 18,000 men. It is supposed that Lee will try to escape thro the South Mountain into Virginia, but his pontoon train at Williamsport has been burnt by Gen'l French[32] & the rains have swollen the Potomac. Gen'l Longstreet is a prisoner in our hands.[33] The battle was a dreadful one—loss on our side said to be 20,000, on the other 30,000, tho these figures were probably exaggerated. We have taken from 10,000 to 15,000 prisoners.

JULY 7, 1863 | Got a copy of the *New York Tribune* last night which contained a notice of a book just published by Mrs. Kemble. It is a series of letters written to a friend during her first visit to her husband's plantation in Georgia.[34] They describe plantation life there and the condition & treatment of the Negroes and reveal terrible secrets of the prison house. Filth, squalor, cruelty, & wretchedness are painted in very strong colors, as well as the discomfort & inconvenience of Butler's own house. When these letters were written, she also wrote a journal which soon after her return she published,[35] greatly to Butler's vexation, who bought up all the copies he could & tried to suppress it. I remember hearing at the time that her conduct at the plantation had enraged Butler & the overseers & caused much dissatisfaction among neighboring gentlemen as she put dangerous notions into the minds of the slaves. These letters are now printed for the first time, partly, I suppose, for the sake of annoying Butler, partly to aid the cause of abolition, & partly for the money they will bring. I am surprised at the picture they draw of the miserable condition of the Negroes, which is very discreditable to Butler.

31. Gen. Darius N. Couch (1822-97) commanded in Pennsylvania and turned out the militia for the Gettysburg campaign.

32. Gen. William H. French (1815-81), a native of Maryland and an 1837 graduate of West Point, commanded the Harpers Ferry district during the Gettysburg campaign.

33. A false rumor, Confederate Gen. James Longstreet (1821-1904) was not captured.

34. Frances Anne Kemble, *Journal of a Residence on a Georgian Plantation* (New York, 1863).

35. *Journal of a Residence in America* (Philadelphia, 1835).

JULY 8, 1863 | Papers full of news of the surrender of Vicksburg,[36] the flight of Lee, & the rejoicings in Phila. . . . The abolitionists are trying to make what they can out of the enlistment of Negro soldiers & are likely to cause a reaction & injure their own cause & the real interest of the Negro. There is a camp of a colored regiment at Chelten Hills[37] & speeches have been made to them by Kelley, Fred. Douglass,[38] &c., reported in today's paper. The orators claim equality for the Negro race, the right of suffrage, &c. All this is as absurd as it is dangerous.

JULY 10, 1863 | The difficulties of the war are likely to be complicated by the fact that the French have now virtually conquered Mexico. The Emperor will no doubt desire to make of it a French province like Algeria, tho it will be far more valuable, both from its extent, its fertility, its mineral wealth, and its position, commanding as it does the Gulf of Mexico and the transit between the Atlantic & the Pacific. This acquisition is one result of our civil war, and to retain it the Emperor has a direct interest in causing the war to end only in a separation of North & South. Should the Union be restored, the traditional & avowed policy of the United States is opposed to his keeping Mexico as it would have prevented his obtaining it.

JULY 12, 1863 | At 2 drove up to Alverthorpe to inquire after the children.[39] They are all doing well. Am sorry I went for Fisher would talk about slavery & the war & was more outrageous than ever. He shows no consideration whatever for others, but assumes the right to denounce with unmeasured abuse & violence of language everything which they respect & value. I shall not go to the house again, except for very special reasons. It is better that intercourse should cease, if

36. Gen. Grant gained full control of the Mississippi River by his capture of Vicksburg on July 4, 1863.
37. Camp William Penn.
38. Frederick Douglass (1817[?]-95), the son of a white father and a slave woman, escaped slavery in Maryland to become a noted abolitionist orator, author, and newspaper editor.
39. Helen and Maria were suffering from typhoid fever.

the rules of courtesy cannot be maintained. When the war is over, old acquaintance & friendship may be resumed, which cannot be the case if, whilst it lasts, people who differ wholly in their sentiments discuss it with warmth & say things which cannot be forgotten.

JULY 16, 1863 | On Monday commenced a terrible riot in the city of New York. It began by resistance to the draft, & it was soon evident that it had been organized on a most formidable scale. The mob numbered many thousands, there was not sufficient military force ready to oppose them, and the whole city seemed at their mercy. The rioters were of the lowest class, they plundered & burnt private houses in the most fashionable parts of the city, robbed & beat unoffending persons in the streets & the passenger cars, tore up the railroad tracks, attempted to destroy the gasworks, murdered & hung to lamp posts Negroes wherever they could be found, destroyed whole squares of Negro houses, killing women & children & committed every sort of fiendish atrocity that a French mob could have done in the worst period of the revolution. As in France, numbers of women joined these ruffians & incited them to deeds of cruelty. This state of things continued till last night when the arrival of some New York regiments sent hastily from the Army of the Potomac restored quiet.

The real authors of this mischief are the demagogues of the Democratic Party, whose incendiary harangues have inflamed the people and given to the rabble a pretext for disorder. They have been told that the war was unjust, that it is waged wholly for the abolition of slavery, that Mr. Lincoln is a tyrant, that the suspension of the writ of habeas corpus & the conscription are unconstitutional & that the liberties of the country are in danger. The Democrats are determined to cause anarchy in the North, if they can, in order to serve the South, with which they expect to revive their old alliance, with slavery as its basis. These demagogues are the true ringleaders of the riot & one of them, Seymour, is the governor of the state. His speech to the mob was really an apology for their conduct & they cheered him loudly. Had they confined themselves to resisting the draft, they would have met no opposition from him, but when they plundered & burnt the best parts of the city & began to rob & murder people in the streets indiscriminately, Democrats & others, he thought it time to interfere.

JULY 19, 1863 | We went for a few moments to Medary. Sally is at Long Branch. Harry told us that Geo. Cadwalader has been appointed to the command of the troops in Phila. This looks as if trouble was expected here. Should resistance be made, the mob would probably be aided by the disaffected of the people in the interior of the state.[40]

JULY 21, 1863 | Edw'd Ingersoll here in the afternoon. He brought a letter from Willy dated at Vicksburg on the 7th. He had been one of the garrison there during the siege & speaks of his sufferings as very severe, reduced to eat mule & horse flesh. Charles, he says, had become interested in a tannery & was therefore exempt from military duty. He was about to go home, having been paroled, & expected to find all the Negroes on the plantation gone & that the family would be reduced to penury. . . .[41] Received today a pamphlet published for general circulation by the Union League on the subject of enlisting colored troops, which contains among other things my article of June 24 entitled "Our Black Army."[42]

JULY 25, 1863 | In the evening drove Bet & Sidney to Fern Hill & had a pleasant visit. The McKeans are going in a few days to Sharon & were very kind in asking me to accompany them.[43] Mr. McK. said he had no doubt the water, air & baths there would do my gout a great deal of good, perhaps cure it for a time. I must do something, for it is

---

40. Alarmed by the New York draft riots, Secretary of War Stanton, on the day before the Philadelphia draft was to be drawn, ordered Gen. George Cadwalader to Philadelphia as military commander. There was no disturbance in the city during the draft.

41. Willy and Charles were sons of John Ingersoll who had moved to Mississippi.

42. Fisher's article was also reprinted by the New England Loyal Publication Company.

43. The Sharon Springs, which rose about ten miles from the Palatine Bridge in the Mohawk Valley, were thought to have qualities similar to those of Virginia's White Sulphur Springs.

becoming a serious affair. I am never free from pain and sometimes suffer very much. If I can, therefore, I will go to Sharon, but not till the middle of next month, as I must stay here to attend to selling my wheat, peaches, &c.

AUGUST 5, 1863 | Called at Lippincott's. He gave me acct. sales & proceeds of my book to July 1. He has sold 400 copies. One of his clerks told me the book is alive & they sell 3 or 4 copies a week. I hope to get out of the scrape without loss, and I think with considerable gain of reputation.

AUGUST 20, 1863 | At 1½ drove with Bet & Sidney to see Mrs. Jno. Butler at her place on Chelten Hill. Had a great deal of talk. Altho she is in part a southern woman, and the war has greatly injured her estate, altho her father & some of her brothers are in the South, also great sufferers by the war and all violent secessionists, she is loyal to the Union & the government. She approves of emancipation. She says Mrs. Kemble's description of the treatment of the Negroes & their condition on the Butler estate is true, & she ought to know as she owns half the property, or did before the war, & has frequently resided on the estate. I fear her income is so much reduced that she will not be able to live at her place, a great misfortune to her as she likes it very much. She never expects to get anything more from her property in Georgia.

AUGUST 31, 1863 | Parties are now preparing for the electioneering campaign in this state, as a governor is to be chosen in October. Curtin, the present governor, is the candidate of the Union Party. The interest of this election is great, for if carried by the Democrats the consequences will be very serious, not only in reference to the war, but to the order & security of society. Went to town. Attended to various business & came out at 4½. Miller McKim in the car. He is a noted abolitionist, an intelligent and I think an honest & sincere man. He went last year to Beaufort, near Charleston, to assist in organizing plans for the employment & education of the Negroes freed by our army.[44] He told me that he had an opportunity of discovering the habits of gentlemen in the treatment of their Negroes, & that all that he had before heard or imagined of cruelty was surpassed by the reality & that some of the worst cases were those of concubines, mulattoes, who suffered from the jealousy of the wives of their masters. He mentioned two beautiful mulatto girls whose statements of barbarous cruelty were so shocking that he could not believe them and had their persons examined by a lady of his party, who found on their lacerated backs full confirmation of their dismal story. The parties whose names he mentioned were ladies of some of the best families. I have often heard that concubinage was a source of much domestic unhappiness in the South, but I never before heard that injured wives revenged themselves in this way on the innocent victims of their husbands' crime.

SEPTEMBER 5, 1863 | Went to Mount Harmon on Wednesday. When I got to Middletown could not obtain a conveyance as all were engaged for a camp meeting in the neighborhood. Was obliged to go in the stage to Cecilton & to hire the stage driver to take me to the farm.... Young Edward Jones drove by, son of my old friend Commodore Jacob Jones[45] & now living at his father's farm, about a mile from Cecilton. He is a violent secessionist and was arrested & imprisoned in Fort Warren a year ago, charged with seditious practices. "What is the reason," said Ford,[46] speaking of him, "that secessionists are always arrogant, overbearing & regardless of the feelings of others? Union men are not so." "Because," said I, "they feel that they are in the wrong." I might have added that slavery educates men to pride and arrogance.

---

44. James Miller McKim (1810–74), a Presbyterian minister and abolitionist, edited the *Pennsylvania Freeman* and was an official of the Pennsylvania Anti-Slavery Society. In 1862, he organized the Philadelphia Port Relief Committee to provide for the wants of 10,000 liberated slaves.

45. Commodore Jacob Jones won fame in the War of 1812, when, in command of the *Wasp*, he captured the *Frolic*. Edward was his son.

46. George A. Ford, storekeeper at Cecilton.

The prices this year, notwithstanding a full crop, have been high, higher than they were last year with half a crop. The reason is that far more peaches have this year been "canned" than ever before. The demand for canned fruit increases rapidly; they are sent all over the world, and the supply cannot keep pace with the demand because the area of supply is limited by nature. Consequently, I feel convinced that peaches will continue to be at least as profitable as they now are, as long as I can raise them. The profit I believe will be from $60 to $150 per acre, according to the prices & the crop. This is far better than grain or tobacco or anything else that my land will grow. I have therefore determined to plant more trees until I have 200 acres. I shall try to have that many in the ground next year. In four years afterwards, if no mischance occurs, & the business continues as it now is, they will pay me an income of $15,000 to $20,000, a great result truly, which would enable me to leave a comfortable estate for Bet & Sidney, now the chief object of my life. . . . Had a satisfactory visit and came up on Thursday morning.

Went yesterday . . . to pay a long intended visit to my cousin, Deborah Wharton. Her daughter Annie has been for the last six months or more ill with consumption and now it is thought has but a short time to live.[47] Annie is a delightful creature, admirable in character and very beautiful, one of the most beautiful women I ever saw. Her face combines regularity of features with expression. She has glorious dark hazel eyes, a sweet smile, a fine complexion, dark hair, a true Grecian contour of head, nose, mouth, & chin exquisitely chiselled. If she had more roundness to her graceful figure she would be perfect. Since boyhood, my intercourse with her family, tho always very friendly, has been slight and I never saw Annie till she grew up and since, but seldom, tho always with great pleasure & admiration. I heard of her illness last winter, called afterwards at their house in town, heard of her from time to time from members of the family and

---

47. Deborah Fisher married William Wharton (1790-1856), by whom she had ten children, including Joseph Wharton (1826-1909), manufacturer and philanthropist after whom the University of Pennsylvania's Wharton School is named. Anna, or Annie, born in 1834, was Deborah's next to youngest child.

today executed my purpose of going to see them at their countryseat.[48] It is an old place, surrounded by fine trees, on a lane leading to the Ridge Road, near Mr. Robert Ralston's & the Church of St. James the Less. I remember being there when I was a boy. When we got to the house a carriage was at the door & cousin Deborah came out & told us that she was just going to drive with Annie. Whilst she spoke, Annie appeared, carried by two women and looking radiantly beautiful. As soon as she saw us, she gave us a smiling & cordial welcome. I went to the carriage when she was in. She was reclining on pillows. She shook hands with me and said she was a great deal better and certainly her brilliant eyes, beaming smile and animated voice did not betoken disease. Nevertheless, her cheek was pale, her person thin and the very brightness of her eye & the spiritual expression of her face were marks of the progress of the insidious disease, which thus often decks its victims in beauty for the grave. It was a sad sight, which impressed both Bet & myself very much, & which I shall never forget.

SEPTEMBER 16, 1863 | In the paper this morning appeared a proclamation by the President suspending the writ of habeas corpus throughout the U. S. *in accordance with the act of Congress* of March last, that is to say, *not* by executive but by legislative authority. This is a very important step as it settles the question whether the President or Congress has the power to suspend the privilege of the writ and settles it wisely in my judgment. There was great danger that it would be decided the other way. I am glad to see the views I advocated in my chapter on executive power, in the *Trial of the Constitution,* prevail.

SEPTEMBER 19, 1863 | There has been a discussion of the President's proclamation suspending the writ of habeas corpus before Jno. Cadwalader, U. S. district judge, in which he declared it to be constitutional. He made a similar decision a few weeks ago in relation to the

---

48. This was Bellevue, a pre-Revolutionary house, though much added to later, which was purchased by Charles Wharton in 1796. Anna Wharton, the Annie here described by Fisher, wrote a little book about the place for her nieces and nephews, *Bellevue, For the Children* (Philadelphia, Christmas 1862).

Conscription Act. He is a Democrat. These two opinions, therefore, will have weight with his party & take from the demagogues two of their chief topics of declamation & agitation. The wisdom of the principle of making the judiciary independent is illustrated by the conduct of Cadwalader & Woodward.[49] The former, a U. S. judge, holds his office during good behavior & has, tho an eager partizan, withdrawn from active or ostensible participation in politics and administered his office without party bias, whilst Woodward, a state judge, elected by the people for a term of years, is at this moment a candidate for the place of governor of the state.

OCTOBER 1, 1863 | At 12 went to [L. R.] Koecker's, the dentist, by appointment. [E. B.] Gardette, the best in town, to whom I have gone when necessary for more than 30 years, is now sick & unable to practice &, as he has made a large fortune, will probably give up practice. Koecker found two teeth needed plugging instead of one as I supposed. They were jaw teeth, furthest back & a difficult & tedious job, but not very painful. He kept me nearly two hours.

OCTOBER 12, 1863 | Tomorrow is election day. A governor, state legislature, judge of the Supreme Court, &c., are to be chosen. The candidate of the Union Party is Curtin, the present governor, who has displayed energy, activity & zeal in sustaining the administration and carrying out all measures necessary to promote the war. His moral character is, I fancy, not very good, but better than could be expected for a governor of Penna. The candidate of the Democrats is Woodward, a judge of the state Supreme Court, who nevertheless has become the candidate of a party, a fact in itself sufficient to prove his unfitness for the office he seeks, as it shows that he cannot appreciate the duties or proprieties of the one he holds. He sympathizes wholly with the rebellion, its motives, passions and purposes, justifies it, advocates the right of secession and defends slavery as a divine and

---

49. George W. Woodward (1809-75) was an associate justice on the Supreme Court of Pennsylvania from 1852 to 1863, and chief justice from 1863 to 1867. In 1863 he was the unsuccessful Democratic candidate for governor of Pennsylvania.

beneficent institution that should be fostered and extended. The election is very important.

OCTOBER 14, 1863 | The election was quiet & orderly, a fact due less to the temper of the Democrats than to the ample police & military force in readiness to quell any attempt at violence. Such precautions are necessary now. The Union Party carried the city by almost 7000 majority and from the returns received there is reason to believe have carried the state.

OCTOBER 27, 1863 | Got a letter from Mr. Ch. Eliot Norton announcing that he and Mr. Lowell have become editors of the *North American Review* & asking me to write for it.[50] Went to town and attended to some business. In the evening, Mr. & Mrs. Wm. Ashhurst came out to tea. She is always agreeable & he is a very good fellow. Afterwards, Sarah Wister came bringing Mr. Miller McKim, who is a neighbor of hers and a good deal at her house. I have known him slightly for a long time, but never visited him nor he me. He is a noted abolitionist of the extreme school & is or was the editor of an abolitionist paper.[51] He is . . . very mild & moderate in his language & intelligent & well informed. The time was when a visit from him would have been very unwelcome to us, but the war has changed our notions in regard to slavery and, like most others, if we are not now abolitionists, in the old sense, we are emancipationists & wish to see slavery destroyed since it has attempted to destroy the nation. Therefore, we were well content to see Mr. McKim. The term "abolitionist" has ceased to be one of reproach.

NOVEMBER 1, 1863 | Began this morning notes for an article on slavery as sanctioned by the Bible, which perhaps I may finish for the *N.*

---

50. The first issue of the *North American Review* under the editorship of Charles Eliot Norton and James Russell Lowell appeared in January 1864.
51. McKim had succeeded John Greenleaf Whittier as editor of the *Pennsylvania Freeman.*

Am. Review. Am pleased to find the view I have always taken of slavery sustained by Goldwin Smith's argument.[52] In all I have written, I have contended that slavery or servitude for life was a human relation, suitable between man & man where great disparity existed of moral and intellectual power, but that chattel slavery, which degraded a man to an article of merchandize, was a violation of all rights. By the Hebrew law, the slave was regarded not as a thing, but as a person. He was a dependent, a domestic servant & one of the family of his master. Rome & Greece made property of men & so do our southern states.

NOVEMBER 3, 1863 | Wister here in the evening. The medicine he gave me caused me an agreeable mental excitement, which I mentioned to Bet. The reason was that Indian hemp, or Hasheesh, was one of its ingredients. I have read of its wonderful powers over the mind & spirits, but never tried it before. It is certainly a very pleasant way of curing gout.

NOVEMBER 12, 1863 | The news is that three of the judges of the Supreme Court of this state, Woodward, Lowrie, and Thompson, Democrats, have declared the Conscription Act unconstitutional & therefore void.[53] They form a majority of the Court. Two other judges gave dissenting opinions. The three former are partizans; Woodward was the candidate of the Democratic Party for governor at the last election. The object of this opinion is to oppose the government in the prosecution of the war. Its probable effect will be a collision between the civil

---

52. Fisher had recently read Goldwin Smith's book, *Does the Bible Sanction American Slavery?* (Cambridge, 1863).

53. The conscription case was *Kneedler v. Lane*. The Supreme Court of Pennsylvania was made up of four Democrats and one Republican. Chief Justice Walter H. Lowrie, a Democrat, was elected to the bench in 1851. The other Democrats were George W. Woodward, who joined the bench in 1852, and James Thompson and William Strong, both elected in 1857. The lone Republican, John M. Read, was elected to the court in 1858. By 1863 Strong had moved into the Republican camp; in 1870 he was appointed to the Supreme court of the United States by Ulysses S. Grant.

authorities of the state & the government, a result which the Democrats have tried to bring about.[54] A desired pretext is now afforded to the mob to resist the draft and, under color of that purpose, to commit every sort of outrage against person & property as they did in the City of New York last July and as they are now doing in the mining counties of this state, where the Irish workmen are banded together by thousands, armed, and have established a reign of terror. They have murdered several of the coal operators, dictate to the owners of the mines, and hold under their control the supply of coal for private use in this city, for all factories & mills and for the steamers and workshops of the government.

NOVEMBER 13, 1863 | Some weeks ago, John Lewis, whose grandfather once owned this place, asked my permission to have some photographic views taken of it. This morning he came with the artist. They took views from six different points and in one of the views, Bet, Lewis & myself are introduced, standing at the porch, with Daniel[55] hard by holding Delly, saddled. We regretted very much that we could not have Sidney, but he was at school. When he returned, he with Bridget, John Leonard & his mother, went to town to visit the Academy of Natural Sciences, where there is a very large & valuable collection of stuffed birds & other animals.

NOVEMBER 20, 1863 | There was yesterday a large meeting at Gettysburg to consecrate a cemetery for the interment of our soldiers who fell in the battles of the 1st, 2nd & 3rd of last July at that place. The President, Mr. Seward, governors of several states, other official persons, and a large concourse were assembled & the proceedings seem to have been dignified & impressive. The orator was Mr. Edward Everett. His speech was long but commonplace, tho well written & appropriate. Mr. Seward made a good speech, Mr. Lincoln a very short

---

54. No collision took place. In October Chief Justice Lowrie failed in his bid for reelection to the court and his term expired in December. A Republican, Daniel Agnew, took his place. In January 1864, again by a vote of 3 to 2, the court reversed itself on the constitutionality of the Conscription Act.

55. Daniel was the gardener at Forest Hill.

one, but to the point and marked by his pithy sense, quaintness, & good feeling.

DECEMBER 14, 1863 | In the morning read the papers and a pamphlet written in 1861, by Bishop Hopkins of Vermont, entitled, *Bible View of Slavery*.[56] It was republished here by a committee of the Democratic Party to influence the election last October. I never read the whole of it before. It is written with skill, but is full of fallacies, sophistries & misstatements. I cannot think it is the result of honest conviction or if it be, it shows great want of reasoning power & the ability to perceive truth.

DECEMBER 23, 1863 | Th. 18 at 9 o'clock, rose only to 22. I like it and always feel better in such weather. Our house perfectly warm & comfortable throughout by aid of the furnace. I have an air-tight coal stove in my library, another in the nursery, and another in the west piazza room, which Bet uses as a boudoir. Wood fires are made in the dining room & parlor about 4 o'clock. There is a flue from the furnace in the parlor, another in the entry & another in the east piazza room, which is my dressing room, and these suffice in the coldest weather.

DECEMBER 25, 1863 | The same fine weather. Th. 22 at 9 o'clock. Last night Sidney was so excited at the expectation of Christkinkle's visit & of the good things he was to bring him that it was long before he went to sleep. He woke about 11 o'clock, and, rising in his bed, got sight of the toys on a table. He would not be satisfied unless he got some of them in bed with him & was with difficulty kept in bed himself & did not go to sleep for two hours. In the morning, he was greatly delighted at seeing all the pretty things which he still believes are brought by Christkinkle, tho I think his faith is not so firm as it used to be. At 1 o'clock started on Robin to pay a visit at Alverthorpe. Had a delightful

---

56. In 1861 Episcopal Bishop John Henry Hopkins of Vermont published a pamphlet which sustained slavery on religious grounds. This pamphlet, retitled *Bible View of Slavery*, was issued in 1863 as a Democratic campaign document, and Pennsylvania was flooded with it.

ride, roads good, country beautiful & weather perfect. Saw them all, except Helen who was skating on the pond. Miss Rutledge[57] still there, a very pleasing girl. Not much allusion was made to public affairs. Fisher, however, could not help predicting all sorts of disasters, financial & other, from the rule of this administration, which he declared to be utterly unprincipled and corrupt. He spoke of his rents, however, as having risen for the most part to their former standard, but his expenses have greatly increased. He said it cost him $2000 a month to live & that now he had to support several persons besides his family—Mrs. Arthur Middleton, who is abroad, & Kitty, his wife's sister, who is here insane, and an insane son of Henry A. Middleton, in the hospital, none of whom get anything from S. Carolina. I fancy the list of such dependents is likely to be enlarged. Fisher does all this, I have no doubt, liberally and generously.

DECEMBER 30, 1863 | Attended to some business in town. Called to see Mrs. Deborah Wharton. She spoke a great deal about Annie & with the calmness & deep feeling which might be expected from *her.* Annie's sweetness, serenity, perfect resignation & joyful hope to the last moment she described as "glorious," as was the radiant beauty of her countenance.[58] She fell a sacrifice to her exertions for the sick & wounded soldiers. Against all advice & entreaty, she would go to the hospitals where she exerted herself in nursing the men & even in cooking for them beyond her strength. She took cold, which became pneumonia and afterwards consumption. She was greatly excited by the war & knew well many young men who went to the army, some of whom were killed. When I think of the efforts made by this delicate & fair young creature, I feel ashamed of my own selfish indolence. She was a rare being.

> As the clock strikes the hour, how often we say,
> "Time flies," when tis we that are passing away.

---

57. A Southern girl who was visiting the Joshua Francis Fishers.
58. Annie had died on November 20, 1863.

~1864~

JANUARY 2, 1864 | Got the January number of the *North American Review*. My article on Goldwin Smith's book, entitled "The Bible & Slavery," the 2nd in the number. Read it. Mr. Norton has made some alterations & omitted some passages, but nothing of importance.

JANUARY 5, 1864 | Quite a snowstorm all day yesterday. We got in ice enough to half fill the ice house.

JANUARY 7, 1864 | Forgot to mention that yesterday, at 3 o'clock, Sidney went to a Twelfth-night children's party at Dr. Wister's. He came home highly delighted. Signor Blitz, the celebrated ventriloquist & performer of sleight of hand, with his wonderful trained canary birds was there and marvellous were the stories that Sidney had to tell of what he & they did.

FEBRUARY 12, 1864 | Delightful, clear weather. Th. 30 to 40. Went to town in the carriage with Bet, chiefly to call on Mr. Geo. W. Curtis, who is here to deliver a lecture this evening. Went to Newhall's countinghouse to see Field, to learn where to find Mr. Curtis. He was staying at Field's house in 18th St. below Locust. Went up there & found him. Sat with him for an hour in the library. He has recently been to Washington & had much conversation with Seward, Sumner,[1] & Mr.

---

1. Charles Sumner (1811-74), a Republican, was U.S. senator from Massachusetts from 1851 to 1874.

Lincoln. Seward, he says, despairs of the success of democracy & has lost faith in the intelligence of the people. Sumner thinks the true way to restore the South to the Union is to extend the suffrage to the Negroes, after they are emancipated, as a counteracting power to that of their former masters, who will, he thinks, never again be loyal to the Union, but a disaffected element, always ready to intrigue with a foreign enemy. Such an enemy is likely to be found in France, if she obtains the control of Mexico, a very probable event. Mr. Lincoln has faith in the vitality of the nation and the ability of the people to meet and dispose of all difficult questions as they arise. Curtis spoke in the highest possible terms of Mr. Lincoln, of his sagacity, firmness of purpose, unostentatious performance of duty, high-minded & pure integrity, and wonderful power to perceive the real wishes of the people. I told him that I took some credit to myself for having appreciated Mr. L.'s character from the first, and that my praise of him in the *Trial of the Constitution,* which some considered excessive at the time, has been justified. "Yes," he said, "fully."

FEBRUARY 19, 1864 | Elizabeth Fisher was here yesterday and invited us to a skating party at Wakefield, given by Frank Wister.[2] The company to meet there at 11 o'clock & go to Thorp's dam, a mile distant, to skate & return to Wakefield to dinner at 6. Skating is now a fashionable amusement for ladies as well as gentlemen in New York, Boston, & here. It affords an opportunity for the display of grace, beauty, and a becoming toilette, & for love making also, & is equal in all these excitements to a ball, besides having the advantage of healthy exercise in the open air. At 1 we went, Bet leaving Sidney & me & going to see Edward Ingersoll who is still suffering very much from sciatica. We found a gay party assembled at the house—fashionable girls, scarlet dresses—such as never before met under its roof, very different indeed from its Quaker inmates of former generations. Miss Lina Peters, a handsome, showy girl, a daughter of Frank Peters,[3] was there. Miss

2. Col. Francis Wister (1841–1905).
3. Lina was evidently Evelyn Willing Peters, daughter of Francis Peters (1817–61).

Nannie Wadsworth, whom I had not seen since she was a child, not a beauty, tho like her mother, some Miss Cadwaladers, &c., there. We walked to the pond, a very large one. The ice was in capital order and I watched them for about an hour, enjoying their graceful movements and the spectacle of youth, gayety and pleasure they presented. Sidney & I left them and came back at 4, having had a delightful walk thro the woods that skirt the meadows all the way to the pond.

FEBRUARY 23, 1864 | An opinion has been given in the Dist. Court for the city on the question of the constitutionality of the legal tender notes, Hare & Stroud, Union men, in favor of it, and Sharswood, Democrat, against it. Hare's opinion was published in the *North American* yesterday & today; Sharswood's in *The Age*, a Democratic paper, this morning. It seems now established in practice that the judges construe the Constitution according to their political feelings, that the Constitution therefore varies with political majorities *on the bench*, & that consequently the supreme law wants the essential attribute of stability.

MARCH 2, 1864 | This is my birthday. I am now 55 years old. I do not feel old. I have more enjoyment of life than I ever had, notwithstanding the gout. Increasing knowledge adds to intellectual pleasures, and habit only makes my dear wife dearer to me every day, whilst as Sidney grows older he becomes an object of greater interest. I have leisure & comfort with a fair prospect of a larger income. I am not tormented with a desire for fame or fortune, content with the small measure of each that I enjoy, and willing to increase each by voluntary and agreeable labor. Bet & I agreed today that we are leading a life of Arcadian felicity. But over it hangs the inevitable doom. It must cease at some time; it may cease at any time. One of us must die. What then will life be worth to the other? I scarcely dare wish that I may go first, yet cannot face the thought of losing her. I did not expect to live so long. My brothers, younger than myself, are both gone. How long shall I be here? Not many years I think, for so my gout warns me, and those may be years of physical suffering, as indeed the present are to some extent. At any rate, this mysterious life is rapidly flying away and this mysterious me is sure ere long not to be, or to be something unknown in an unknown sphere. It should reconcile us to death that no one would wish to live in this world forever, that what we call death has really no existence for us, for we are not conscious of it if we die wholly, and if we do not, death is the commencement of a new life. When we think of the dead we do not think of them as losers by death. Those that remain are the losers. The world, beautiful & delightful as it is, has its dark side, and life is dominated by fear & care & pain, so both are well lost, even if exchanged for eternal sleep. We would not live here forever, but we would not die today.

MARCH 4, 1864 | At 4½ drove over to Somerville. The guests were Dr. [Edward] Peace & Dr. [Charles] Carter. The latter is from Virginia, one of the old Carter family. He married here Miss Pauline Davis, a daughter of Mr. Samuel Davis of Natchez, Miss., one of the richest men in the state. He came to live in Phila: some 20 years ago or more, and I knew him & his wife very intimately. They both died about 10 years ago, very suddenly, within a few days of each other. Their other daughter, Celestine, married Dr. [William Byrd] Page, also from Virginia. Mr. Davis left an immense estate in plantations & Negroes in Louisiana & Mississippi. Both Page & Carter were obliged to go there when the war broke out to prevent the confiscation of their property. Carter has just returned, and he gave us some interesting information about the state of affairs in the South, which has the merit of being authentic. He says the privation & suffering around Natchez, which has not been devastated to any great extent by the armies, was chiefly among people of property, caused by the loss of articles supplied by commerce—luxuries & refinements for the most part—and by the desertion of household servants. The plantations supplied them with meat & bread. In some cases, the stock & Negroes were carried off from plantations, by which the owners were prevented from planting a crop of cotton. He himself kept his Negroes & put in a crop last year, which, tho a small one, paid him, because of the high price as well as his average crop, 1,150 bales. He paid his Negroes wages, as other planters are glad to do. Wages are very high, $25 per month. Everyone considers slavery at an end & is preparing for the new state of things. Most of the planters in Miss. & Louisiana are Union men & have been from the first and are anxious to restore the Union. Secession was the work of politicians, & afterwards the passions engendered by war or military force compelled or excited all classes to join in the rebellion. The majority would gladly come back but for the threat of confiscation hanging over them. "But," said I, "they can escape that by taking advantage of the amnesty proclamation." "The chief officers," he replied, "are excepted from that, and these the people do not like to desert." He seems perfectly satisfied that slavery is destroyed, tho he is so large an owner, & thinks the consequent prosperity will compensate the loss.

MARCH 10, 1864 | Called at F. & M. Bank to see Mr. Mercer to ask him some questions in relation to legal tender notes, etc. He thinks the system of National Banks, established by Congress, is capable of being made a powerful and dangerous engine of party influence. No doubt. Unfortunately in this country every sort of power is used for party purposes. Genl. Jackson[4] tried so to use the Bk of U. S. He was resisted & finding that he could not bend the Bank to serve his designs, he broke it. In the contest, the Bank in self-defense did become a party engine. So will any bank become or any national system that may be devised.

MARCH 11, 1864 | Had a good deal of gout today. Wister has prescribed a new remedy, the salts of Vichy, which, he says, is much used in England. At home all day reading & making notes for the article I am writing on the legal tender currency. Whether I shall finish it, I do not know, nor is it of much consequence.

MARCH 16, 1864 | Mr. and Mrs. J. F. Fisher here. They would talk about the war, tho Bet & I tried to avoid the subject & they uttered a great deal of treasonable nonsense, Mrs. F. exulting much in the successful defence of Charleston & both expressing the hope & belief that the rebels will eventually triumph, showing themselves, indeed,

---

4. President Andrew Jackson.

thorough partizans of the South in all its most extravagant claims, & denouncing with unmeasured bitterness Mr. Lincoln, the government, and the northern people. The first, according to Fisher, is an ignorant blackguard, the second corrupt & tyrannical, the last a mere mob. Liberty is destroyed, he said, all security for property at an end, refined & gentlemanlike life henceforward impossible, & he wished his children were all dead rather than see them live in such a country & under such a government. He vociferated a great deal more of such trash, the only effect of which must be, & indeed has been, to deprive him of all influence among sensible people and of the respect of his friends. Everyone laughs at him. Times like these lift & try character & test intellect & moral worth.

MARCH 18, 1864 | Genl. Grant has assumed command of the national armies and is to make his headquarters with the Army of the Potomac, leaving Sherman[5] in command in the southwest. The operations of the spring campaign will soon begin in earnest & much depends on their success. It is the last throw of the dice for the rebels.

MARCH 25, 1864 | Got a note this morning from Mr. T. C. Henry of Germantown, on behalf of the Union League, asking me to deliver a lecture in Germantown in aid of some ladies' hospital society.[6] Will inquire about the matter & perhaps may accept the invitation. I could write a lecture suitable for such an occasion without much trouble & it would at any rate put some money in the purse of the hospital. I have done so little & others have done so much for such objects, that I feel as if I ought to make some effort.

---

5. William T. Sherman (1820-91), a graduate of the U.S. Military Academy in 1840, rose to the rank of major general during the Civil War and achieved everlasting fame for his 1864 taking of Atlanta and his subsequent March to the Sea.

6. Thomas Charlton Henry (1828-90), a prominent businessman and brother of Mayor Alexander Henry, was assisting the Committee on Orations and Lectures of the Great Central Fair at Philadelphia for the Sanitary Commission, which was seeking to raise money by sponsoring lectures "in every city, town, or village, whose population is sufficiently large."

MARCH 28, 1864 | Called to see Field at Mr. Newhall's countinghouse, Race above 4th. Mr. Newhall gave me a memoir of his son, Walter S. Newhall, written by Mrs. Owen Wister.[7] He was a captain of the 3rd Penna. Cavalry, joined the army when the war broke out, served with great distinction both in the West and in Virginia, was severely wounded last summer at the battle of Gettysburg. When he got well, returned to duty and last December was drowned in Virginia by his horse falling on him whilst fording a creek. He had been to see his brother in a neighboring camp and they were both, the next day, to have come home to pass Christmas with their family who live in Manheim St., Germantown. His death caused a great deal of feeling at the time, as he was universally beloved & respected.

Went to see Mr. T. C. Henry about the lecture. Told him that I would not be able to write one as I found it was to be delivered in a month, but that if the committee chose I would read one of those I wrote about 25 years ago for the Athenian Institute, tho perhaps it would not be considered appropriate, as now everyone is expected on such occasions to speak about the war. Mr. Henry seemed to think it would do very well & said he would consult the committee. I am almost sorry I made the offer, as I dislike notoriety.

APRIL 2, 1864 | Wrote to Meredith at Bet's request to ask him if he had any autographs of Taylor, Harrison, Buchanan, &c., to spare. She wants them for Mrs. Bernard Henry, who is making up a book of autographs of the Presidents for the great fair for the Sanitary Commission, which is to come off in June & for which extensive preparations are making. Women of all ranks are busily at work. I recd a letter some days ago from Mrs. Isabella James, wife of Th. P. James, wholesale druggist, with whom I have a slight acquaintance, saying that she is making a poet's album & requesting me to contribute something to it. I understand she has made a similar request to authors of celebrity, Tennyson included, so I am put in good company. Wrote to

---

7. Sarah Butler Wister, *Walter S. Newhall. A Memoir* (Philadelphia: Published for the Benefit of the Sanitary Commission, 1864). Fisher wrote a notice of this book which appeared in the *North American* on June 17, 1864.

her this morning that if I could find anything I had written not published, which by a little touching up I could make at all worth her acceptance, I would send it to her. Got a note from Mr. T. C. Henry saying that the committee of the Union League accepted my offer to read a lecture at Germantown in aid of the Ladies' Hospital. I shall select a lecture I wrote for the Athenian Institute & delivered at the Musical Fund Hall in 1841 on the Crusades.[8]

APRIL 6, 1864 | I usually breakfast about 8½, a pleasant meal, not hurried thro but lengthened by charming talk with Bet & Sidney, then a visit to the stable or garden and a conference with Cornelius & Daniel,[9] then newspapers, scribblement in this diary, writing letters if necessary, and these little affairs bring me to 12 or 1 o'clock. I then, if I do not go to town, sit down to my task, if I have one on hand, and I am always happier when I have one, and write till 3, when, if the weather is fair, I ride or drive, &, if not, write till 4½ or 5, when we dine. In the evening, talk with Bet & Sidney, light reading for an hour or two, sometimes a nap on the sofa in the parlor, & to bed at 10 o'clock. I am satisfied & happy with this sort of life and require no external excitement, tho an occasional visit to or from friends is very agreeable. Neither do I dislike the little external business which the management of my small estate gives, nor an occasional trip to Mount Harmon. It is pleasant also to receive, as I do from time to time, tokens that my writings are well received by some judicious people & that my easy labors are not wholly in vain. The only alloy to all this enjoyment at present is the gout. I am never free from pain. Sometimes I suffer severe pain, and at all times I am partially a cripple; I have not the full & free use of legs and arms. I cannot look forward to any cure, but only to partial & temporary alleviation of this malady, and I may be called on to endure its most dreadful forms.

---

8. The sequel to this is found in the diary entry for May 6, when Fisher learned from Henry that the committee for the lecture could not get a hall until June, which was too late.

9. Cornelius Shelly was Fisher's farmer at Forest Hill; Daniel, his gardener.

APRIL 8, 1864 | Miss Fanny Butler called. She came down from Germantown in the passenger car & walked over from the Rising Sun. It was a P. P. C. [*pour prendre congé*] visit as she is going in a few days to Europe, where she expects to remain with her mother, Mrs. Kemble, for a year, and to visit Italy with her next winter. Miss Fanny is a very charming person, gay, graceful, thorobred, clever, cultivated, & more than pretty. She has a good figure & an expressive face, beautiful hair, & good features. I intended to ride & stop at Wakefield, but instead drove her home to Dr. Wister's, which compensated the loss of my ride. Called at Wakefield on my way back. Mrs. J. F. Fisher there, in good humour & good spirits. Fisher, with Helen & Maria, is at Boston, where, Mrs. F. said, he found even more *agreeable* people than on his former visit. By agreeable she meant sympathizers with the rebellion & defenders of the South.

APRIL 10, 1864 | Edward Ingersoll here in the afternoon. He expressed his treasonable sentiments with revolting shamelessness. The folly of the opinions he boastfully uttered was almost equal to their criminality. It is very painful to have relations with such men and that he & those like him should be Bet's brothers & Sidney's uncles. The course they have taken is a great distress to Bet.

APRIL 13, 1864 | Forgot to mention that on Monday I received a courteous letter from Mr. Chase, Secretary of the Treasury, saying that he would send me the reports I requested & giving me his views on some points relating to the currency.

APRIL 19, 1864 | Went to Mount Harmon on Saturday. The weather was cloudy and soon after I started from Middletown it began to rain & continued to rain hard almost all the time till I got to the farm. I did very well, however, as I had a buffalo skin & the wagon had a top. Found a good fire in the parlor and everything clean & comfortable. Walked about the lawn. By moving a fence & diminishing the size of the barnyard, half an acre has been added to what we call the lane-lawn. The tomato plants have been transplanted to the 2nd hothouse & looked very well. Three plows were running in the home field where we are to plant potatoes, watermelons, &c. Men were at work raking the lawn. Altogether it was a busy, prosperous scene & the place looked neat & in good order. The wheat looks well, so also the grass. Cattle & horses thriving. Dined at 5 on a shad caught in our river and as I sat after dinner & smoked my pipe by a bright fire in my comfortable parlor had a pleasant feeling of proprietorship & satisfaction in the place which belonged to my fathers, but which in its present state I have created.

APRIL 23, 1864 | Intended to work at the article [*A National Currency*] this morning, but first Edward & then Charles Ingersoll came and devastated the day, besides disgusting me & distressing Bet by their talk. Edward was more excessive in his opinions than usual. He declared that the southern people were right. That slavery was attacked & they were justified in rebellion. That slavery was a divine institution, but whether right or wrong, was protected by the Constitution which was our supreme law, behind which no one could go. That no one had a right to speak against slavery. That the South would prevail and the Union be restored in the blood of abolitionists. That ere long the war would be brought into the North & array father against son, brother against brother, but that in the end, after anarchy & violence, the Democrats & the South would prevail & slavery be more firmly established than ever, and much more of such rabid trash. What he said reveals the sentiments of many of his party, for he is by no means alone in his opinions. . . . His notion that there is no higher law than the Constitution & that freedom of speech should be suppressed for the sake of slavery shows what his spiritual nature is made of.

APRIL 25, 1864 | Thought I would try to write some verses for Mrs. James' poet's album. I had not rhymed before for three years, I think. Accomplished three stanzas of 9 lines each, which I read to Bet and Elizabeth Fisher, who paid us a visit this morning. They approved them very much. In the evening added two more stanzas. The subject is the part woman plays in this war, by nursing the sick in hospitals, by supplying clothes, delicacies, &c. to the Sanitary Commission, by stimulating & encouraging men to join the army. The instances of effort, self-denial, & true heroism among the women are numberless and would furnish material for a thousand romances. The theme is worthy far better treatment than I can give it. I shall send the verses to Mrs. James.

APRIL 30, 1864 | People are now universally talking about the approaching fair for the Sanitary Commission, and many very busy working for it, among them Betty, who is on a committee. The New York fair made one million 10 thousand dollars. Ours is expected to do half as much at least, and another is to come off soon in Baltimore. The expenses of the Sanitary Commission are about $50,000 per month, so that if it gets from these three & other sources $1,800,000, it will have enough for three years. It is not expected that the war will last that long or, indeed, one year longer. What then is to be done with the surplus? Betty suggests that it be invested as a fund for wounded soldiers & the families of the killed. This I suppose will be done. It would have an excellent effect on the army.

MAY 2, 1864 | Went to town. Called to see Mrs. Barton. This is her day for receiving. Found several ladies with her, all talking about the fair, for which Mrs. Barton is very busy. She showed me a very beautiful lace handkerchief, exquisite in design & workmanship, made at Brussels, to be sold at the fair, price $300. It cost about $100 in Brussels. . . . Went to McMichael's. Some weeks ago he asked me to write an address, to be circulated by the Union League, to promote the election of Mr. Lincoln. Asked him this morning by what authority he gave me the invitation. He said as chairman of a committee of the League appointed for the purpose. He said that if I wrote it by the 7th of June it would be time enough. Told him I would do it, and I shall do it as well as I can, for I think the election of Mr. Lincoln essential to the cause of the country.

MAY 3, 1864 | I asked Dickinson Logan the other evening for an autograph to send to Mrs. James, as I know that he has many among the papers of the family connected with Revolutionary times & men,

Washington, Jefferson, Franklin, Jno. Dickinson, &c. He promised to give me one to be selected by his wife & this morning I received it: a letter from John Dickinson introducing General Ch. Lee to Richard Henry Lee, the grandfather [*actually, a cousin of Lee's grandfather*] of the Lee now in command of the Confederate Army in Virginia.[10]

MAY 10, 1864 | Read with much regret the account in the morning's paper of the death of James Wadsworth. He was a brigadier general in the Army of the Potomac, and was killed in the dreadful battle of Friday at the head of his men when leading them on to attack one of the strongest positions of the enemy. He had just given the order to charge & was riding in front, waving his hat, when a ball struck him in the forehead & he fell dead. His fall caused his men to waver & they were driven back, so that his body remained for a time in the hands of the enemy, but it was soon after recovered. As soon as the war broke out, Wadsworth joined the army and has remained in active service ever since. He was at the battle of Bull Run. Afterwards he was military governor of Washington, then on duty in the southwest. He was at the battle of Gettysburg, where he displayed his accustomed gallantry & was one of those who exhorted Meade to pursue & attack Lee on his retreat, which, it is now generally believed, would have caused the destruction of the rebel army. Wadsworth's talents, character, & early training were exactly suited to the life of a soldier, & for important & responsible position, tho not for the highest command. He had administrative & practical ability, a restless love of action & excitement, great personal courage, habits of physical exertion & endurance. He was bred to country pursuits & large farming in the West & was accustomed in early life to hunting excursions in the wilderness, where he often spent weeks in the forest, sleeping on the ground & depending on his rifle for food. He inherited a magnificent estate near Geneseo, his father having been one of the early settlers of western New York, & purchased immense tracts of land which rose in

---

10. This manuscript was offered at $2.50 in *A Priced Catalogue of Autographs . . . for Sale at the Grand Central Fair for the U.S. Sanitary Commission* (Philadelphia, 1864), 15.

value with the settlement of the country & became a noble fortune of many thousand acres. He could drive to Rochester, 30 miles, by making one turn thro cultivated farms on his own land when I was at Geneseo in 1837. James married Mary Wharton, the most beautiful woman of her day. I knew her & him & all his family intimately many years ago and was in the habit of seeing them constantly. I have been at Geneseo twice, once in 1837, during the old gentleman's life, and again in 1847, at James' house. All are now dead that I saw there (except Mrs. Wadsworth)—his father, his sister, his brother William & now himself.

MAY 17, 1864 | At home all day. Resumed writing the article on the currency, which I am anxious now to finish. It is too long. I have already written 87 pages. Condensation is a difficult part of writing. I like to have elbow room.

MAY 20, 1864 | Drove up to Wakefield at 3. Mrs. James there. Evidently an intelligent woman, far from handsome or young but of agreeable manners. Betty had a large quantity of old relics, autographs, books, letters, Continental money, &c, to show her & give her. They are family accumulations. She gave me a quantity of Continental money & two books that belonged to my grandfather Thomas Fisher. One of the books is a treatise on maritime law by Charles Malloy, printed in 1722, the other a French translation of Wm. Penn's *No Cross, No Crown*, 1746. Mrs. James thanked me for the autograph & for my verses. She says I will be in good company, as she has contributions from Longfellow, Whittier, Holmes, Bryant, Miss Howit, Kingsly, &c.

JUNE 1, 1864 | Grant advances towards Richmond & is successful in every encounter with [the] enemy. So also Sherman advances towards Atlanta and Genl. Johnston recedes before him. Grant's object seems to be to fight & defeat Lee outside of Richmond & thus prevent his entering the place, which is said to be strongly fortified, so that if Lee can get into it a long siege might be necessary. If Lee can be driven away, the town, I suppose, could be easily taken. Worked at the address all the morning with much satisfaction. Wrote to Severson.

Walked over to the post office with Sidney at 4½. The sun was very hot, the road dusty, & I came back tired and exhausted. I move with pain & am easily tired now. Dinner revived me.

JUNE 7, 1864 | The great fair for the Sanitary Commission opened today. It is held in Logan Square, which is covered in for the occasion, and no doubt will be very grand & successful. The convention of the Union party for the nomination of a candidate for the President meet today in Baltimore. That they will nominate Mr. Lincoln without serious opposition is considered certain, and that he will be elected by a large majority equally certain. He has gained the confidence of the country so entirely that he is the only one who can be nominated with any chance of success. His personal character has secured this result more than anything else. No one doubts his unselfish purity of motive & entire probity.

JUNE 11, 1864 | At three went to the fair. It is at Logan Square and is well worth seeing. The buildings are chiefly long & lofty galleries with Gothic roofs. These are very numerous. Two or three are large rotundas, the restaurant, the horticultural room, the smoking divan, &c., all are profusely decorated with flags & flowers & lined on each side with counters containing articles for sale & exhibition in infinite variety—dry goods, glass, china, hardware, books, engravings, army pictures, curiosities, relics, fancy work, &c., &c. I went to Mrs. James' apartment for "autographs, relics & curiosities." She showed me the "Poet's Album." It is a thick volume elegantly bound. I copied Emerson's contribution of 8 lines. Longfellow, Whittier, Holmes, Bryant, Lowell were among the writers. The book sold for $500. There were a good many autographs & other relics of Washington. The horticultural room was very splendid, but everything else was eclipsed far by the gallery of pictures, 500 feet long. The walls are covered with paintings large & small, none of them bad or mediocre, many admirable works of art, much the best I have ever seen. They were contributed from private collections in New York, Boston, & this city, & many more were offered than could be received. I have never been abroad & have therefore never seen anything approaching this collection before. I was greatly interested & delighted and shall go as often as I can to study it. I spent an hour merely in a cursory examination, walking once up one side & down the other, pausing before anything that especially attracted my attention, without a catalogue. Was particularly struck with a large picture, the size of life, of a group of deer in the mountains. It must, I think, be by [John] Landseer, or an excellent copy. It is full of truth & expression. The beautiful animals stand before you alive & breathing & gazing at you with their lustrous eyes, looking as if they would bound away at a motion of your hand. "The Heart of the Andes" was there, which I had seen before, & another by the same artist, Church,[11] a scene in the Rocky Mountains, very grand & also beautiful. There is a very touching picture of Lady Jane Grey[12] led to execution, another of a scene in the prison during the French Revolution when the officer is reading the names of those selected for immediate execution, another of a group of Christians before the gate of the Roman amphitheatre who are about to be thrust in to the wild beasts, another of the Derby day in England. These are all very large & there are many others as large. Then there are countless landscapes, faces, figures, groups, interiors, animals, &c., &c. I propose to examine them at leisure. The rooms were full, but not crowded unpleasantly, so vast is the space. The throng was well dressed & respectable in its appearance, good humored & polite. I saw but three persons that I knew. Upwards of $500,000 have been received already. These fairs & the Sanitary Commission are miracles of American spirit, energy, & beauty. Nothing like them has ever been seen in the world before. The Sanitary Commission have spent ten millions in relieving the sick & wounded soldiers, & millions are flowing into their treasury. All voluntary subscriptions, from all classes of the people, rich & poor. All the immense labor of superintending the arrangement of the innumerable

---

11. Frederick E. Church (1826-1900), an American artist who had visited Ecuador and Colombia in 1853 and 1857.

12. Lady Jane Grey (1537-54) was Queen of England for nine days in 1553 in an unsuccessful attempt to prevent Mary Tudor, a Catholic, from ascending to the throne. In 1554 she was beheaded for high treason.

things of this fair, of managing its myriad details & of selling the articles is performed by volunteers, ladies & gentlemen many of them, all of them highly respectable people. What prosperity, what wealth, what a fund of intelligence, public spirit, right feeling & good taste does it show. Got a lunch & came out by the Germantown steam car, at 6, Daniel meeting me at the station.

JUNE 16, 1864 | There is good news from Virginia. Grant has crossed the Chickahominy & the James River with his whole force without opposition, & is now in connection with Butler, south of Richmond. He has thus turned Lee's strong position. He has united his force to that of Butler. Hunter, Averell, &c., are north of Richmond.[13] They have destroyed many railroads on which Lee depended for supplies. All this is considered very favorable, but much is to be done before Richmond can be taken. Went to town at 12 to get some cabbage seed, &c., for Mount Harmon. Mr. Lincoln arrived today to visit the fair. Saw McMichael who said my address was now entirely satisfactory to him & he doubted not would be so to the committee, to whom he should at once submit it. The committee has 75 members. He asked me to join him & some members of the Union League who were to go at 3½ to pay their respects to Mr. Lincoln at the Continental Hotel. As I wished much to see him & might not again have an opportunity, determined to go. At the time appointed, I was at the Continental & went with McMichael & others to a room where Lincoln & his party were at table, having just finished dinner. [Charles] Gibbons on the part of the League invited the President, who rose to receive us, to visit the League House this evening. McMichael then presented me. Nothing was said beyond the ordinary salutations & shaking hands. I had all that I wanted, an opportunity to see & observe the man. Was much pleased by his countenance, voice & manner. He is tall, slender, not awkward & uncouth as has been represented, well dressed in black, self-possessed & easy, frank & cordial. The pictures of him do

---

13. Gen. David Hunter (1802–86) commanded the Union forces in the Shenandoah Valley. Gen. William W. Averell (1832–1900), an 1855 graduate of West Point, commanded the 2nd Cavalry Division.

great injustice to his face. His features are irregular & would be coarse but for their expression, which is genial, animated & kind. He looked somewhat pale & languid & there is a soft shade of melancholy in his smile & in his eyes. Altogether an honest, intelligent, amiable countenance, calculated to inspire respect, confidence & regard. His voice, too, is clear & manly. Am very glad I have seen him. His whole bearing & aspect confirm the opinion I had formed of him. Mrs. Lincoln I did not admire. She is stout, by no means handsome, her face has a sharp look & she is far from thorobred in her appearance. There were several other gentlemen & ladies in the party, whose looks I did not particularly notice. In a few moments, Mr. Lincoln went in to another room to receive the City Councils. We followed. The room was crowded. The mayor made a very happy & well-turned speech, to which Mr. L. made a short & fitting reply. Some of the members of Council were very coarse, vulgar-looking men. At 4, the President started for the fair in a handsome barouche & 4 grey horses, well turned out, furnished by [Samuel R.] Phillips, the saddler & harness maker, who has got a large fortune by government contracts to supply accoutrements for the cavalry. From a window, I saw Mr. Lincoln enter the carriage. The crowd around was immense, the shouting vociferous.

JUNE 28, 1864 | Mrs. Logan looks badly & suffers much from asthma. She is going to Bordentown tomorrow, where she will remain a week & then go to Richfield, a place 30 miles beyond Sharon, for the summer. It is decided that I go to Sharon.[14] Everyone thinks I ought to go as the bathing & drinking the water may probably benefit the gout. It is a hateful exile from all my best enjoyments, but I think I ought to go. I shall go alone, as to take Bet & Sidney would involve much trouble & expense & we would leave this place in the hands of servants, none of them of a very trustworthy kind. . . . It is hard to leave home for three weeks, to miss three weeks of happiness.

14. Fisher went to Richfield instead, since he could not get the accommodations he wanted at Sharon.

JUNE 30, 1864 | Met Geo. Smith on the road. He was just from town. He said there was news that Chase had resigned & Governor Tod[15] of Ohio appointed in his place. This event I should think would have a very injurious effect on financial affairs at this time. The country had much confidence in Chase. Tod I knew some years ago. He was an acquaintance of Henry's & I met him often at Brookwood, a rather coarse & uneducated man of business, clever, intelligent & of practical, administrative ability, tho hardly, I should judge, fit for such a place as Secretary of the Treasury at such a moment as this.

JULY 1, 1864 | The news of Mr. Chase's resignation in the paper this morning. The community were taken by surprise. The cause is said to be that Mr. Lincoln refused to appoint someone selected by Chase for an office in New York. This I fancy was rather the occasion than the cause. When Chase permitted his name, some months ago, to be used as a candidate for the presidency, he placed himself in a false, because unfriendly, position towards Mr. Lincoln. He could not be at once a rival & a subordinate or even co-laborer. The failure of the attempt & Lincoln's signal success were not calculated to soften Chase's temper, which is said to be arrogant and dictatorial. . . . Mr. Tod refused the appointment. It was a mistake in Lincoln to offer it to him. Went to town. Saw McMichael. News came that Mr. Fessenden of Maine had been appointed & immediately & unanimously confirmed by the Senate.[16] He is chairman of the Finance Committee of the Senate. McMichael says he is better fitted for the place than Chase. His appointment gives general satisfaction.

JULY 2, 1864 | Went to town. Attended to some business. Hollis has employed Mr. Geo. Biddle as counsel for the estate instead of Gerhard.[17] A good selection. Got the July number of the *North American*

---

15. David Tod (1805-68), a War Democrat, was governor of Ohio from 1862 to 1864.

16. William Pitt Fessenden (1806-69), a Whig and later Republican, was a U.S. congressman from Maine in the 1840s and U.S. senator from 1854 to 1869, with a brief interval in 1864 and 1865 when he resigned to serve as secretary of the treasury.

17. Benjamin Gerhard had died in June 1864.

Review. My article is the 7th & is entitled "A National Currency." Read it coming out in the car. It occupies 41 pages. Did not notice the repetitions which struck me when I last read it in MS. I think Mr. Norton has omitted some parts & thus improved it.

JULY 4, 1864 | It is the great anniversary of the birth of democracy in the western world, & is very appropriately celebrated by license & brute noise—guns, pistols, crackers, & squibs thro the day, fireworks, drunkenness & brawls at night. As a general rule, 30 or 40 houses are set on fire in town every 4th of July, and the constant noise of crackers, etc., is enough to drive a nervous person frantic. Out here, we hear something of the uproar & thro the day the reports of guns were heard all around us. It was very bearable, however, compared with our experiences in town, which I remember with horror.

Sidney had been invited to spend the day at Brookwood & Bet took him up there at 10 o'clock. At 6 in the evening she & I drove up for him. Found him on the lawn with Geo. Smith's children, Charley & Sally, & with Jim & Jane Hewson & Ellen, playing croquet, in which he joined with great eagerness & activity. He is always glad to be at Brookwood & with his cousins there, & they seem glad to have him. They ought to be, as he is the only cousin they have, & he is a lively, bright boy, evidently fond of their society. He has the air of being perfectly at home & at ease among them. It is a great pleasure to me to see them together & to think that he may find friends & companions in them thro life, as he has no brother or sister. What I can do to promote their intimacy I shall. They are all of *my* family likely to influence him hereafter & as he is all they have outside their own circle, it seems to be very natural that they should make much of him. How it will be there is no telling, so much depends on individual character & circumstances. Sidney on his mother's side has many cousins, very nice & promising, some of them. After tea, Geo. Smith came and we had a display of fireworks, and from the piazza we could see the rockets rising in the distance in quick succession. Mrs. Atherton was well & in good spirits, Liedy gracious, little Maud animated & sparkling, the boys boisterous & merry, & I sat among them thinking of those who were gone.

JULY 6, 1864 | The capture of the *Alabama* by the *Kearsarge* produced a sensation in England as the former was in reality an English-built vessel, & manned by Englishmen chiefly under the shameful system of technical neutrality but real sympathy with the rebels & aid to their cause pursued, since the war began, by the British government, and for which a day of reckoning will come ere long. The combat was a very brilliant one, lasted an hour, the vessels were never nearer to each other than a quarter of a mile, our ship lost no men & had only 2 or 3 wounded, the *Alabama* had many killed, & when she sunk, a number of her crew & the captain, Semmes,[18] were in the water. The English yacht, the *Deerhound*, was near at hand, watching the fight, & at the request of Captain [John A.] Winslow of the *Kearsarge* assisted his boats in rescuing the men of the *Alabama* from drowning. The *Deerhound* did this with cordial good will &, among others, picked up Semmes &, instead of delivering them to Winslow as lawful prisoners, took them to England, where Semmes was received with demonstrations of respect. Such is the story and if true presents a case for the notice of our government. Should our civil war terminate successfully, a war with England is very likely to grow out of the ill-feeling caused by her course towards us during the present trouble.

JULY 13, 1864 | Mr. J. R. Ingersoll & Miss Wilcocks here for a few minutes in the afternoon. The latter brought to Bet a diary kept by her mother, Mrs. Sam. Wilcocks, before her marriage. She was a Miss Manigault, a So. Carolina family. Mr. Wilcocks was Bet's uncle. Read some of the diary. It gives an agreeable picture of society in Phila: of that day & a pleasant impression of the writer.[19]

18. Capt. Raphael Semmes (1809-77), a native of Maryland, settled in Mobile, Alabama, after the Mexican War. In 1861 he was made a commander in the Confederate Navy, and he had an important commerce raiding career during the war. This conflict took place on June 19, 1864, off Cherbourg, France.

19. The diary of Harriet Manigault from 1813 until her marriage in 1816 to Samuel Wilcocks was presented to the Historical Society of Pennsylvania by Anna W. Ingersoll in 1960.

JULY 16, 1864 | Got a letter from Severson with the unpleasant intelligence that the house at Mount Harmon was burnt down on Wednesday. The men were all in the harvest field, a mile off, so that nothing could be done to save it. They got out some of the furniture. The fire originated, Severson thinks, in a loft over the kitchen where the Negro hands sleep, from their carelessness. He begs me to come down at once. I shall go this afternoon to Middletown, sleep there & drive to the farm tomorrow morning. The house is insured for $3,000, but it would cost $10,000 to build one like it. It was a very comfortable brick house, 50 feet by 33, with a wing containing two good rooms, well finished, with high ceilings, four rooms & a hall on each floor. The disaster has occurred in the midst of our busiest season, when peaches are to pick, truck to get to market, wheat to thresh, &c., so that there will doubtless be a heavy loss independent of the loss of the house. Where the hands are to be put I cannot tell. So ends my pleasure of Mount Harmon, for I cannot afford to build another house as good, or one that will give me the accommodation it afforded. So ends, too, I fear, my hope of making a good profit from the farm this year. The drought has destroyed a large portion of my crops, prices are falling, and now the question is, can the crops the drought may leave be gathered? Certainly not without much additional expense. I am likely to have trouble enough on my hands just now, but feel strong enough to work thro or at least try my best. Independent of the cost, it is painful to lose the old house where my grandfather lived, & which is associated with so much of my past life.

JULY 18, 1864 | On Saturday afternoon left town in $4^{1}/_{2}$ train. Got to Middletown at $6^{1}/_{2}$. Went to Lippincott's tavern, a large, convenient brick building erected last year near the railroad station. It is very clean & comfortable & well kept. Got a good room & supper. In the evening happened to meet Major Jones, as he is called, an eccentric, well-known old man, a farmer once, but now living in the village, & told him that my house had been burned & that I was going down to make arrangements to rebuild it & provide accommodations meanwhile for the hands. He entered into the subject at once & offered to introduce me to an excellent carpenter, David Maxwell, who lived in the town & had built some of the best houses in the neighborhood. He built Mr. Ward's house some years ago and I heard him highly spoken of at the time. We went to see him & he offered to drive me down to the farm the next day & give me his advice.

On Sunday morning we started in a comfortable covered wagon & good horse & got to the farm about 10 o'clock, weather still dry, bright sun & cool air, the country all the way showing the effects of the long drought. As we drove up the avenue, we saw on the lane lawn under the trees two large tents made of carpets thrown over a frame of boards. There Severson & his family had lived since the fire. Various articles of furniture were strewn about & nearby were the blackened walls of the house with the ground around it covered with ashes and cinders. Severson & Eli received us. The former looked worn & nervous. He ran a mile from the harvest field when he heard the fire & then worked with others to save his & my furniture, which in such weather, with all the attendant excitement & subsequent discomfort, was a severe effort for a man in delicate health. He says all the men behaved admirably. He had fitted up the old quarter, used by me as a carpenter shop, in my grandfather's time as a servant's house, whence its name, by putting down a floor etc as a place for himself & his family to live in. It is tolerably comfortable, at any rate is shelter. He had built a hut, big enough for a cooking stove and a bed for the cook, which serves as a kitchen. The hands are placed about in various out buildings, stables, barn & the three cottages. At this season laboring men can sleep anywhere. All the arrangements seemed well made & Severson said the work of the farm could go on without interruption.

All this examined, discussed with Maxwell the plan for rebuilding. The walls are all standing, inside & outside, & can be used again, which will save much expense and also make it necessary to put up another house of the same size & much the same plan. The only alterations I propose are to make the wing two stories high, instead of one as before, and to divide the lower story into a large kitchen with an entry containing a good pantry & a staircase, instead of two rooms as before. I thus get two good bedrooms above & two large closets, one above & one below, all great conveniences at small additional expense. The cost of the whole will be, Maxwell said, at a rough estimate,

$6,000. The building was insured for $3,000, so that my loss will be $3,000, and for this I get a new & better house than the old.

JULY 22, 1864 | Read Riethmuller[20] in the morning. Was delighted with his portrait of Jefferson, whom I always detested. He was a man of practical talents but without the slightest claim to genius or those qualities of mind which enable one to perceive general truth or spiritual things at all. He was a materialist and an infidel. Neither could he perceive moral truth or beauty. He was devoid of moral sensibility and honor, thoroughly selfish & capable of any meanness or perfidy to gain his ends. He was imbued with the principles of the French Revolution, approved of its horrors & excesses, was a Jacobin in his opinions, & the enemy of order, law & just authority. Yet this man became the leader of the Democratic Party in this country, was indeed its founder, and, backed by the mob, proved too strong for Washington & Hamilton, & impressed his influence so deeply on the country that it remains to the present day. He is still worshipped by all true Democrats, who in their hearts prefer him to Washington, whilst the fine character & high intellect of Hamilton, who was emphatically the organizing mind of the Revolution, and who, more than any other, framed the Constitution, is known only to the cultivated few.

JULY 26, 1864 | Maxwell, my carpenter from Middletown, came about 11 o'clock this morning with a plan for the new house & estimates. It will cost much more than he supposed at first—$10,500. The price of everything, he said, labor & materials, is now three times or twice as high as before the war. Was much disappointed.

JULY 27, 1864 | Called to see the mayor, Mr. Henry, about a matter which has caused me much annoyance & to which I called his attention some weeks ago. On our lane & opposite to this place are a number of small houses. Some of them are decent dwellings and occupied by respectable working people. One, however, a miserable hovel, is

---

20. Christopher James Riethmuller, *The Life and Times of Alexander Hamilton* (London, 1864).

inhabited by a person named Strouss, a wretch who has been in prison, who was driven out of Nicetown Lane as a nuisance and who has two or three girls in his house who are prostitutes. The place has for some time been the resort of convalescent soldiers from the neighboring hospital at Stenton. These soldiers & other rowdies, probably not soldiers but wearing a uniform, have been for months the pest of the neighborhood. I hear from several that they rob gardens & poultry houses in all directions, they have attacked & beaten unoffending men on the roads, & some days ago a squad of them broke into Cowperthwaite's house, hard by on this lane, & robbed it in broad day.

JULY 29, 1864 | Daniel told me that last night the police came with a wagon to Strouss' house on the lane & took away him & his family & inmates. A good riddance & prompt work on the part of the mayor.

JULY 31, 1864 | Dined at 3 in order to drive up to Alverthorpe. Started at 4½. Saw Fisher & his wife, Helen & the two boys, who are at home for the holidays. Spent a pleasant evening, not much being said about the war. Fisher declared that Grant & Sherman were both now virtually defeated. Miss Wilcocks got a wrong story about Oliver Middleton's being in Fort Delaware. He was killed in battle last May. He was the only son of Mrs. Fisher's brother Oliver. Fisher said that Harry Middleton is totally ruined. Fisher, as I came away, gave me a pamphlet he has just written, entitled *The Cruelties of War*. It is intended for limited private circulation only. He was not so excited as he used to be on the subject.

AUGUST 1, 1864 | The news is that a party of rebels entered Pennsylvania & on Saturday *burned* Chambersburg, a large & flourishing town. They demanded 100,000 in gold or $500,000 in greenbacks & the demand not being immediately complied with set fire to the place, without giving the people time to carry anything away. The barbarous act shows what a bitter spirit is animating the contest as it is prolonged.

1864

In the morning read Fisher's pamphlet under the tree, where there was a slight breeze to temper the heat. As a mere literary performance it is creditable, as the style is good and he shows scholarship & intelligence. As an argument, it is utterly weak & senseless. It is written with passionate advocacy of the South and is intemperate, one-sided, unfair and abusive of the northern people, army, government & cause. He shows himself wholly unable to appreciate the motives, principles or necessities involved in the war. It is too hot to discuss the opinions he sets forth & not worth while. I regret very much he has written the pamphlet. It is calculated to injure him in the judgment of all rational men & it is so very offensive in its language & spirit that it may get him into personal difficulty. . . . This is the most disagreeable season of the year—the period of flies, mosquitoes, bats, heat, dust, drought & harvest. I prefer greatly the cold & snow of winter.

Wrote this afternoon to Maxwell, the carpenter, informing him that . . . I had directed Severson to speak to some one else. The loss of my old house cuts me off from a very pleasant portion of my past life.

AUGUST 9, 1864 | The carpenter came. We discussed his plan; he agreed to several modifications & finally we signed a contract by which he is to rebuild the main building, finish a part of the cellar as a basement kitchen, and build a shed room on the east side of the house under which the doors from basement, kitchen, & dining room are to open, & which is large enough for a wash house, 8 by 15, for $4,500. Paid him $1,000 on account. . . . The carpenter's name is Andrew T. Brown. He lives at Fredericktown on the Sassafras. . . .

AUGUST 11, 1864 | Farragut has taken one of the principal forts in Mobile Bay & another was blown up by the enemy.[21] General Averell's victory is confirmed.[22] Sheridan has been placed in command of the

21. David G. Farragut (1801-70) entered the U.S. Navy at the age of nine and saw action in both the War of 1812 and the Mexican War. During the Civil War he took New Orleans (1862) and Mobile Bay (1864).

22. In an action at Moorefield, Va., Gen. Averell was reported to have taken five hundred prisoners.

country on the Potomac & the Susquehanna, so I suppose we shall have no more raids.[23] The true way to protect Pennsylvania & Maryland is to defend the Potomac.

AUGUST 13, 1864 | Paid Sherman in full for printing *The Trial of the Constitution*. The work has cost me so far about $350 more than I have received. My literary efforts have certainly been far from successful financially. There are about 450 copies on hand. If they sell, which is very doubtful, they will bring me out square.

SEPTEMBER 30, 1864 | I left home on Wednesday, August 17, at 10½ o'clock, & drove to the Kensington depot to take the 11¼ train for N. York, feeling very gloomy at the thought that four weeks must elapse before I should see Forest Hill[24] & Bet & Sidney again. The weather was oppressively hot. In the car were a number of dirty, miserable-looking invalid soldiers and several rowdies with faces like bulldogs, who were very near getting up a fight. Some of the party pulled off their coats & some their boots. The car, however, was not crowded, we got to New York in good time, 4 hours, &, but for the heat, the journey would have been comfortable enough. I transferred myself & luggage to the steamer *St. John*, the night boat to Albany, a really splendid vessel of immense size & furnished with lavish cost. Could not get a stateroom, but took a berth to myself, a little room, smaller than a stateroom. Arrived in Albany the next morning at 5 o'clock after an uncomfortable night. Went to the Delavan Hotel, a fine house, much enlarged & improved since I saw it last. Got a bath & a capital breakfast, everything in the establishment elegant & comfortable, quite equal in style to any hotel in Philadelphia. Started in the car at 7½ and, after a pleasant run thro the smiling valley of the Mohawk, got to Herkimer about 11. The weather was cool, there was

---

23. Philip H. Sheridan (1831–88), an 1853 graduate of the U.S. Military Academy, rose to the rank of major general during the war and received lasting fame for his burning of Virginia's Shenandoah Valley in 1864.

24. Forest Hill, previously the summer home of Charles Jared Ingersoll and now the residence of the diarist, was on Rising Sun Lane near the intersection of Germantown Avenue and Old York Road. The house was still standing in the 1890s.

no dust, the scenery wild & picturesque, & the railroad & car excellent. The country had a thriving appearance, good farmhouses, neat & pretty villages every 6 or 8 miles, trains crowded, all things indicating prosperity & progress, and yet we are in the midst of an immense civil war. From Herkimer stages run to Richfield, 14 miles, old-fashioned four-horse coaches on C springs. As they were crowded, I proposed to a gentlemanlike-looking young man to join me in taking a private carriage, &, he assenting, we drove very comfortably to the Springs over a succession of steep hills, each commanding a fine view of rich valleys & wooded slopes. Arrived at Richfield, & went to the Spring House, where I expected to find Dickinson Logan, to whom I had written to secure me a room. Was informed that he had gone to Sharon before my letter reached him & that the house was full. Was recommended to a boardinghouse opposite, kept by Mr. M. K. Hosford. Went there & got a good room downstairs. It is a small house, clean & well kept, & Hosford proved very attentive & obliging. My room had a good bed, bureau, rocking chair, &c. Was soon established & the next day Hosford offered me an adjoining vacant room as a sitting room, which proved a great luxury as there I could read & write & smoke & be alone when I pleased. Felt pretty forlorn the first day, being wholly among strangers. Mrs. Leonard was at the Spring House. I did not know her, but I knew her husband slightly, & her daughter was a friend of Liedy's. In the evening called to see her. She was very gracious & is a pleasing woman. She has suffered greatly from rheumatism & been much benefitted by the waters. The next morning I saw on the piazza of the American Hotel Mr. John Hodge of Philadelphia. He is an intimate of Mr. J. R. Ingersoll, & I knew him slightly & knew also his brother, Mr. Wm. Hodge of Washington, whom I often used to meet at Henry's. He greeted me with great kindness. I saw him afterwards every day till he went & liked him much, a worthy, amiable, intelligent old gentleman of 80 years, full of reminiscences of old times, & the old people I used to know when I was young. He introduced me to several N. York gentlemen, Howland, Bruen & Mr. Jacob LeRoy, the latter a very respectable person, once an intimate of Geo. Smith's father. I soon made as many acquaintances as I wished. There were some pleasant people at Hosford's with whom I got to be on very friendly terms, Mr. & Mrs. Goodyear & two daughters from New Haven, Mr. & Mrs. Gautier, Dr. & Mrs. Parisim of New York, Mr. P. a cousin of Mrs. Warren, the mother of Mrs. Edw. Ingersoll. Mr. Goodyear is the brother of the person who discovered the process of vulcanizing India rubber which has proved so extensively useful in its various application to the arts.[25] His family seem to have a genius for invention. His father introduced, many years ago, a patent pitchfork, which soon became the only pitchfork employed. He lately brought out the metallic tips for boys' shoes, from which he is reaping now very large profits & he has just invented an India rubber stopper for bottles, which promises to supersede cork for certain purposes & from which he expects great results. . . .

In a day or two, the attractions of Richfield produced their effect, more especially after I began to get letters from Bet, and my homesickness disappeared.[26] The beauty of the country, the delightful temperature, the comfortable living, the pleasant society, which was pleasant tho by no means of the highest order, made my visit agreeable, more especially as I got a letter every day from home & heard nothing but good news. I soon fell into an easy routine & the days passed rapidly. Breakfast at 8 to 9, the newspaper & pipe as at home, a walk, bathing at 11, talk on the piazza at one of the hotels or a walk, dinner at 1½, at 3 a letter from Bet & writing one to her, reading in my little sitting room, an evening walk, tea at 7, then conversation & the newspapers which came from N. York at 8. I read Hawthorne's *Our Old Home*, and *Leisure Hours in Town*, by the Country Parson, whilst I was there. Both pleasant books.

Richfield is a neat, pretty Yankee village. Like all Yankee villages, it looks new, thriving, prosperous & comfortable & has no traces of poverty in the aspect of any of its houses or people. Many new houses are building, all look so fresh that they seem just finished. Each dwelling stands some 20 to 30 feet back from the street or road, isolated in

---

25. The Goodyear whom Fisher met was evidently Charles Goodyear (1833-96), president of the American Shoetip Company, and a son, not the brother, of Charles Goodyear (1800-60), the founder of the rubber industry in the United States.

26. Eleven of his wife's letters during this period are in the Fisher Collection at the Historical Society. She called him George, whereas his brother had called him Sid.

a little lot, enclosed by a picket fence & adorned with trees & shrubbery. The street is wide, with sidewalks of stone or plank, shaded by rows of sugar maples. The town lies among hills, which almost encircle it. The ground is undulating. The hills are richly wooded & the rolling land covered with grass, as dairy farming prevails exclusively throughout this region, except that a few acres are devoted to growing hops. The scenery is very beautiful. Every few miles there is a lake or lakelet, so that the charm of water is added to the woods & green slopes. Schuyler's Lake is a mile and 1/2 from the village & is 5 miles long by one road surrounded by lofty hills. Otsego Lake & Cooperstown are 15 miles off. I went there with Mr. and Mrs. Gautier & was much delighted with its beauty & with the scenery along the road. Cooperstown is a flourishing village situated at the head of the lake, which is nine miles long & one or two wide, with irregular shore outline, & lies among mountains. We went to see the site of Cooper's house which was burnt some years ago. It was in a lot of about three acres with a front on the village street. The lot has some good trees on it & is overgrown with bushes & weeds. It does not now belong to his family. In a pretty cemetery about a mile from the town, the people of the place have erected to his memory a marble monument, 30 feet high, with a statue of Leatherstocking on the top. His remains are in the churchyard. We dined at Tunnicliff's, a tavern on the shore of the lake, celebrated for its fish dinners, & found it worthy its reputation.

I bathed every day except Sunday, and the day I went to Cooperstown. I also drank 4 or 5 tumblers of the water daily. It smells & tastes very strongly of sulphur & is a nauseous dose, tho cool & clear & becomes less disagreeable after a time. My general health was excellent all the time & the gout better after the first week, tho I had pain every day. I was told by everyone that I would feel the effects of the water after I got home. I took 20 baths. I left Richfield on Monday 12th at 1½ o'clock in the afternoon in the stage for Herkimer, thence by the railroad to Albany, & there went on board the *Hendrick Hudson* steamer at 7½ for N. York. I had telegraphed for a stateroom. The boat was excessively crowded & as the tide was low did not start till 12 o'clock, so that we did not get to N. York till 12 the next day. I went on deck just as we entered the Highlands and enjoyed the noble scenery of the river thence to the city. Countless country houses cover the right bank all the way down. They are in every variety of style, some costly & grand, all comfortable & well kept. They are the summer abodes of the rich men of N. York &, therefore, many of them, of very vulgar & common people & their beauty & expense imply neither taste nor cultivation on the part of their owners. Upstart wealth, often enormous wealth, is the characteristic of N. York. An intelligent Scotch gentleman on board, who lives on the river, pointed out to me some of the finest places. One was owned by a man who had made his fortune in the ribbon trade, another, a grey castle with turrets, surrounded by fine trees, by a vendor of pills. Edwin Forrest, the actor, built one imitation of a feudal castle, & Bennett, the editor of the *N. York Herald*, erected a splendid house, the dome of which is just visible above a surrounding wood, & his yacht lies in the stream near the shore. Further up the river, however, the estates are larger & the society better. Some of the old families yet retain their land, & the newcomers are people of education & refinement.

Since my return the weather has been delightful until the last two or three days, when it has rained or been raw & cold. I have resumed ordinary habits. Bet & I have paid visits to friends & neighbors, Wakefield, Brookwood, Champlost,[27] Mr. J. R. Ingersoll, the Blights, Mr. Leonard, & Mr. Jno. Williams, the two last we have never visited before. Severson has been up. My hopes of having a good income & of getting out of my money difficulties this year have been sadly disappointed because of the drought and the very low price of peaches & the fly in the wheat. These have caused a loss of at least $6000, to which must be added the loss by the burning of the house. As a consequence, so far from being able to pay all my debts I shall owe more at the end of the year than at the beginning. This is a great disappointment, but I must bear it & try to do better hereafter. It is somewhat compensated by the prospect of considerably increased income. Bet's

---

27. Champlost, built by the Fox family about 1770, was located diagonally across Green Lane from Brookwood and was near Fern Rock Station. It was torn down in 1901 or 1902.

will be a good deal larger & I shall have 70 acres in peaches next year. We are not likely always to have such a drought, as that of this year was the worst I have ever known, except that of 1838, nor always fly in the wheat, nor every year a house burnt with insufficient insurance.

Soon after my return I had a conversation with Mr. S. A. Mercer, pres. of the Farmers & Mechanics Bank, who told me that there was an effort making by himself and others to induce the state banks to become national banks under the Act of Congress, & thru issue of a national currency. He was pleased to say that he thought my article on that subject in the July number of the *N. Am. Review* was calculated to promote the success of this movement & that he & some other gentlemen proposed to reprint it. I was, of course, gratified by the compliment. In subsequent interviews with him & Lippincott, it was arranged that the latter would publish the article, not in pamphlet but book form, and offer it for sale to help defray the cost of publication. He will print 500 copies, of which about 200 will be distributed gratuitously. I wrote to Mr. Norton, requesting him to ask the consent of Crosley & Nicholls (now Crosley & Airesworth), the publishers of the *Review*, which was promptly given, & I suppose the book will be out in a week or two.

Mr. McMichael, a few days after I came back, submitted to the committee of the Union League the address I wrote for them last May in favor of the re-election of Mr. Lincoln. It was approved. A few alterations were suggested & made by McMichael, which are of no importance.

OCTOBER 3, 1864 | Got from Is. S. Loyd $1000, the principal of my mortgage on the Florence. It was the last item of property that I owned besides Mount Harmon & the stock there, and it must go to pay debts. Regret is useless, however, or I could say much on this topic. Twenty-five years ago I was worth *at least* twenty thousand dollars independent of the farm—now I am worth only the farm. Much of this sum, it must be said, went to improve the farm, which I suppose may now be considered worth $40,000. So that I am about as rich as I was at first. With prudence & economy, however, I might have kept the $20,000 & the farm. Well, I have lived comfortably &

agreeably all this time & the money has not been spent for nothing. I have had a good deal for it.

OCTOBER 11, 1864 | Some days ago, young John Meigs, a son of Montgomery Meigs, a very brave & intelligent officer who had served with distinction from the beginning of the war, was killed by guerillas in [the Shenandoah] valley.[28] He was of Sheridan's army. As a punishment for this deed, Sheridan burned all the houses within a circuit of 5 miles from the spot where it was committed. Retribution is fast overtaking the southern people for their atrocities, but how much of it falls on the innocent, on women & children! How many families, educated in comfort & refinement, have been made homeless & destitute. The only consolation for the thought of all this misery is that the war cannot last much longer.

Went to town. Found a proof of the article on the currency at the office & corrected it. It is the last. Found also 25 copies of my address for the Union League. It is very neatly printed & in a pamphlet of about 30 pages. Went to the Penna. Life Ins. Co. to borrow money. Saw Mr. Hutchinson.[29] He told me that money was very tight, that they had applications for more than they could lend at 1 pr. ct. per month & that it was impossible to let me have it. This was a great disappointment as I had counted on him. Went to the Bories.[30] They said it was out of the line of their business to lend money without collateral security or a responsible endorser, but they would like to oblige me & would give me an answer tomorrow. This would not do for me, as the money must be paid tomorrow without fail. I was greatly perplexed & alarmed, for not to pay it would involve very

---

28. John Rodgers Meigs (1841-64), son of Union Quartermaster General Montgomery C. Meigs, graduated from West Point in 1863. Twice cited for gallantry and meritorious services, and brevetted major, he was killed on October 3, 1864, near Harrisonburg, Va. His grave marker, which is in the shadow of his father's grave at Arlington National Cemetery, portrays him in bronze, dead on the battlefield.

29. I. Pemberton Hutchinson was a director of the Pennsylvania Company for Insurances on Lives and Granting Annuities, 304 Walnut Street.

30. Charles L. and Henry P. Borie, bill brokers, 3 Merchants Exchange.

serious consequences. I went to consult Ch. Muirheid.[31] He could not help me. I happened to think of Mr. [John G.] Fell, whom I had met that morning in the street. I know him very well & he was a friend of Henry's. He has recently made an enormous fortune, 12 millions it is said, and is receiving now $3,000 per day from his coal investments. Muirheid said at once that he was sure Fell would gladly lend me the money. I went to him, explained the case, & he promised to let me have it tomorrow. It was a great relief.

OCTOBER 14, 1864 | My gout is much better. I think my trip to Richfield did me good.

OCTOBER 17, 1864 | Some weeks ago Mr. Hollis mentioned to me that a question arose as to the construction of that clause of Henry's will which provides for releasing my debt to his estate. That debt is on his books and must therefore come before the auditor. The will provides that the executors shall cancel & release the debt charged on his books to me. The will is dated May 12th, 1858. The question is, does it release money lent subsequent to that date? If it does not, I owe the estate over $4000. There can be no doubt of his intention to release it, for he expressed that intention to me and also to Hollis shortly before his death. Hollis has taken the opinion of Mr. G. W. Biddle, who is counsel to the estate. He has decided that the clause in the will refers only to money due at its date, & that his declaration to Hollis afterwards does not amount to a re-publication, because it can be proved by one witness only—Hollis. Such is no doubt the law. Hollis handed me the opinion this morning. I would be most glad to pay this money and the whole debt, if I was able. But I am not able. . . .[32] Got at the Farmers & Mechanics Bank a copy of my article on the currency, published today. It makes a neat little pamphlet of 83 pages.[33]

31. Charles H. Muirheid, conveyancer, 203 S. Sixth Street.
32. The debt was afterward, January 10, 1865, released by P. C. Hollis and H. P. Muirheid, executors.
33. Sidney George Fisher, *A National Currency* (Philadelphia, 1864).

OCTOBER 25, 1864 | On Friday I paid a visit to Hetty Wistar & she gave me photograph copies of pictures of my great uncle Miers Fisher & his wife. He was called the Quaker lawyer & was eminent in his profession & is said to have been an accomplished man, intimate with Franklin & other celebrities of the day. He & his two brothers, Saml. R. and my grandfather Thomas Fisher, were men of high respectability in their day, of good estate & much esteemed for their virtues. They belonged to the old Quaker aristocracy of Philadelphia and lived with comfort & sober elegance, kept their carriage & country houses. Ury, a place near Frankford, belonging to Miers, The Cliffs on the Schuylkill to Samuel, and Wakefield to my grandfather, who built the house there. The land he got with his wife, Sarah Logan. He was called the Quaker Gentleman because of the neatness of his dress, the elegance & courtesy of his manners, & his handsome establishment, which must have been luxurious for those days, judging by the plate & furniture he left & by what I have heard from those who knew him. He drove fine horses & two menservants always waited at dinner. The descendants of Thomas & Samuel hold their own in social position, but those of Miers have not been so fortunate, tho recently one of his grandsons has made a large fortune in California, is said to be a worthy man and is likely to buy Ury & live there.

OCTOBER 26, 1864 | The election of Lincoln will be a great blow to the rebels. They count largely on the success of McClellan & are virtually in league with his party. Should he be elected, they would expect peace on their own terms, and they declare that nothing short of separation would satisfy them. They are mistaken, however, in this as they have been in all other calculations. The great majority of the northern people of both parties are determined to restore the Union, the larger portion of the Democrats believing that it can be restored & the war stopped by making concessions to the southern people, by universal amnesty & by maintaining slavery or rather by refusing to destroy it. All that the leaders of that party care for is power, and, when they got it, they would be forced to continue the war should the South refuse still to return to the Union. But the success of the Democrats would be a great gain to the South. Some efforts for peace would be made, our troops would be discouraged, the rebel hopes revived, perhaps there would be an armistice which would give them time to recover strength & invite European intervention in their favor, if they still determined on independence and if, hopeless of success, they agreed upon reconstruction, they could have it almost on their own terms, slavery & the right of secession included. It is impossible to say what disaster the success of McClellan would bring. What would the army say, which is almost unanimous against him & for the war, at degrading terms of peace now that victory is assured and almost within their grasp? And would the northern people consent that the immense sacrifices of the war should be made in vain? Two things are necessary for a permanent & satisfactory peace—the utter destruction of the military power of the rebels & the actual emancipation of all the slaves.

OCTOBER 28, 1864 | Got a very kind letter from Joshua Fisher. His state of mind, or rather of feeling, about the war is morbid & deplorable. I sent him some time ago my Union League address, without mentioning that I wrote it. In his letter he says: "I think the writer as much deluded as Titania and with an object much less worthy admiration."

NOVEMBER 8, 1864 | Went over to the Rising Sun at 1 o'clock to vote. There was no crowd. A few drunken men were shouting for McClellan. This is the important day which is to decide the fate of the country, or rather to register a foregone conclusion, for there is no doubt that Lincoln will be elected, probably by large majorities.

NOVEMBER 9, 1864 | Lincoln is elected by a large majority. All the New England states & the great West went for him. So also Penna: & Maryland. N. York is doubtful, being claimed by both parties. The majority in the city of N. York was 36,000 for McClellan, but it is hoped that this will be overcome by the country vote. The Democrats got N. Jersey & Delaware. Went to town. Attended to some business. Called to see Clark Hare to ask him to dine here some day this week. Told him that now that Lincoln was elected I should feel at liberty to criticize his measures & oppose such as I did not approve. That, before the election, the important matter was to get the Union party in power, or rather to keep them in. But that power is always abused by a party & the danger now was from excessive & extreme ideas & measures. That I feared the fanaticism of the abolitionists, advocates of Negro equality, Negro suffrage, etc. I said that I thought that he & other influential men in the Union League, which is now very powerful, might do much in guiding public opinion toward moderate counsels. He agreed entirely with my views and thought that the extreme abolition element of the party likely to do great mischief, that the closeness of the election in the Middle States proved the necessity for caution & moderation on the ground of policy alone, but that he was afraid the tendency of the League was very strongly in favor of the most radical doctrines. I was surprised to hear this and it confirmed my judgment not to join it, as I was asked to do when it was established.

NOVEMBER 21, 1864 | Sherman has been heard from. He is marching in two divisions on Macon & Augusta, having, it is said, *burnt* Atlanta. The belief is that he is going to Charleston or Savannah and his progress thro S. Carolina & Georgetown will no doubt be marked by desolation. Our invasion of the South is almost as terrible as Cromwell's invasion of Ireland. The only thing we can say is that the southern people have brought it on themselves. They had not the excuse for rebellion that the Irish had, for a more wicked & unprovoked attempt to destroy a great nation never was made.

NOVEMBER 22, 1864 | Suffered very much all day from rheumatism. I fear the influence of Richfield is wearing out.

NOVEMBER 28, 1864 | Gout worse. I can, however, walk about, but am never free from pain. It is most severe at night & when I wake in the morning. It is difficult to get out of bed & to dress. The pain is chiefly in my shoulders, back, knees, & fingers. My hope of having a comfortable winter is not likely to be realized. Got a note today from Field, inviting me to dine tomorrow to meet Mr. Goldwin Smith.[34]

34. Goldwin Smith (1823-1910), professor of modern history at Oxford University, had come to America in September bringing to the North a message of sympathy

NOVEMBER 29, 1864 | At 2 drove to town with Bet in the carriage. At 4 went to Field's. Mr. Goldwin Smith is a tall, thin man, dark hair & eyebrows, well-cut features, rather handsome. His manners are cold & formal. There seems to be nothing genial about him. Nevertheless, he was courteous & gentlemanlike. We had a good deal of talk about the war, the prospects of the country, the nature of our government, the abuses of the English government, &c. He is a very warm Union man & an advocate of democracy. He fully agreed with me, however, as to the dangers of universal suffrage, & that these arose chiefly from the Irish, which here as in England were a nuisance. I spoke of the corruptions of our government. He said that they had corruption in England, tho in a different form, the influence of the court & aristocracy. He said that no nation in the world could sustain such a war as our people & government have sustained this, & that the election of Lincoln by so large a majority was a proof of the sound moral sentiment of the people & rendered it certain that the Union would be restored & preserved. In England, he said, 5/6ths of the people are disfranchised and disaffected & that nothing but the lavish use of influence of the government on Parliament kept such an "old roué & adulterer" as Palmerston in office. That a change must come at last & whether it should be sudden & violent, or gradual & peaceful, was the only question. He has just returned from Washington & the front, saw & liked much Genls. Butler & Grant and Mr. Lincoln. He saw some of our soldiers from the southern prisons & had no words that could describe the ghastly spectacle of these poor, living skeletons. He said that he could clasp the arm of one of them, above the elbow, with his thumb & finger & did. On the whole was disappointed in Goldwin. Doubtless he has fine talents, highly cultivated, but he has not genius & seems rather hard & cold.

from England. He was later to teach at Cornell, take an American wife, and settle in Toronto.

~1865~

APRIL 5, 1865 | A long gap in my diary. The last volume closed Nov. 30th. I suffered so much from gout then that I felt no inclination to write or make any exertion. Soon afterwards the pain increased so much that I could not come down stairs. I sent for Dr. Wister. He ordered me to stay in bed, which I did from the 4th of December till the 20th of Jan'y. I had an acute attack of rheumatic gout, chiefly in my right knee, tho there was much swelling & pain in the other. I suffered a good deal for the first week or ten days; afterwards, I was free from pain when I did not move a leg. Slowly I got better & on the 20th I got up & could hobble into my dressing room. On the 23rd I came down stairs & on 27th went to town in the carriage to attend to some business. Since then I have been getting very slowly better, but am far from well. I have a great deal of pain, especially at night, in my knees, shoulders, neck & wrists. I walk with difficulty & perform every little necessary operation with difficulty & pain, such as dressing, carving, eating, rising from or sitting upon a chair, getting in & out of a carriage &c. In short, I am a cripple, tho not quite helpless yet. My general health has been good, I have a good appetite & generally sleep well. Wister has fed me up & stimulated my system. I drink ale & whiskey every day for dinner & take quinine and cod-liver oil. I cannot say that I have spent an unpleasant winter. . . .

Public affairs have been more satisfactory. I think the rebellion is now virtually crushed & that before many days we shall have peace. . . . When Sidney came from school he said that Richmond was taken & that in Germantown bells were ringing & flags flying. At $3\frac{1}{2}$

Jim [Fisher] stopped here on his pony on his way home. He came to tell us that Richmond was taken & the town (Philada) in a state of wild excitement, Chesnut St. crowded, firemen parading & sounding steam whistles, guns firing & bells ringing. And so it was all over the country. The people feel that the nation has been victorious, that the great rebellion has been put down, that the country & the government have been saved. Truly it is a glorious event & a signal triumph of truth & justice over a foul treason & a wicked cause.

During the winter two men of note have departed, Edw'd Everett and Geo. M. Dallas, neither of them ranking in the highest order of ability, but each eminent in his way. I have met Mr. Everett occasionally, but never liked his cold, formal manners. Mr. Dallas I knew very well from the time I was admitted to the bar, & was a frequent visitor at his house. He was very gracious & kind in his manners, had the air & breeding of a gentleman, was handsome, a tall well-made figure, pleasing countenance, white hair, was worthy & amiable in all private relations, but he was a Democrat and a demagogue.

In January I received a note from Joshua Fisher announcing the engagement of his daughter Helen to young John Cadwalader, a son of Jno Cadwalader, Judge of the Dist. Court of the U. S. It is a very fair match. The young man is very amiable, good looking & gentlemanlike, & comes of an old & distinguished family. He is a lawyer & will have influence to push him forward. Whether he has the talents necessary for success, I do not know. Fisher is more violent & extravagant in his opinions about the war than ever, indeed I really think he is a monomaniac on the subject. He told me the other day that the Middletons are all ruined, that Middleton Place was burned, that all the gentlemen were reduced to poverty, and mentioned the case of a lady, the wife of a judge, who was selling ground nuts & cakes at the corner of the streets of Savannah to our soldiers, & of a gentleman, whom I knew, who was selling pies. I doubt these stories.

APRIL 6, 1865 | Went to town chiefly to try to get one or two men to send down to Severson. Labor is very scarce & wages high. He wrote me a day or two ago that hands were asking $20 & $25 per mo. & that he could find none at that & asked me to send him two. I had heard recently that discharged soldiers of our army and rebel deserters were coming in great numbers North & that they were eagerly sought as laborers by farmers & others & one or two instances were mentioned in which rebel deserters had proved satisfactory. They are anxious to get employment & will accept moderate wages. I went to the Volunteer Refreshment Saloon at the foot of Washington St., where these people are collected. The officer in charge told me that they were getting them everyday in large numbers, & that they were eagerly sought by farmers & immediately got places. I saw one only, a young Virginian, who was engaged, but I did not go at the proper hour.

APRIL 8, 1865 | Sam & Mary Fox[1] & Eliz'th Fisher dined with us. We invited them some days ago. The Foxes have become rich. Mary has a large interest in the Bloomsburgh Iron Works, which has become very valuable, paying her an income of $12,000. Sam last summer invested $200 in an oil co. & soon afterwards sold his shares for $44,000. The oil of Penna. has added immensely to the wealth of the state, almost as much as coal or iron. It has been discovered in many places west of the mountains, hundreds of companies have been formed to make wells, many of which have been successful & some individuals have made enormous fortunes.

APRIL 10, 1865 | Drizzling rain all day. Great news this morning. Yesterday Gen'l Lee surrendered himself & his whole army to Gen'l Grant.

APRIL 11, 1865 | Read an article on Reconstruction in last number of *N. Am. Review*. The writer advocates conferring the right of suffrage on the Negroes, North & South. This absurd plan gains supporters. The abolitionists cannot bear to lose so fruitful a theme of excitement as the position of the Negro race, so that now, having emancipated him, they propose going a step further by granting him political

---

1. Mary Rodman Fisher, a daughter of William Logan Fisher and a cousin of the diarist, married Samuel M. Fox in 1849.

power. Already universal suffrage is acknowledged by all thinking men to be the chief source of danger to our government because of the ignorance & recklessness of the mob which is thus brought to bear on our politics, yet these fanatics wish to add the mass of the abject & degraded Negro population to make, what was already bad enough, a great deal worse. The men who are doing this belong to the conservative classes, whilst those who oppose the scheme are the Democrats, each contradicting thus the principles of its own party for the sake of partizan success, the Republicans, because they hope to gain the Negro vote in the South & elsewhere in the next elections, the Democrats, because if they advocated Negro suffrage they would lose the Irish vote. Such motives sway the leaders & managers of parties, & those who care chiefly for party victory, who are a large number, whilst others take sides according to passion, prejudice, & the influence of social position & education.

APRIL 15, 1865 | Calamitous news indeed this morning and a sad interruption to the joyful hopes inspired by late events. The national exultation at the prospects of peace & union has been suddenly converted into alarm & grief. Mr. Lincoln & Mr. Seward have been assassinated. Mr. Lincoln is dead & Mr. Seward, it is supposed, mortally wounded.[2] This morning, about 8 o'clock, Sidney knocked at my dressing room door, "Father," he said, "Lincoln is shot." "Nonsense, child, how did you hear that?" "It is true, Cornelius heard it at the village. He was shot because he tried to shoot Seward." I was bathing. Bet soon came to the door & said that Cornelius had brought the news from the village that the President had been killed, adding that she thought the story probable enough as he went about everywhere, with the utmost confidence, alone. She had sent to the village for the paper, as ours is not delivered before 11 o'clock. In a little while, when I was half dressed, she brought the paper and read to me, half crying & in a tremulous voice, the sad & terrible story.

 I felt for some time a mere dull & stupefied sense of calamity. What disasters, what wide-spread misfortune may not these events produce.

2. Seward's wounds were not mortal.

A vague feeling of coming ill & real sorrow for Mr. Lincoln, deprived me of the power to think & reason on the subject. I felt as tho I had lost a personal friend, for indeed I have & so has every honest man in the country. Bet said she was as much agitated as if she had lost a relation. Mr. Lincoln's character was so kind, so generous, so noble, that he inspired personal attachment in those who can appreciate such qualities, malignant & bitter hatred, however, in southern people & Democrats, who saw with envy the popularity he acquired, the affectionate respect that was generally expressed for him & his growing fame at home and abroad. He was indeed the great man of the period. On his integrity, constancy, capacity, the hopes of the country rested. He possessed the entire confidence of the people. His perfect uprightness & purity of purpose were beyond all doubt. His ability to comprehend all the questions before the country & to deal with them in an efficient, practical manner, his firmness & purpose & strength of will, were equally well known, whilst his frank, easy, animated manners and conversation, his entire freedom from vanity, or pride, or self-seeking or apparent consciousness of his position, except as to its duties, won all hearts. His death is a terrible loss to the country, perhaps even a greater loss to the South than to the North, for Mr. Lincoln's humanity & kindness of heart stood between them and the party of the North who urge measures of vengeance & severity. The southern people have murdered their best friend, as they are likely to find ere long. The feelings of good will & conciliation, which were spreading thro the North at the hopes of speedy peace, will now be checked & converted in the minds of many into resentment & rage.

Dr. Wister came about 3 o'clock. He ordered a new pill for me, but I have but little hope & I fancy he has little. We had a great deal of talk about this deplorable event. He says the people everywhere seem stunned and overwhelmed, the windows of the houses in Germantown & the city bowed & draped in black, everybody in the streets looking sad & depressed, in striking contrast with the hilarious cheerful expression of all faces a few days ago, or indeed yesterday. Bet, who went up to Germantown to [Dr. Louis] Jack, the dentist, remarked this when she returned. In the afternoon, I sent Daniel up Germantown for an evening paper. Not one to be had, all sold. He said that he heard that the Mayor had ordered out the police to protect the office of the *Age*, a Democratic paper from the mob. Very likely. The forbearance of the people has been wonderful. The Democrats in their speeches & their press have denounced the war & its motives & purposes, gloried in every rebel victory, mourned over their defeats, vilified the North, abused every officer of the government and above all Mr. Lincoln, on whom they have lavished every epithet of scorn & contempt; he was a usurper, a tyrant, a blackguard, a ruffian, a buffoon, a gorilla, a kangaroo, & his administration was worse than an eastern despotism. They have been permitted to do this without check or molestation, thus refuting their own charges. At length, Mr. Lincoln has been murdered by a Democrat in the execution of a plot made by Democrats. That a leading Democratic paper or leading demagogue of the party should require at such a moment the protection of the police is not surprizing.

APRIL 17, 1865 | Drove to town with Bet. Festoons of black cloth hanging from the windows of almost every house, shutters closed, flags in all directions with black streamers, portraits of Lincoln draped in crepe in hundreds of windows. The city quiet & has been, except the attempted attack on the *Age* office, which the police prevented. The windows of the houses of leading Democrats all bowed. The Mayor sent them notice that unless they gave this external mark of respect to the popular sentiment he would not be answerable for the consequences. Joshua Fisher's house bowed among the rest, which must have been a bitter pill for him to swallow.

APRIL 21, 1865 | Dr. Wister here in the morning. He prescribed a new remedy as I get no better under the present treatment. He told me that Edward Ingersoll had made in New York another violent speech, a few days ago, against the government, advocating the repudiation of the national debt. The war he said against the South & slavery was a violation of the Constitution, therefore the debt contracted to sustain the war was unconstitutional. The speech, Wister said, was published today & had excited very strong feeling against him so that he was in danger of being mobbed.

Bet brought out the *Evening Bulletin*. It contains a short article about Edward's speech, headed "The Ingersoll and Booth doctrine." It then says that on Thursday, the evening before the murder of the President, Edward Ingersoll at a dinner given in New York by the Anti-Abolition State Rights Society made a speech & with many other seditious and traitorous sentiments said: "I yield to no man in sympathy for the people of the South, a gallant people struggling nobly for their liberty against as sordid & vile a tyranny as ever proposed the degradation of our race, nay I go further & with Jefferson, Madison, & Livingston embrace the doctrine of secession as an American doctrine, without which American institutions cannot permanently live." The article significantly adds, "Shall such a *traitor* be allowed to dwell with and among us of Phila." Such an intimation at a moment of profound excitement like the present is ominous of trouble. What indeed can a man expect who has the audacity publicly to utter such sentiments in the midst of civil war. It is in accordance with his usual conversation. Some months ago he made another speech, in which he counselled open resistance to the government. It seems to me that the government ought to put some restraint upon practices which if they could succeed would overturn its authority. Here is a man who is permitted openly to advocate resistance to the laws & the destruction of the national credit, & yet talks of tyranny. I really think that to arrest him would be the best thing for *him* that the government could do. It might save his life.

APRIL 22, 1865 | The article in yesterday's paper about Edward made Bet very uneasy. This morning she determined to go to see Anna & Mrs. McKean. I had business in Germantown & went also, hoping to see Mr. McKean[3] & have some conference with him on the subject. We went first to Edward's house. He was out but Anna was at home. In a short time Mr. & Mrs. McKean drove up, she having just arrived from Troy. Mr. McKean came into the parlor where I was sitting alone. I asked him if he did not think Edward Ingersoll in a very dangerous position. He said that he did. That on Saturday a friend

3. Thomas McKean (1842–98).

called on him to say that one of the mob which, on the day the news of the murder reached here, surrounded the *Age* office & were prevented from attacking it by the police, read to the crowd extracts from a speech made by Edward last January, in which he advised resistance to the government, and denounced him in such violent terms that Mr. McKean's informant feared that he would be attacked. Several other intimations to the same effect had been given to McKean, & there can be no doubt that but for his influence & that of his family violence would have been committed ere this. . . . The people of Germantown are greatly incensed and McKean said he knew that a number of respectable men intended, in a few days, to write to Edward, requiring him to disclaim his disloyal sentiments or quit the neighborhood. So the matter is likely now soon to be brought to an issue.

APRIL 24, 1865 | The paper full of accounts of the reception of Mr. Lincoln's remains. Windows closed, 30,000 people at the station when the train arrived, a great procession, appropriate ceremonies at the Hall, guards everywhere to preserve order, and a file of people that reached almost to the Schuylkill going in turn to look at his face. This began at 6 o'clock yesterday & continued till evening, thousands waiting patiently for hours.

APRIL 27, 1865 | The catastrophe I have so long dreaded for Edward & Charles Ingersoll has at length occurred. Bet & I drove to town this morning at 12. I stopped at the office where Hollis told me that Edward had been arrested, as H & I supposed by Federal authority. I drove with Bet at once to Charles'. On our way, Wm. Rotch Wister stopped us & said that this morning Edw'd came in by the 9 o'clock train of the Germantown railroad. When it got to the station at 9th & Green, the passengers as they got out began to hoot at Edward & denounce him as a traitor. They followed him in this manner for a short distance when he turned & faced them. A certain Capt'n Withington, of Germantown, officer in a Penna: regiment, then advanced to him & with some abusive epithets demanded an apology to the people for the treasonable sentiments he had uttered. Edward told him to "go to hell." They both had canes & immediately began to exchange blows, the crowd surrounding them, flourishing their sticks & encouraging Withington. Edward very soon stepped back a few paces & drew a pistol. The crowd retreated for a moment &, fortunately, two police officers stepped up, took him in charge & conducted him to a station house. Having heard this story from Wister, we went on to Charles'. I went into his office where I found him with Peter McCall, consulting as to the best course for Edward to take. He was then safe, being in charge of the police, where they wished him to remain for the present. I told them that such was the feeling of indignation he had excited, that his life would be in danger if he appeared in public now, in the street, in a car, on the road near or in Germantown, and that if he returned to his house it would surely be attacked by the mob. I thought therefore that the only thing left for him to do was to go away for a time; that he might go to a farm he had recently bought in Montgy Co. or to Troy or anywhere, till the excitement subsided, which it would probably do ere long, as new events were constantly occurring to engage public attention. McCall agreed to this. Charles hesitated, evidently anxious that Edward should do nothing unworthy of a gentleman, by yielding to illegal persecution. Edward behaved very well this morning & showed pluck. He confronted the crowd, he fought the bragging Captn. Withington & got the better of him, as Tom McKean told me, who was present & stood by Edw'd manfully, and when he was taken before the magistrate, who bound him over in $2,000 on the charge of carrying concealed weapons, more to protect him from the mob than anything else, he told the excited mob in the office, when accused of having a pistol, "Yes, & when I drew it, you ran like sheep," which drew forth a fresh explosion of rage.

Having heard all these facts, Bet determined to go to see Anna, so we drove out to her house. Bet found her quiet, calm, & defiant, not disposed to talk but reserved & cold. We then went over to Mr. McKean's, where we got a lunch, as it was 5 o'clock & we had had no dinner. About 6½ o'clock Mr. Chas. Borie came out. He told us that the police station where Edw'd was had been surrounded all the afternoon by a mob, tho it was so well guarded by a large force that he was in no danger. That just before he left town, Charles Ingersoll came up to the station or near it intending to visit his brother; that he had been recognized by the mob & attacked & terribly beaten & had been taken home covered with blood by three policemen in a carriage. During the day, John T. Montgomery & Manlius Evans, both well known "Copperheads," had gone out to inform Anna of what had happened to Edward. She had sent in by them her son Warren with a carpet bag containing clothes &c for his father. They arrived about the time that the mob attacked Charles. Evans escaped but Montgomery was roughly handled & would have fared worse but for the presence of Warren, for even a ruffianly mob respects a child. Warren came out to Mr. McKean's whilst we were there & so did Anna & her children & spent the night, not feeling entirely safe in her own house, or rather because Mr. and Mrs. McKean wished her to come & said that she must either come to them or they would go to her. When Mr. McKean heard of the attack on Charles, he drove over to Mr. Henry's, the Mayor, who lives on School House Lane & who immediately went to town.

APRIL 28, 1865 | Drove to town at 12 with Bet. Left her at Charles'. Went down the street on business. Called at Geo. M. Wharton's, who is one of the advisers about Edward's affair, being a leading "Copperhead."[4] He said that Edward would go away for a time, where, he would not say as it was thought better that his friends generally should be able to say that they did not know where he was. I told him that I thought so too & would rather not know. Went to Charles'. Saw Mr. [John M.] Thomas. He said that Charles' appearance was horrible when he was brought home; his face swollen out of all human shape; his shirt & waistcoat drenched in blood. The mob dragged him out of the carriage, beat him over the head & stamped upon him. The policemen allowed them to do it for a time & then, merely to save his life, interfered. They in truth sympathized with the mob. Charles is not dangerously hurt as no vital point is injured. He will probably soon get well, tho erysipelas is feared. Bet saw him & was much shocked

---

4. George M. Wharton (1806-70), a Philadelphia lawyer, was a vice president of the Central Democratic Club in Philadelphia.

at his appearance. His spirits are good & he is not in the least cast down.

APRIL 29, 1865 | Edward was released on bail last evening, came out to his house, saw his family, & then drove away to his place of refuge, wherever that is. He was very reluctant to go, seemed much distressed at the brutal treatment that Charles had received, & said that he had been grossly insulted by the police whilst in their custody. Nevertheless, they did protect him from a mob whose passions they shared.

MAY 3, 1865 | The paper says the government has discovered a plot to burn Phila: & other northern cities. It was discovered by means of a letter dropped by a suspected person while pursued by the police. This city was to have been burned on Monday last. It is believed that 800 persons are concerned in the plot and that it originated with rebel refugees in Canada & was approved in the South. This war seems to have developed a devilish spirit that plans crimes on a scale as big as the war itself. Went to town. At the office met Pierce Butler who told me that he dined yesterday with Geo. Cadwalader who said that on Sunday the city government was in a state of great excitement & that he had all the troops under arms on Monday night in consequence of the notice of the plot sent from Washington.

On Monday Eliz'th Fisher invited us to go to Wakefield this evening to meet Mr. and Mrs. John Wister, who returned from Europe a few weeks ago. I went at 8 o'clock, Bet going with me to the door, but drove on to see Anna. Moreover, she did not care to go into company just now. There was quite a party & I had a pleasant evening. . . . Young John Cadwalader, who is to marry Helen Fisher, there. I spoke to him about Fisher, said I thought him morbid about public affairs & that if they continued to prey on his mind, as they have done, he will die. He said that they all felt the importance of diverting Fisher's mind towards other subjects as it was evident that he was unduly excited. He said that Middleton Place had been burned with everything in it, library, pictures, &c, and that the vaults in the family graveyard had been opened & the bones scattered, but that this was done not by our troops but by the Middleton Negroes, a number of whom had been brought up from the plantation at Combahee when Charleston surrendered. There were no doubt some shocking things done by the Negroes on many estates at that time.

MAY 5, 1865 | Yesterday, a bill was brought into the City Councils, offering a reward of $500 for the discovery of the persons who attacked Chas. Ingersoll. It was lost by a strict party vote, the Democrats, usually the advocates of mob law, voting for it; the Republicans, representing the conservative sentiment of the country, voting against it. This shows, if indeed anything were needed to show, how completely party spirit rules over principle. There was quite a debate in which Charles was spoken of with much severity as having been himself the advocate of mob law & as having outraged the patriotic feelings of the community (both true), and that the government was not bound to protect him and others like him from the consequences of their own folly. These people did not seem capable of rising above the particular case & of seeing that Charles was not of the slightest consequence compared to the general principles involved, & that the mob, when they struck at him, struck at the security of all rights. The conduct of Councils withdraws, so far as they can, the protection of the law from every man & invites the mob to further violence by impliedly sanctioning what they have already done. This vote of the Councils reveals the condition of our society. That we are really & virtually living under mob law, notwithstanding the show of order that is ordinarily represented.

Dr. Wister was here this morning & mentioned a case in point. Pierce Butler is living at the smaller of the two houses on his estate up the York Road near Branchtown. The house stands very near the road. The windows were not bowed because of Mr. Lincoln's death. He is known to sympathize with the South, but he is also known to be very quiet on the subject, even in private conversation. A number of laboring men, a few days ago, determined to attack his house. Mr. Morris Davis, a noted abolitionist who lives in the neighborhood, happened to hear of it. He went among them & had influence enough to keep them quiet. Dr. Wister says he has just heard of Avon Springs as superior to Richfield. He thinks I must go there or to Richfield for the summer, that it is not a question of choice. This sounds almost like a sentence of death. I *cannot* take Bet & Sidney, because of the expense. To go alone would be a miserable thing for me & for her, separation for three months. It was bad enough last year for four weeks. We seem to have fallen on evil days & to be caught in a net of trouble. Money difficulties, disease, necessary absence from home, Bet's brothers in a position painful to her & the future uncertain both of public & of our little private affairs, present a complication of circumstances such as I have not before encountered.

MAY 23, 1865 | Joshua Fisher here this morning. Much more moderate in his manner & language than heretofore. The logic of recent events has no doubt had its effect on his mind. He says that Middleton Place was burned by their own Negroes indeed, but they were in our army and under the command of white officers, who first plundered the house. Middleton, that is to say Williams, anticipating such an event, had sent his wife & children with a quantity of luggage to a small house he had hired in some small village in the interior. She was met by a party of raiders & robbed of everything. He followed by another route, with luggage also. He was robbed & escaped into a swampy woods, where he remained till half-starved, & what had become of him Fisher did not seem exactly to know. They are all ruined & suffering from actual destitution of the common necessaries of life. Harry & his wife are coming here & Fisher expects them at Alverthorpe every day. She is going to her family in England. Harry is to remain here, as he cannot go to her family for a support & he has literally nothing. "I must give him a room in my house," said Fisher, "& make him an allowance." He already supports a son of Russell Middleton in the Insane Asylum here, Mrs. Fisher's sister Kitty, also insane, & Mrs. Arthur Middleton in Paris. He must do something for Williams, for he cannot let him & his family starve, so that his generosity will be somewhat exercised. I think he will respond liberally to these calls, at the same time very unwillingly, for Fisher loves money & has a special affection for the "handsome surplus" of income which is necessary for executing his plans. Far more painful than for him to give will be the hard task for them of accepting, gentlemen, as they are, proud of their birth & position & inherited wealth, belonging to the old noblesse of S. Carolina. I feel for Williams especially, an amiable good fellow. It must be very bitter to lose a fine, old, ancestral house like Middleton Place, with library, paintings, plate, &c, and to be driven out homeless & penniless.

MAY 24, 1865 | In the evening looked over a volume of my diary in 1839. Was not pleased. The follies of youth are I think well exchanged for the infirmities of age. I would not, if I could, go back to those days of blindness, ignorance, & passion.

JUNE 5, 1865 | Drove to the station of Balto. railroad at $3^{1}/_{4}$. The cars left at $3^{1}/_{2}$. Got very comfortably to Middletown at 6. Not far from Middletown met a train coming up, filled with soldiers. They were Ohio & Illinois troops from a camp at Camden, Delaware. A more disgusting and brutal looking gang I never saw. They were dirty & ferocious animals. I felt greatly shocked. . . . Staid all night at Lippincott's tavern at Middletown . . . & the next morning started for Mt. Harmon at 8 o'clock in a wagon with a good horse & a boy to drive, hired from a man who now has Mullin's livery stable, he having died last winter. The weather was delightful & I had a pleasant drive. The day, Thursday, had been appointed by the President for National Fasting, humiliation, & prayer, in commemoration of the death of Mr. Lincoln, and it was observed throughout the country. The Negroes regarded it as a holiday. I met many groups on the road in gay attire and happy smiling faces. I stopped & spoke to two men a mile or two below Cecilton, good-looking fellows, well dressed & jet black. "Well boys, where are you going." "Going to meeting Sir." "But why do you go?" "Cause this thanksgiving day sir." "It is indeed. Well, what are you going to give thanks for." "For our liberties sir," said both smiling. . . .

Got to the farm about 10 o'clock. All the hands except two old men were away, "thanksgiving." The appearance of the place is much changed. . . . The house itself is much altered outside. It has a projecting roof with brackets, the roughcasting in several places is broken, disclosing patches of brick, there is no porch in front or piazza back as before, only simple steps to the hall doors & all the wood work is painted Spanish brown. Instead of the wing containing two good rooms, there is a small shed for a kitchen. When I entered, the hall & my parlor had a strangely novel & familiar look. The size & shape & outlook the same, the coloring & finishing different. The woodwork is painted French grey, there are no cornices & wainscotts as before & the tall mantelpiece painted black in the parlor is replaced by a low wooden one of grey. The windows however are better than the old, as the panes of glass are larger and afford a better view of the landscape.

JUNE 8, 1865 | It seems our fate never to get rid of the Negro question. No sooner have we abolished slavery than a party, which seems [to] be growing in power, proposes Negro suffrage, so that the problem—What shall we do with the Negro?—seems as far from being settled as ever. In fact, it is *incapable* of any solution that will satisfy both North & South, because of the permanent difference of race. No position for the Negro that would please the South would agree with enlightened opinion in the North. But how can the North enforce its views? Only by such an exertion of the power of the general government as would be inconsistent with its plan & theory. The South, moreover, when restoration is fully accomplished, will again hold the balance of power, will make another bargain with a northern party, as they did before, the condition of which will be as before—support in all southern plans for governing the Negro race, and again the South may control the country. I can see no way out of these difficulties consistent with the preservation of the Union & free government.

JULY 2, 1865 | Before I went to town this morning, whilst I was sitting reading the papers in the north piazza, Charley Ingersoll[5] made his appearance. He looked unaltered, except that he was browner. He was a surgeon in the rebel army almost from the beginning of the war and has seen a good deal of hardship which has done him no injury apparently as his health is excellent & his manners improved. Peace has not softened his feelings, for he is very bitter against the North.

5. Dr. Charles J. Ingersoll, son of John Ingersoll.

He dined with us. He says that at the plantation the family have not suffered during the war as some 12 or 15 Negroes remained, enough for household servants & to cultivate provision crops, and they had plenty of everything except the luxuries supplied by commerce. Charley in the first year of the war sold Negroes enough to pay $20,000 of debt, leaving only $6,000, & they have now a few bales of cotton left, so that for the present they are not in want. The future is the trouble. Charley has come on to discuss with his uncles plans for the property & the family.

JULY 4, 1865 | My "nonsense verses," written some weeks or months (I forget which) ago, about the people in Green Lane have been generally read, as anything personal about people's acquaintances will be, & I am told generally liked. I may as well copy them here as they are descriptive of what forms now part of our surroundings & important influences on our life, fleeting, & soon to change, like all the rest, so that before long few will be left who can understand them.

GREEN LANE
There is a great Duke of Medary,
Of Lincoln he grew very weary,
So he crossed o'er the sea
To enjoy Liberty,
Leaving country & home & Medary.[6]

A Duchess there is of Medary,
She is brilliant & gay as a fairy,
When she went away
Her neighbors did say,
Come back very soon to Medary.

And there is Charles Fox, Lord of Champlost,
A prince of good fellows as all know,
They call him a Judge,
But that is all fudge,
He's just honest Charley of Champlost.

6. Harry and Sally Ingersoll of Medary had sailed for Europe in May 1864.

There is Lady Mary of Champlost,[7]
A nicer old place no one *can* show,
But the charm of the place
Is the kindness & grace
Of this excellent Ladye of Champlost.

At Warriston lives Mr. Smith.
For wisdom he's grown quite a myth.
Greenlaners declare
That none can compare
With this wonderful, wise Mr. Smith.[8]

He's blessed with a good wife named Mary;
Her kindness was ne'er known to vary.
Such dinners & teas,
Elsewhere no one sees,
As those of this house-wifely Mary.

At Brookwood there lives a dear lady,
Whose years, not whose manners, are shady,
Her smile is so bright,
Her eye full of light,
You cannot but love this dear lady.[9]

There is Liedy Fisher of Brookwood.
They say she both is & doth look good.
But no one can tell,
So apart doth she dwell,
Much about this young Liedy of Brookwood.

JULY 5, 1865 | All thought it very wrong in me to go alone to Richfield, that both Bet & I would be so much happier if she & Sidney went too. I said I knew that, but could not afford the expense. Dickinson

---

7. Mary Fox, sister of Charles P. Fox.
8. George R. Smith's Warriston adjoined the Medary and Brookwood properties.
9. Mrs. Humphrey Atherton, grandmother of the diarist's Fisher nieces and nephews of Brookwood.

[Logan] offered to lend me the money till next year's peach crop. Everyone no doubt thinks it very odd that I go alone, & Bet is very anxious to go with me, but on the whole I think it better she should stay at home, for other reasons beside the expense. We have no confidential servants with whom to trust the house, or the farm, horses, &c. Bet will be a thousand times more comfortable here, as she hates watering places and travelling. It will be a satisfaction to me to think of her & Sidney in our own house with good servants, which we have now, near Dr. Wister & surrounded by relations & friends, almost as great as it would be to have her at such a place as Richfield, which I know she would not like, where there is no doctor, & to reach & return from which she & Sidney must run all the risks of steamboats & railroads, now not a few, as almost every paper has an account of some accident. Besides all this, is the question of expense, a most serious one to us just now. If all goes right, the tedious two months will come to an end at last.

JULY 8, 1865 | Received this morning from Ticknor & Fields, Boston, publishers of the *North American Review,* a cheque for $40 for my article in the number for this month, on Duties on Exports.

JULY 15, 1865 | Called at Lippincott's to order a copy of the *Trial of the Constitution* sent to *The Nation,* a new journal just issued in N. York to be conducted on the plan of the English *Saturday Review & Spectator* & to be published weekly. It is intended to discuss politics & literature & to be, if possible, of a high character, over $100,000 of stock having been subscribed to get it up. Some weeks ago Mr. Chas. J. Stillé met me in the street & spoke of it to me, saying the editor was in town & wished to see me, to invite me to contribute an article from time to time. I told Mr. Stillé to say to him that most probably I would do so, as I liked occasionally to have my say on public affairs & preferred writing for a magazine than for a newspaper. On the strength of this my name is advertised in the list of contributors. I am in pretty good company.

OCTOBER 1, 1865 | I left home at 10$^{1}/_{2}$ o'clock on Monday morning July 17th, drove to the Walnut St. ferry, reached N. York about 4 o'clock, went on board the *St. John* steamer, where I secured a stateroom, had a comfortable night, got to Albany at 6, breakfasted, left in the cars at 7½ & got to Richfield at about 2 o'clock.

I need not say much about my visit to Richfield, as my life there was nearly a repetition of what it was last year, with a change of the dramatis personae. . . .

My habits were those of watering place life, when one goes for health & not for pleasure to a quiet resort like Richfield. In the morning I read the newspapers, talked, walked, & bathed. We dined at 2. In the afternoon at 3 I got *always* a letter from Bet, the great event of the day for me. This I answered *always*. Then reading in my pleasant retired cottage, where I could be alone when I pleased, and then a walk. In the evening the drawing room, where we generally had music & sometimes dancing. . . .

My health was not improved so much as I expected. I got gradually better, a good deal better, but not so that I could walk without limping or go up & down stairs, or rise from or sit down on a chair without pain in my knees. I was not as well as I was last year at Richfield. Nevertheless, there was decided improvement which has continued. I left Richfield on Sep. 8, the company at the Spring House being reduced to two or three. I went down the North river in the new steamer, the *Dean Richmond*, built after the plan of the *St. John* and very sumptuous & costly as well as comfortable. These boats pay enormous profits. The *St. John* cost $750,000 & cleared that sum last year, & I was told the *Dean Richmond* cost as much & had already paid for herself when I came home in her. I arrived early the next morning at N. York but did not leave my stateroom till 8 o'clock. I then walked up to Delmonico's corner of Chambers St & Broadway & got breakfast. I then thought I would pay a visit to the Editor of the *Nation*, as he had invited me to write for it. Went to the office, 130 Nassau St. He was up stairs in a comfortable well-furnished room. He is a young man, good manners & appearance.[10] He received me very courteously, said the paper was succeeding beyond his expectations, would be

---

10. Edwin L. Godkin (1831-1902), born in Ireland of English stock, came to America in 1856. He assumed the editorship of the *Nation* on its founding in 1865.

glad to receive contributions from me, that they paid for *all* contributions. I told him that I should accept the money tho it was not my motive in writing; that I had a great deal of leisure & liked the occupation & was glad of an opportunity such as the *Nation* afforded of expressing my opinions from time to time on public affairs. I agreed to write, as soon as I got home, an article on the best means of preventing railroad accidents, which for the last three or four months had been so numerous & destructive. Left New York by the 11 o'clock train, reached the Kensington station at 3, found Daniel waiting for me with the carriage and in half an hour was once more at home. It was Sidney's birthday, the 9th, when he was 9 years old & he had a party. Edward Ingersoll's children, Jim & Maud, Charley & Sally Smith, Fanny Logan, etc. Geo. Smith & Liedy were here also. How glad I was to see them all & to be at home & how comfortable & pleasant everything looked, & what a delight to see Bet & Sidney & hear their voices need not be told.

The most important event that has happened in our circle during my absence is that Geo. Smith has sold his place in Green Lane. He is so intimately connected with & so important to the people there, to Brookwood, Medary, & Champlost, that it will make a great difference to them. Miss Fox is quite indignant & considers herself wronged and Brookwood is in grief. I regret it very much too. It is a break in our circle of friends, an important influence withdrawn & one house the less to visit at where we were sure of welcome. George's chief reason for selling is no doubt the expense of such a place & of a town house too, now when the cost of living has so greatly increased. An income quite sufficient before the war is inadequate now. He thinks of going abroad in the spring. So everything around us changes.

As to my own affairs, they are bad enough. It is the old story of disappointment. Half the wheat crop destroyed by rust, only half a crop of peaches, or indeed less. I will not enlarge upon it. The result is that I am unable to pay my debts out of income and as I cannot go on forever having my notes renewed at bank, I must get a permanent loan on *mortgage!* A sad result & very painful & mortifying to me, but it must be done.

Last week I wrote an article about railroad accidents & sent it on Friday Sep. 22 to the editor of the *Nation*. It is entitled The National Highways.

OCTOBER 8, 1865 | On Tuesday received a polite letter from Mr. Edwin L. Godkin, editor of the *Nation*, saying that my article would appear the following Thursday, which it did, & on Friday I rec'd $10 for it, which is $5 per column, liberal pay. I sent the same day I rec'd Mr. Godkin's letter Article No. 2 on the same subject. . . .

Had some talk with Charles [Ingersoll], who advocated with arguments ludicrously absurd the new movements just set afoot by the working classes in favor of making 8 hours a legal day's work. In "old times" it was 15, then 12, more recently 10, and now the laboring people, stimulated by high wages & the consciousness of power caused by a great demand for labor in all departments, ask 8 hours with the same wages paid for 10. They demand a law to this effect & denounce any one who opposes them as a monarchist & an enemy to Republican Liberty. Their claims have been recognized by the Democratic Party & made one of the issues at the next election. Indeed the probability is that the whole scheme was suggested by the demagogues of that party as a partizan measure to bring over the American working classes to their side; the foreigners they have already. . . .

Writers on political economy have generally spoken of the advantages of high wages as a means of elevating the condition of the laboring classes. They never had our experience in the matter, which proves that high wages are generally a curse, not to society merely but to the laborer. Their effect is idleness, dissipation, insolence to employers, riots, & violence. Very few are found to save their earnings & accumulate property, but they spend recklessly and at the end of the year are as poor as ever. That high wages instead of stimulating should diminish production, is a result that few would anticipate.

OCTOBER 10, 1865 | Got a note from Mr. Godkin asking for an article on the 8 hour labor movement. In my letter to him of last Tuesday I asked him if he would like to have an article on that subject.[11] This is

---

11. This article appeared in the *Nation* later in the month.

election day for mayor, &c. Voted at the Rising Sun. McMichael is the candidate for Mayor, Mr. Henry having refused to serve any longer. I doubt much whether McMichael is the right man for such an office in these times. Mr. Henry was eminently fitted for the place, and never before was the city so well governed as during his administration. He was re-elected three times, & would have been again had he not refused the nomination. A committee of the 8 hour labor faction waited on McMichael and S. M. Fox, the Democratic candidate, to know their respective opinions on that subject before the election. Fox promised them his support. McMichael gave them no definite answer, but expressed in general terms his desires for the elevation of the laboring classes.

OCTOBER 13, 1865 | Went with Bet in the evening to Champlost. Julia Fisher & her daughters there. The old house looked very comfortable with its blazing wood fires, profusion of light & well-kept old-fashioned furniture. Spent a very pleasant evening, for Julia & Bet were full of animation & talk & one of the girls gave us some music on the piano. Among other things we laughed about was the irritation Geo. Smith showed at my nonsense verses on Green Lane. He did not at all like what I said about himself & his wife. I told them of a verse he had written in retaliation & which he repeated to me at his house last Sunday.

> There was an old man of Mount Harmon,
> Who by verse tried to carry a farm on,
> But his crops & his verse
> Were not worth a curse,
> This seedy old man of Mount Harmon.

This was rather coarse. Bet did not like the profanity and for the 4th line substituted

> Put no cash in his purse.

And I wrote the following, which expresses George's idea, at least more poetically, & so they all thought:

A *Poet* there was of Mount Harmon
Who, dreamingly carried his farm on,
'Twas so dream-like, it seems
All his profits were dreams,
And a dream too will soon be Mount Harmon.

A melancholy prophecy which may perhaps be realized, but not if I can help it.

OCTOBER 18, 1865 | Went to town. Saw [Charles H.] Muirheid. He has failed to get me the money I wanted, $10,000 on mortgage of Mount Harmon. No one is willing as a matter of business to invest money on mortgage out of the state. I told him that as the property was ample security & the investment a safe one, I did not wish him to go to any of my acquaintances, who might probably lend the money as a favor to me, & he mentioned several whom he felt sure would do so. Some days ago, George Smith told Stewardson that he would lend me the money with pleasure. But I was averse to establishing the relation of debtor & creditor between us. The question now is, however, since I *must* have the money, shall I accept such a favor, for it appears that it *is* a favor, from an old friend who knows all about my affairs & *offers* willingly to do what someone else might do reluctantly. As there can be no doubt on this point, I told Muirheid that he might let Stewardson say as much to George. How much it worries me to have to mortgage Mt. Harmon at all, and then to get the money in this way, I cannot express.

OCTOBER 19, 1865 | The Irish part of our population are holding meetings to support what is called Fenianism in Ireland. This is a popular agitation to get up a rebellion against the English government & make Ireland an independent nation. It caused no serious alarm, tho the ministry have taken summary & prompt measures to prevent any outbreak, apparently with success. Here, efforts are made to sustain the intended insurgents by their countrymen. There are secret societies and conclaves & assistance in men & money is promised.

OCTOBER 21, 1865 | The demand for labor is so great that it injures the laborers by rendering them independent, indifferent, & careless. A man who knows that he can at any time get a place is, of course, less anxious to please than one who knows that if turned out of his place it would be almost impossible for him to get another as good. This cause is acting on the whole laboring class throughout the country & its effects are constant demands for high wages & less work. The result is diminished production & the increased cost of all the necessaries of life, so that people of moderate incomes are subjected to much suffering. They are going to Europe in large numbers to economize or rather to live as well as they did here before the war, which they can do, it is said, notwithstanding the rate of exchange. The very rich go also to enjoy pleasures & luxuries which this country does not furnish, works of art, good cooking, good roads, good servants, & all the manifold advantages of long civilization & aristocratic government. Europe was never so full of Americans as at present. On the other hand the poor & laboring classes of Europe are coming hither in greater numbers than ever before, attracted by the high wages & immense demand for labor which now prevail, by cheap land and by what they call liberty. So these two streams of emigration cross each other on the ocean, the one to escape poverty, the other to enjoy wealth....

NOVEMBER 5, 1865 | On the 26th, Muirheid told me that he had made other fruitless efforts to get the money & would that afternoon go out to Geo Smith's & settle the question whether it was to be got from him. He stopped here on his way back & left a note from George enclosing a cheque for $3,000, promising the balance, $4,000, in a few days. The next evening, I went up to see him. He was very kind in his rough way. Said he thought my affairs looked unpromising, did not see how I was to get income to live in my present manner, was very willing to lend me the money, would not take a mortgage, my note was enough, and acquiesced in my plan of getting the money on mortgage elsewhere as soon as I could to repay him. Altogether, he behaved very well.

NOVEMBER 16, 1865 | The *Nation* came this afternoon. My 2nd article on the National Highways in it, considerably cut down, however, which is very annoying.[12] Indeed it destroys so much of the pleasure of writing, that I think I will give it up, except perhaps on topics which can easily be treated in a small space. The *Nation* improves I think in quality & gains in circulation, so that, for one who likes now & then to express his opinions in print, access to it is worth having, and as the editor publishes my articles, I take it for granted that he is willing to receive them.

NOVEMBER 27, 1865 | At 3 drove up to Wakefield. Aunt Sarah very low. Was invited to her room, where a number of the family were assembled. She breathed with difficulty & her face was much distorted. She was however perfectly conscious & her mind clear. She answered when spoken to but so indistinctly that it was difficult to understand her. I went to the bedside & took her hand & Mary told her who I was. She said "How is thee," & when I bade her good-bye, "I shall soon be gone." A little before I came she had said she knew she was dying, but did not shrink & would soon be with Lindley & Charley & her husband. Will she? That is the important question. That she does not think it a doubtful one is a great consolation.

NOVEMBER 30, 1865 | A message from Betty this morning that Aunt Sarah died this morning at 6 o'clock. Another old friend gone, the last of that generation of my family. I have no uncles nor aunts, nor brothers, and my nearest relations outside of home are a nephew & nieces and first cousins. Aunt Sarah was nearly 81 years old. She was my Uncle William's second wife. Her name was Lindley. She was of a respectable but very plain Chester County Quaker family, whose social position was much below that of my uncle, whereas his first wife was a Rodman of New Bedford, one of the best and most influential families there. She made him a most excellent wife however & was a

---

12. Fisher's third article on "The National Highways" appeared in the *Nation* in January 1866.

mother to his first wife's children. She was a woman of great intelligence, her mind was cultivated by reading and her conversation highly agreeable.

DECEMBER 4, 1865 | Drove up to Wakefield in the carriage at 11 to go to Aunt Sarah's funeral. Went up stairs to her room where I had so lately seen her & where the members of the family were assembled. Sat at there nearly an hour. According to the custom of Friends, there was some preaching, if it may so be called, by Mrs. Deborah Wharton & Lucretia Mott. The latter is a noted female abolitionist & lives on the York Road, a worthy respectable woman enough & a visitor at Wakefield. I went in a carriage with Joshua Fisher & Mifflin Wistar. There were, of course, no ceremonies at the grave, unless standing around it in solemn silence till it was filled be a ceremony. I think it as impressive as the church service. And so that was the last of Aunt Sarah. . . . Those whom I considered old are now all gone & we have become the old people.

EPILOGUE

Sidney George Fisher died at the age of sixty-two on July 25, 1871, three days after making his final diary entry. For a while, his widow and child lived with the Edward Ingersolls, but Mrs. Fisher, not wishing to be dependent on her brother, soon moved to lodgings in Germantown, where she survived her husband by less than a year, dying in May 1872. It would be more comforting to believe that she died of a broken heart than to accept her son's bitter and unlikely diagnosis—*starvation!* The son, who spelled his first name Sydney, was educated at St. Paul's School, Concord, New Hampshire, Trinity College, and Harvard Law School. Later, he was to serve many years on Trinity's board of trustees and to interrupt his legal practice in favor of writing numerous books on American history. The diarist would have taken solace could he have but known that his son was to retain ownership of Mount Harmon all his life. Indeed, so far as physical possessions were concerned, about the only ones held by Sydney George Fisher at the time of his death, which occurred on February 22, 1927, were Mount Harmon and his father's diaries, still stored in the walnut chest made for them in 1866.

FISHERS AND INGERSOLLS

The following brief outline is intended to clarify the identities and relationships of the numerous Fishers and Ingersolls whose names appear in the diary.

THE FISHER FAMILY

Joshua Fisher (1707-83), a notable Quaker merchant of Philadelphia, had four sons—Thomas, Samuel Rowland, Miers, and Jabez Maud,

of these

Thomas Fisher (1741-1810) married Sarah Logan (1751-96) and built Wakefield on land he purchased in 1799. He had five children, of whom the youngest, Esther, died unmarried in 1849. The other children were:

1. Joshua Fisher (1775-1806), who married Elizabeth Powel Francis (Mrs. E. P. F. in the diary). The Joshua Fishers had one child, Joshua Francis Fisher (1807-73), usually referred to as "Fisher" by the diarist. He married Eliza Middleton of South Carolina, built Alverthorpe near Jenkintown, and had six children: Elizabeth Francis (Lilly), who married R. Patterson Kane; Sophia Georgiana, who married Eckley B. Coxe; Mary Helen, who married John Cadwalader Jr.; Maria Middleton, who married Brinton Coxe; George Harrison, who married Betsey Riddle; and Henry Middleton, who married Mary Elwyn Wharton.

2. Hannah Logan Fisher (1777-1846), who married James Smith and had three children: Sarah Fisher (Sally), an eccentric; Rebecca Darby, an eccentric and troublemaker; and Esther Fisher (Hetty), who married Dr. Mifflin Wistar.

3. William Logan Fisher (1781-1862), who inherited Wakefield and married Mary Rodman of New Bedford, by whom he had three children: Thomas Rodman, an unsuccessful businessman; Sarah Logan, who married William Wister and lived at Belfield; and Elizabeth Rodman (Betty), who was very kind to the diarist. Secondly, William Logan Fisher married Sarah Lindley and had three more children: Lindley; Charles William; and Mary Rodman, who married Samuel M. Fox.

4. James Logan Fisher (1783-1814), who married Ann Eliza George (1785-1821), daughter of Sidney George Jr., of Mount Harmon, Cecil County, Maryland. (By a later wife Sidney George Jr., also had a daughter, Phoebe, who married Moses Bradford.) James Logan Fisher and his wife had three sons:

    a) Sidney George Fisher (March 2, 1809-July 25, 1871), the diarist, who married Elizabeth Ingersoll on May 28, 1851. The Fishers had one child, Sydney George Fisher (1856-1927), the historian.

    b) Dr. James Logan Fisher (1811-33), who died in Paris.

    c) Charles Henry Fisher (1814-62), called Henry, the family millionaire who built Brookwood and who married Sarah Ann Atherton, by whom he had six children, only one of whom married: Emily Atherton (1838-48); Eliza (Liedy) George (1841-1916), the head of the Brookwood family after her father's death; Ellen (1845-1903), who was crippled, evidently by polio, in 1849; Mary Dyre (1848-1848); James Logan (1849-1925), who married Mary Wilcocks Ingersoll, daughter of Edward Ingersoll; and Maud (1858-1932), the last occupant of Brookwood.

THE INGERSOLL FAMILY

This family, which immigrated to Salem, Massachusetts, in 1629, had its Philadelphia beginnings in 1771, when Jared Ingersoll moved there from Connecticut. He had but one child, Jared Ingersoll Jr. (1749–

1822), a celebrated member of the Philadelphia Bar and the father of three lawyer sons, the youngest of whom, Edward, is barely mentioned in the diary.

1. Charles Jared Ingersoll (1782-1862) was the oldest son of Jared Ingersoll Jr. He married Mary Wilcocks (1784-1862) and was the father of nine children.

a) Charles Ingersoll (1805-82), who married Susan C. Brown of New Orleans and sired a family of daughters: Adele C. (Delly), who married John Moylan Thomas; Ann, who married Dr. James Howell Hutchinson; Elizabeth (Betty) Wilcocks, who married Arthur Amory; Kate, who married Dr. Frank Maury.

b) Alexander Wilcocks Ingersoll (1807-89), a promising young man who went insane and spent most of his life in an institution.

c) Harry Ingersoll (1809-86), who married the wealthy Sarah Emlen Roberts and gave up the Navy to live at Medary. His only child, George Roberts Ingersoll, was killed in a railroad accident in 1855.

d) John Ingersoll (1811-59), who became a planter in Mississippi and married Margaretta Smith, by whom he had three children: Dr. Charles J. Ingersoll, who served in the Confederate Army; William (Willy), also a Confederate soldier; Helen, who several times visited the diarist. Secondly, John married Mrs. Sarah Griffin and had two more daughters.

e) Benjamin Wilcocks Ingersoll (1813-59), a successful businessman who died unmarried in Rome.

f) Elizabeth Ingersoll (1815-72), who married Sidney George Fisher, the diarist, and was the mother of the historian, Sydney George Fisher.

g) Edward Ingersoll (1817-93), who married Anna C. Warren, of Troy. Their children were: Stephen Warren (1851-84), who married Josephine Bond; Mary Wilcocks (1852-1905), who married James Logan Fisher; Phoebe Warren (1854-1937), who married Harry Wilcocks McCall; Anna Warren (1855-1945), who married Charles Morton Smith; Charles Edward (1860-1932), who married Henrietta A. Sturgis; Henry McKean (1862-1943); Jane Hobart (1865-1951).

h) Ann Wilcocks Ingersoll (1822-56), who married Dr. John Forsyth Meigs and had eight children.

2. Joseph Reed Ingersoll (1786-1868), younger brother of Charles Jared Ingersoll, the progenitor of the above generations, married Ann Wilcocks (1781-1831), a sister of Mrs. Charles Jared Ingersoll. They had three children, two sons who died young and a daughter, Mary, who died unmarried in 1842 at the age of twenty-six, after which his niece, Mary Wilcocks, kept house for him until his death.

COUNTRYSEATS

Alverthorpe was built by Joshua Francis Fisher in 1850-51 on Meeting House Road near Jenkintown. The house was torn down in 1936.

Brookwood was built by Charles Henry Fisher in 1851 on Green Lane and County Line. The house was torn down in the 1930s.

Butler Place, built in 1791 and acquired in 1810 by Major Pierce Butler, was on the west side of Old York Road at a site opposite the Widener Home for Crippled Children. It was last occupied by the Owen Wister family and was torn down in the late 1920s.

Champlost, built by the Fox family about 1770, was located diagonally across Green Lane from Brookwood and was near Fern Rock Station. It was torn down in 1901 or 1902.

Clermont was a Ridgway family property located close to the northern limits of Philadelphia and near Forest Hill. In the diarist's time it was occupied by the John Rhea Bartons.

Fern Hill was built by Henry Pratt McKean in 1849-50 on what later became McKean Avenue, Germantown. The house was demolished in 1913.

Forest Hill, the summer home of Charles Jared Ingersoll and later the residence of the diarist, was on Rising Sun Lane near the intersection of Germantown Avenue and Old York Road. The house was still standing in the 1890s.

Medary was built by the Harry Ingersolls in 1847 on Green Lane near Fern Rock Station and next to Brookwood. C. Morton Smith inherited the property in 1892 and sold it about 1910.

Somerville, on the west side of Germantown Avenue, opposite the Fair Hill Burying ground and extending to Broad Street, was erected early in the nineteenth century by Albanus Charles Logan, and was later occupied by Dr. J. Dickinson Logan.

Stenton, built by James Logan in 1728, still stands at what is now Eighteenth and Courtland Streets. Owned by the city, it is under the care of the Pennsylvania Society of Colonial Dames of America.

Wakefield was built about 1798 by the diarist's grandfather, Thomas Fisher, and was subsequently the residence of the diarist's uncle, William Logan Fisher. It was inherited by the Fox family who ultimately sold it to the city. Wakefield stood near Lindley Avenue and Ogontz Avenue, what is now Wakefield Park, until 1985, when it was torn down.

Mount Harmon was the diarist's plantation on the Sassafras River in Cecil County, Maryland. Originally part of a 350-acre land grant to Godfrey Harmon from the second Lord Baltimore, in 1651, Mount Harmon was a tobacco plantation in the seventeenth and eighteenth centuries. The diarist inherited the property, which had been his grandfather's home, from his mother, and it remained in the family until the death of his son, Sydney George Fisher, in 1927. Since 1997, Mount Harmon has been owned by the Friends of Mount Harmon, Inc. It is still open to the public, and is approximately 75 miles from Center City Philadelphia.

Index

abolitionists, 3-4, 7-8. *See also* slavery
   Beecher, 66-67
   Brown, 18, 26
   "chattel" slavery, 206-7
   conservatives' view of, 17-18
   Curtis, 19, 123-24, 193, 211-12
   Douglass, 198
   Kane, 92n110
   Kemble, 32n45, 45, 82, 134, 197, 201, 219
   McKim, 202
   Mott, 168, 273
   Negro soldiers enlisted by, 198
   Pennsylvania Anti-Slavery Society, 202n44
Academy of Natural Sciences, 208
Adams, John Quincy, 125
Agassiz, Elizabeth Cabot Cary, 135
Agassiz, Jean Louis Rodolphe, 81, 135
The Age, 189, 213
Agnew, Daniel, 208n54
Alabama (warship), 230
Alexandria, Virginia, Marshall House in, 93-94
Allibone, Samuel A., 26
Alverthorpe country seat, 59, 109, 198, 209-10, 234, 279
American flag. *See also* flag
   Lincoln raises, in Philadelphia, 75
   symbol of loyalty, 84
American Philosophical Society, 40
Anderson, Robert, 83
Antietam, battle of, 172
Arkansas, reluctant to secede, 72

Arlington National Cemetery, 242
Army of Potomac
   Chancellorsville defeat, 189
   critical of government, 183
   Hooker, 189
   inactivity of, 134-35
   McClellan, 130, 134-35, 145-46, 151, 164, 166
   Meade, 195-96
   Wadsworth, 115, 222-23
Ashhurst, William Henry, 19
Atherton, Humphrey, 264
Atherton, Sarah Ann, 38n52, 117, 146
Averell, William W., 226, 235

Bache, Francis Markoe, 110, 115
Baldwin, Matthias, 179
Baltimore
   1860 Union Party convention, 34-35
   civil v. military law in, 94-95
   wealthy secessionists in, 158
Baltimore & Wilmington Railroad, 73, 86, 143
banks. *See also* business; currency
   bankruptcy from unpaid Southern debts, 93
   Brown, John A., 148
   Farmers & Mechanics Bank, 241, 243
   Jackson, Andrew, v. Bank of United States, 215
   paper money, 156, 186-87
   secession threatens, 58-59, 81
   state banks to be nationalized, 241
Banks, Nathaniel P., 151, 179

Barclay, Clement C., 118n58
Barnum's exhibition, 79
Barton, John Rhea, 166, 279
Barton, Susan, 166, 221
Bayard, James A., Jr., 135
Baynard, Charles P., 31
Beauregard, Pierre Gustave Toutant, 83, 97–98
Beecher, Henry Ward, 66–67
Bellevue house, 204
Bell, John, 34, 38
The Bible & Slavery (Fisher, S. G.), 211
Bible View of Slavery (Hopkins), 209
Biddle, Charles J., 48, 99–101, 113
Biddle, Craig, 48
  Agricultural Society address by, 24–25
Biddle, George W., 228, 243
Biddle, Henry J., at Richmond, 152–54, 223, 226
Biddle, Nicholas, 25
Binney, Horace
  congressman/Republican, 23–24
  The Privilege of the Writ of Habeas Corpus under the Constitution, 166
Blight, George, 48
Blitz, Antonio, 121, 211
Bloomsburg Iron Works, 250
Boileau, Albert D., 183
Boker, George Henry, 45
Bolivar, Fernando, 102n37
Bolivar, Francis, 101–2, 103
Bolivar, Simon, 102n37
Bonaparte, Joseph, 28n34, 123
Bonaparte, Napoleon, 182
Borie, Adolphe E., 148
Borie, Charles L., 242
Borie, Henry P., 242
Boston. *See North American Review*
Brazil, slaveholding nation, 43
Breckinridge, John Cabell, 37–39
Brooklyn (warship), 71n1
Brookwood country seat, 29–30, 44, 53, 58, 81, 108, 117, 167, 187, 229
Brougham, Henry Peter, 43, 44
Brown, Andrew T., 235
Browning, Elizabeth Barrett, 136
Brown, John
  at Harper's Ferry, 18
  Howe, sympathy for, 26
  Lee's capture of, 194n25
  militant abolitionist, 18
Brown, John A., 148
Buckalew, Charles R., 180
Buell, Don Carlos, Union victories due to, 134–35
Bullitt, John C., 161
Bull Run. *See also* Manassas Junction
  First Battle of, 104–5
  The London Times reports on, 105
  Second Battle of, 166, 182
Burd, Edward Shippen, 30, 152
Burnside, Ambrose E.
  defeat at Fredericksburg, 176–77
  Union victories due to, 134–35
business. *See also* banks; currency; railroad companies
  American Shoetip Company, 238
  bankruptcy from unpaid Southern debts, 93
  Bloomsburg Iron Works, 250
  coal mining, 59, 138, 148, 243
  controlling legislature, 54
  corruption/inefficiency in Washington influencing, 130–31
  currency panic influencing, 156
  du Pont, 36
  fortune from government contracts, 227
  Goodyear rubber company, 238
  national debt influencing, 187
  newspapers controlled by, 54
  sale of American stocks, 126
  secession's influence on, 58–59, 81
  shopkeepers benefit from war, 191
  Wharton, 203n279
  worker's wages, 268
Butler, Benjamin F., 179, 226
Butler family
  Chelton Hill estate, 201
  country seat, 279
Butler, Fanny, 96–97
Butler, Henry, 68
Butler, Pierce, 32, 45, 68, 82. *See also* Kemble, Frances Anne "Fanny"
  arrested for treason, 108
  postwar condition of, 259
  release from prison of, 116
  secessionist, 161–62

Index 283

Cadwalader, George, 18*n*6
  commanding troops in Philadelphia, 200
  Democratic views of, 204-5
  mixture of races anecdote, 18-19
  as Union general, 94
Cadwalader, John, 162
Camac, William, 97
Cameron, Simon, 103, 131
Camp Curtin, 91
Camp William Penn, 198*n*37
Carlisle, Pennsylvania, 194*n*25
Carpenter, George W., Phil Ellena estate of, 28
Cass, Lewis, 22
Central Democratic Club, 180
Chambersburg, Pennsylvania, 193-94, 234
Champlost country seat, 279
  Fox family's, 240
Chancellorsville, Virginia
  Army of Potomac defeat at, 189
  Stonewall Jackson's death in, 195
Charleston, South Carolina, in flames, 84
Chase, Salmon P., 82, 228
Chelton Hill estate, 201
Chew, Ann, 31
Chew, Benjamin, 31*n*41
Chew, Samuel, 31*n*41
Chicago, Historical Society of, 24*n*20
Christianity
  The Bible & Slavery, 211
  Bible View of Slavery, 209
  Dred Scott decision v., 7*n*17
Church, Frederick E., 225
Civil War. *See also specific battle site; specific person*
  European royalty witnessing, 108
  Fort Sumter, 83, 84
  Northern troops in Virginia, 93-94
  class relations. *See* abolitionists; Negroes; rioting; slavery
Clermont country seat, 279. *See also* Barton, John Rhea
Cliveden mansion, 30-31
coal oil
  Heckscher's interest in, 130-31
  Little Schuylkill Navigation, Railroad, and Coal Company, 138, 148
  lucrative investing in, 243
  sperm candles v., 59
Colonial Dames of America, Pennsylvania Society of, 23*n*17
Colorado
  Gilpin, governor of, 80-81*n*8, 87
  Pike's Peak gold region, 81
colored troops. *See* Negroes
Colwell, Stephen, 65
Confederate Army. *See also* soldier; *specific person; specific place*
  Carlisle entered by, 194*n*25
  Chambersburg taken by, 193-94, 234
  destruction of, 245
  Ewell, 195
  Johnston, 97-98
  Lee, 194*n*25, 195-97
  Semmes, 230
  U.S. officers joining, 97-98
Confederate flag, 84
Congregationalist Church, 67*n*88
Congress, suspending habeas corpus, 204-5
Connecticut, Hartford Convention, 184
Connell, Wilmer, 48
Conscription Act
  New York riots against, 200
  Pennsylvanian judges on, 207
  resistance to, 208
conservative class, diarist's view of, 17-18
Constitution
  Kanzas and the Constitution, 5
  as protecting slavery, 61-62
  situations unprovided for by, 78
  The Trial of the Constitution, 9, 10
  wisdom of, 5-6, 9-10, 78
  writ of habeas corpus provided in, 95
Continental Hotel, 47, 112, 179
  Lincoln at, 226
Coppee, Henry, 98-99
"Copperheads," 187
Correa, Jose Francisco, 27
Couch, Darius N., 197
Crosley & Nicholls publishers, 241
The Cruelties of War (Fisher, J. F.), 234, 235
C. Sherman & Son Printers, 176
Cuba, 122*n*66
currency. *See also* banks; business
  Continental, 223
  gold in Colorado, 81

legal tender notes, 213
national, 241
National Banks system, 215
A National Currency, 219-20
panic over, 156
paper money, 156, 186-87
Curtin, Andrew G., 72
  governor/congressman, 47, 47*n*69
  Pennsylvanian armed militia, 83
  Union Party governor, 205
Curtis, George William, 19*n*11
  1864 report from Washington by, 211-12
  abolitionist, 123-24
  on Lincoln, 211-12
  mob attack against, 19, 193

daguerreotype, 79
Dallas-Brougham incident, 44
Dallas, George Mifflin, 249
  Dallas-Brougham incident, 44, 44*n*64
  mayor/attorney general/ambassador/vice president, 43, 43*n*60
  September 1861 anti-secessionist speech, 115-16
Dana, Napoleon Jackson Tecumseh, 195
Davis, Henry Winter, 85
Davis, Jefferson, 74, 110, 180
  Evening Journal praise for, 184
Deerhound (English yacht), 230
Delaware Avenue Market, 163
democracy, 2-3, 9
Democratic party
  Bible View of Slavery used by, 209
  break up of, 34
  Charleston convention/April 1860, 33
  critical of "unconstitutional" government measures, 187
  dividing public opinion, 108
  incendiary propaganda from, 199
  Ingersoll, Charles, opinion of, 145
  meeting to depose Lincoln, 172
  Philadelphia's, 159-60
  Republican Party v., 38
  success in 1861 election, 116-17
  working classes recognized by, 268
Democrats
  The Age, 189, 213
  Binney's view of, 23-24
  Central Democratic Club, 180

as "Copperheads," 187
  diarist's view of, 11, 23, 54, 190
  inciting riots, 193
  mob violence of, 2-3
  treasonous speeches/arrests of, 160-64, 186
Dickinson College, 2
District of Columbia, Wadsworth, 115, 222-23
disunion. *See* secession
Donnel, John R., 57
Douglas, Stephen A., 37-38
Douglass, Frederick, 198
Dred Scott decision, 7*n*17
Duncannon estate, 173-74
du Pont, Henry, 36
du Pont, Henry Algernon, 36
du Pont, Samuel Francis (1803-1865)
  takes Beaufort in South Carolina, 121
  Union victories due to, 134-35
  U.S. Navy captain, 85

elections
  1860 Lincoln elected president, 56-57
  1861 Democrat victory, 116-17
  1861 Pennsylvania state, 116
  1863 Union Party victory in Pennsylvania, 206
  1864 Lincoln re-elected, 244-46
  business interests controlling, 54
  telegraph announcing results, 57
  Union League promoting Lincoln, 221, 241
elevator, 112-13
Eliot, George (Mary Anne "Marian" Evans), 136
Ellsworth, Elmer Ephraim, 94
Emancipation Proclamation, 174. *See also* Negroes; slavery
Emerson, Ralph Waldo, 18*n*4, 81, 136
  conservatives' view of, 17-18
Emory, John, 181
Emory, William H., 181-82
England. *See also* Europe
  Dallas-Brougham incident, 43, 44
  Deerhound yacht incident, 230
  England & the South, 126, 127
  Ingersoll, Charles, quoting English law, 185

Index

Mason and Slidell question, 122, 125–26, 127, 128
Monroe Doctrine disregarded by, 129-30n163
Mr. Dallas and Lord Brougham, 44n64, 49
Prince Albert of, 42-43
Prince of Wales visiting U.S., 47-49
Rush, Richard, minister to, 62n84
South's relationship with, 126, 230
Stillé on Napoleon v., 182
Trollope meets diarist, 135-37
England & the South, 126, 127
Europe. *See also* England; France; Spain
  Americans visiting, 271
  colonization of Americas by, 122
  royalty from, witnessing Civil War, 108
Everett, Edward, 34, 38, 249
  at Gettysburg, 208-9
Ewell, Richard S., 195

Fairmont Park, 121, 122
Farmer's Club, 48
Farmers & Mechanics Bank, 241, 243
Farragut, David G., 235
Federalist, 72
Fell, John G., 148
Felton, Cornelius Conway, 81
Fenianism, 270
Fern Hill country seat, 200, 279
Fern Rock Station, 162n47
Fessenden, William Pitt, 228n16
Fichte, Johann Gottlieb, 192
Field, John W., 123
Fisher, Charles Henry (1814-62), 38, 110, 243, 276. *See also* Brookwood
  business of, 89-90, 120
  death of, 137-44
  plot to assassinate Lincoln told by, 76
Fisher, Deborah, 203
Fisher, Elizabeth "Bet" (diarist's wife), 17
Fisher, Elizabeth Francis "Lily," 92, 119
Fisher, Elizabeth Rodman, 32, 32n44
Fisher, Hannah Logan (1777-1846), 276
Fisher, James Cowles, 122
Fisher, James Logan (1783-1814), 276
Fisher, James Logan (1811-33), 276
Fisher, Joshua (1701-83), 275
Fisher, Joshua (1775-1806), 275

Fisher, Joshua Francis (1807-73), 275. *See also* Alverthorpe
  The Cruelties of War, 234, 235
  opposed to Lincoln/Seward, 186
Fisher, Mary Rodman (diarist's cousin), 250
Fisher, Sidney (diarist's son), 188, 274
Fisher, Sidney George (diarist)
  ancestry of, 244, 275-76
  Civil War forecast by, 4-5
  financial condition of, 36-37, 100, 119, 188, 231, 241-42, 267
  married life of, 94
  poetry of, 151-52, 220-21, 223, 263-64, 270
  published works by
    The Bible & Slavery, 211
    commending Lincoln, 102
    diary, 1, 2n3, 13
    England & the South, 126, 127
    Kanzas and the Constitution, 5
    The Law of the Territories, 5
    The Laws of Race, as Connected with Slavery, 5, 53-56, 81
    Maryland, 93
    Mr. Dallas and Lord Brougham, 44n64, 49
    A National Currency, 219-20
    The National Highways, 268
    Our Black Army, 200
    The Right Men in the Right Places, 100
    The Trial of the Constitution, 9, 10, 174-75
    The True Interest of the Border States, 72-73
    The Writ of Habeas Corpus, 111
  recounting brother's life, 142-43
  views of
    black suffrage, 12
    Constitution, 5-6, 9-10
    death/hereafter, 80, 141-42, 154-55
    Lincoln, 46-47, 77-78, 125
    Lincoln as "unspeakable blessing," 102-3
    Lincoln's character/appearance, 226-27, 252
    mob violence, 2, 5, 109-10
    popular democracy, 2-3, 9
    slavery, 3-9, 17-18, 206-7
    Southern v. Northern interests, 4-8

Fisher, Thomas (1741-1810), 275
Fisher, William Logan (1781-1862), 276
The Five Cotton States and New York; or, Remarks upon the Social and Economical Aspects of the Southern Political Crisis (Colwell), 65*n*87
flag
  American, 75, 84
  Confederate, 84
Ford, George A., 202
Forest Hill country seat, 236
  Cornelius Shelly at, 218*n*9
  "Daniel" gardener at, 208, 218*n*9
  location of, 279-80
Forney, John W., 180
Fort Donelson, Tennessee, captured by Grant, 133
Fort Sumter, South Carolina, 83, 84
Fort Warren, 164
Foster, Henry D., 47
Fox, Charles P., 264
Fox, Mary, 264
Fox, Samuel M., 250, 250*n*1
Fraley, Frederick, 44-45, 148
France. *See also* Europe
  England v. Napoleon, 182
  in Mexico, 198, 212
  Monroe Doctrine disregarded by, 129-30*n*1
  revolution principles of, 233
  supportive of South, 212
Freas, Philip R., 48
Fredericksburg, Virginia, 176-77
Fremont, John C., 151
French, William H., 197

Gerhard, Benjamin, 228
Gerhard, Louisa, 36
Germantown Academy, 102*n*37
Germantown, battle of, 27
Germantown School, 29, 30-31, 31-32
Germantown Telegraph, 24*n*20
Gettysburg, Pennsylvania
  Confederate prisoners of war from, 197
  Everett at, 208-9
  Lee at, 196-97
  Lincoln's address at, 208-9
  Meade at, 196-97
  Seward at, 208-9

Gilpin, Charles, 21
Gilpin, Henry, 20-24, 26-27
Gilpin, Joshua, 21
Gilpin, William, 80-81*n*8, 87
Godkin, Edwin L., 266
Goodyear, Charles (1833-96), 238
Goodyear, Charles (1800-60), 238
gout remedies, 218, 243
  Indian hemp, 207
  salts of Vichy, 215
Grant, Ulysses S.
  advances to Richmond, 223
  assumes command of Union Army, 216
  Butler joins forces with, 226
  Mississippi River gained by, 198*n*36

habeas corpus, 111, 204
  Binney on, 166
  Congress suspending, 204-5
  Constitution on, 95
  Lincoln's suspension of, 94-95, 204-5
Halleck, Henry Wager, 133, 166
Hallowell, Morris, 93
Hare, John Innes Clark, 113, 179
  judge, 112
Harper's Ferry
  Brown, John, revolt at, 18
  destruction of arsenal at, 88
Harrison, Charles W., 48
Hartford Convention, 184
Harvey, James E., 53
Hawthorn, Nathaniel, 136
Hazard, Samuel Jr., 49
"The Heart of the Andes" painting, 225
Heckscher, Charles A., 130-31
Henry, Alexander, 216*n*6, 19
Henry, Thomas Charlton, 217
Herbart, Johann Friedrich, 192
Hickman, John, 170
Hicks, Thomas H., 86*n*16
Historical Society of Pennsylvania, 37, 57, 182
The History of Philosophy in Epitome (Schwegler), 192
History of the United States (Bancroft), 28, 29
Hobart, Jane, 277
Holmes, Oliver Wendell, 81, 151-52
Hooker, Joseph, 189
Hopkins, John Henry, 209

Index

How a Free People Conduct a Long War (Stillé), 182
Howe, Julia Ward, 25–26
Howe, Samuel G., 26
Hunter, David, 226
Hutchinson, I. Pemberton, 242

Ingersoll, Alexander Wilcocks (1807-89), 277
Ingersoll, Ann Wilcocks (1822-56), 230, 278
Ingersoll, Charles (1805-82), 277
　favoring secession, 117
　A Letter to a Friend in a Slave State: By a Citizen of Pennsylvania, 144–45
　slavery as divine institution, 220
　speech incites mob attack upon, 254–57
　treasonous speeches/arrests of, 160–64, 165, 186
Ingersoll, Charles Edward (1860-1932), 277
Ingersoll, Charles Jared (1782-1862), 277
　death/funeral of, 147, 149–51
　father-in-law of diarist/Democrat/congressman, 43
　Forest Hill country seat, 236n24
　Recollections, Historical, Political, Biographical, and Social, 150–51
　Webster's dispute with, 150
Ingersoll, Edward (1817-93), 277
　forecasting North's downfall, 220
　mob attack upon, 254–58
　Personal Liberty and Martial Law: A Review of Some Pamphlets of the Day, 145
Ingersoll, Elizabeth (1815-72), 277
Ingersoll, Harry (1809-86)
　husband of Sally, 277
　Lincoln critic, 165–66
Ingersoll, Jared, Jr. (1749-1822), 276–77
Ingersoll, John (1811-59), 277
Ingersoll, Joseph Reed (1786-1868), 26n26, 278
　stumping for Bell and Everett, 46
Ingersoll, Sarah Emlen "Sally"
　dying sentiment of, 272
　funeral of, 273
　secessionist, 75

Insane Department, Pennsylvania Hospital, 171
inventions
　coal oil lighting, 59, 138, 148, 243
　daguerreotype, 79
　elevator, 112–13
　"greenbacks," 156, 186–87
　sewing machine, 59
　streetcars, 158
　telegraph, 57
Irish Americans
　Fenianism of, 270
　Negroes hated by, 2n4, 169

Jackson, Andrew, 2, 215
Jackson, James W., 93–94
Jackson, John P., 44
Jackson, Thomas Jonathan "Stonewall," 151
　accidental death of, in Chancellorsville, 195
Jacobi, Friedrich H., 192
Jefferson Medical College, Philadelphia, 52n77
Johnston, Joseph E., 97–98
　at Manassas, 104
Jones House, 174
Jones, Jacob, 202
Journal of a Residence on a Georgian Plantation (Kemble), 197
judiciary
　business interests controlling, 54
　Cadwalader, U.S. district judge, 162
　Hare, 112, 113, 179
　Kelley, 165
　Pennsylvania judges on Conscription Act, 207
　Pennsylvania supreme court, 112, 205, 207
　Stroud, 112
July fourth celebration, 1864, 229

Kane, Elisha Kent, 92–93
Kane family, 92–93
Kane, John Klintzing, 92n21
Kane, Robert Patterson, 92, 119
Kane, Thomas Leiper, 92–93
Kansas. *See also* new territories
　Kansas-Nebraska Act, 5, 34
　Kanzas and the Constitution, 5

The Law of the Territories, 5
The Laws of Race, as Connected with Slavery, 5, 53-56, 81
Kansas-Nebraska Act, 5, 34
Kanzas and the Constitution (Fisher, S. G.), 5
Kelley, William D., 165
Kemble, Frances Anne "Fanny," 32*n*45, 45, 82, 219. *See also* Butler, Pierce
  abolitionist, 134, 201
  Journal of a Residence on a Georgian Plantation, 197
King, Charles R., 48
Kirkbride, Thomas S., 171
Kneedler v. Lane, 207
Kuhn, Hartman, 96-97, 179
Kuhn, James Hamilton, 97*n*27
  at Richmond, 152-54, 223, 226

laborers
  demand for, 271
  discharged soldiers as, 250
  Negro, 201-2
  wages, 268
  working class, post-Civil War, 268
Landseer, John, 225
The Law of the Territories (Fisher, S. G.), 5
  Virginia slaveholder's opinion of, 19
The Laws of Race, as Connected with Slavery (Fisher, S. G.), 5
  publishing of, 53-56
  read by Emerson, 81
  white supremacy theme of, 53*n*79
Lee, Robert E.
  captor of Brown, 194*n*26
  at Gettysburg, 196-97
  war strategy of, 195
Lehigh University, 98
A Letter to a Friend in a Slave State: By a Citizen of Pennsylvania (Ingersoll, C.), 144-45
Lewes, George Henry, 136
The Life of George Washington, Commander in Chief of the American Forces (Marshall), 27
Lincoln, Abraham, 228
  1860 election of, 56-57
  1864 re-election of, 244-46
  1865 Commemoration of, 261
  assassination of, 251-53

Confederates' meeting with, 79
Curtis' high regard for, 212
diarist's description of, 226-27
first proclamation for troops, 84
Fisher, Joshua Francis, opposed to, 186
Gettysburg address, 208-9
Gilpin, William, on, 87-88
habeas corpus suspended by, 204-5
inauguration of, 77
mourning after assassination of, 253, 255
nomination of, 35-36, 38, 46
Philadelphia flag-raising by, 75
as President-elect, assassination plot against, 73-74
protector of Southern interests, 125
as "unspeakable blessing to the nation," 102-3
war cabinet meeting, 157
Lincoln, Mary Todd, diarist's description of, 227
Lippencott Publishing Company, 201, 241, 265
Lippencott Tavern, 231
Littell, John S., 31-32
Little Schuylkill Navigation, Railroad, and Coal Company, 138, 148
Logan, Albanus Charles, 40, 101*n*125
Logan, Gustavus, 40*n*54, 41-44
Logan, James, 42
Logan, John Dickinson, 40, 93, 101*n*36
Logan, Maria Dickinson, 40-44
Logan Square Park, 113
Logan, William, 42
The London Times
  diarist's Dallas speech in, 49
  report on Bull Run, 105
Longfellow, Henry Wadsworth, 81, 136
Longstreet, James, 197
Louisiana
  1864 accounts of, 214-15
  reluctant to secede, 72
Lowell, James Russell, 206
Lowrie, Walter H., 207-8
Loyd, Issac S., 122
Ludlow, James R.., 183-84
Lyons, Richard, 107

Magarge, Charles, 87
Malvern Hill battle, 164

Index

Manassas Junction, 115
  amassing of troops at, 103
  First Battle of Bull Run, 104-5
  The London Times reports on, 105
  Second Battle of Bull Run, 166, 182
  Union army defeated at, 104, 134
Manigault, Harriet, 230
Markoe, Francis, 110, 115
Marshall House, 93-94
Maryland, 88
  Antietam battle, 172
  Maryland, 93
  mixture of races in, 18
  North American and United States Gazette article on, 93
  Rebel invasion of, 166
  slaves escaping from, 87
  trade with North, 85
Mason and Slidell question, 122, 125-26, 127, 128
Mason, Elizabeth Margaretta, 31n41
Mason, James Murray, 31, 122
  Mason and Slidell question, 122, 125-26, 127, 128
Massachusetts. *See also North American Review*
  6th Regiment en route to Washington, 86
  regiments of, 88
Maupay, Samuel, 87
Maxwell, David, 231-33, 235
McCall, George A., at Richmond, 152-54, 223, 226
McCalmont, Robert, 19
McClees, James E., 123
McClellan, George Brinton. *See also* Army of Potomac
  Chickahominy to James River, 164
  inactivity on the Potomac, 134-35
  Philadelphia native, 130
  Union commander-in-chief, 130, 145-46, 151, 166
McCrea, James A., 48
McDowell, Irvin, 103, 182
McKean, Henry, 277
McKim, James Miller, 202, 206
McLane, Lydia, 97-98
McMichael, Morton, 26, 48, 98-99, 100, 180
Meade, George Gordon
  Army of Potomac commander, 195-96
  at Richmond, 152-54, 223, 226
  at Gettysburg, 196-97
Medary country seat, 200, 280
  location/sale of, 162n209
Meigs, Charles D., 52, 111
Meigs, John Rogers, guerilla murder of, 242
Meigs, Montgomery C., 111, 242
Mercer, Singleton A., 63, 241
Meredith, William M., 35-36
  attorney general, 95-96
  views on Lincoln, 35-36, 175
Merrick, Samuel V., 48
Merryman, John, 94
Mexico
  European claims in, 122-23
  France in, 198, 212
  Spain in, 129
Middleton, Harry, 59-60
Middleton Place, 121
  Negroes blamed for burning of, 260
Milward, William, 163
Minnesota Regiment, at Bull Run, 104
Mississippi
  1864 accounts of, 214-15
  battle of Vicksburg, 198
  Grant's control of Mississippi River, 198n36
Missouri Compromise, 5
Mobile Bay, Farragut victorious at, 235
mob violence
  Curtis threatened by, 19, 193
  danger of, in North, 109-10
  Democrats', 2-3
  Democrats' meeting inciting, 193
  Ingersoll, Charles, incites, 254-57
  The Palmetto Flag office attacked, 84
  in Philadelphia, 2
  Wister, William, advocating, 101
Monroe Doctrine, 122
  disregarded by France/England, 129-30n1
Monroe, James, 122
Morgan, Charles, 173
Mormons, 92
Morris, E. Joy, 100
Mott, Lucretia Coffin, 168, 273
Mount Harmon, 74, 82, 163, 231
  alleged crop failure at, 100

290　Index

death of Stephen, 141
last possession of diarist, 274
mortgaging of, 270
satisfaction in proprietorship of, 219-20

A National Currency (Fisher, S. G.), 219-20, 229
The Nation journal, 265-67, 272
Nebraska. *See also* new territories
　Kansas-Nebraska Act, 5
Negroes. *See also* slavery
　actual emancipation of, 245
　attempting to join Union troops, 106
　Douglass, 198
　Emancipation Proclamation, 174
　employment/education of freed, 201-2
　equality claimed for, 198
　Irish against, 2n4, 169
　liberated, arriving in Philadelphia, 202n44
　Middleton Place burning blamed on, 260
　New York rioting/atrocities against, 199
　New York Times recommending emancipation for, 107
　Our Black Army, 200
　suffrage for, 12, 212, 250-51, 262
　white supremacist doctrine, 53n79
New Bedford, Rodman family of, 272
New Castle Company Agricultural Society, 45, 50-52
New England
　Hartford Convention, 184
　superiority of, 88
New England Loyal Publication Company, 200
Newhall, Thomas A., 123
Newhall, Walter S., 217
New Orleans, Farragut victorious at, 235
new territories. *See also* slavery
　fugitive slave law, 87
　Kansas/Nebraska, 5, 34
　The Law of the Territories, 5
　The Laws of Race, as Connected with Slavery, 5, 53-56, 81
　Missouri Compromise, 5
　popular sovereignty for, 5
　Seward on, 27

　slaveholder's opinion of *The Law of the Territories*, 19
New York
　diarist visits, 236-40
　draft riots, 200
　rioting/murdering of Negroes in, 199
　Zouaves, 93-94
　New York Herald, predicting Civil War, 52
New York Times, 91
　recommending emancipation, 107
New York Tribune, *Journal of a Residence on a Georgian Plantation* reviewed in, 197
No Cross, No Crown (Penn), 223
North American and United States Gazette, 26
　Maryland in, 93
　Mr. Dallas and Lord Brougham in, 44n64
　The President's Proclamation of September 22 in, 174
　The Writ of Habeas Corpus in, 111
North American Review
　The Bible & Slavery in, 211
　constitutionality of legal tender notes, 213
　Crosley & Nicholls publishers of, 241
　first issue of, 206
　Ticknor & Fields, Boston publishers of, 265
North Carolina, reluctant to secede, 72
Norton, Charles Eliot, 81, 206
　editing *A National Currency*, 229

Ohio, Tod, governor of, 228
Our Black Army (Fisher, S. G.), 200

Palmetto (Confederate) flag, 84
The Palmetto Flag newspaper office, attacked by mob, 84
paper money, 156, 186-87
Patterson, Robert Emmet, 91
　colonel of Pennsylvania infantry, 181
　as Union general, 107
Peace, Edward, 48
Pennsylvania. *See also* Philadelphia
　1861 election, 116
　1863 Union Party victory, 206
　armed militia from, 83

Index   291

Carlisle entered by Confederate forces, 194*n*25
Historical Society of, 24*n*20, 37, 57, 182
A Letter to a Friend in a Slave State: By a Citizen of Pennsylvania, 144-45
Pennsylvania Freeman, 206*n*51
Philadelphia Academy of Music, 47-49
Philadelphia Port Relief Committee, 202*n*44
rebels cross state line into, 166-67, 169
rebels in Chambersburg, 193-94, 234
Society of Colonial Dames of America, 23*n*17
state judiciary on Conscription Act, 207
Strong, supreme court justice of, 207
Pennsylvania Academy of Fine Arts, 24*n*20
Pennsylvania Anti-Slavery Society, 202*n*44
Pennsylvania Freeman, 206*n*51
Pennsylvania Hospital Insane Department, 171
Pennsylvania Life Insurance Company, 242
Pennsylvania Railroad, 172-73
Pennsylvania, University of, 98*n*30
Perry naval brig, 99*n*121
Personal Liberty and Martial Law: A Review of Some Pamphlets of the Day (Ingersoll, E.), 145
Philadelphia. *See also* Pennsylvania
Agricultural Society, 24-25
Cadwalader commanding troops in, 200
Democratic party of, 159-60
First Troop of, 97
Gilpin, mayor of, 21
Henry, mayor of, 19, 216*n*6
home guard defense of, 87
liberated slaves in, 202*n*44
Lincoln flag-raising in, 75
mayor of, 19
mob violence in, 2
Port Relief Committee, 202*n*44
Railroad burnt, 86*n*15
Philadelphia Academy of Music, 47-49
Philadelphia Evening Journal, 183-84
Philadelphia Inquirer, 91

Philadelphia Port Relief Committee, 202*n*44
Phil Ellena estate, 28
Phillips, Samuel, 227
Phillips, Wendell, 18*n*5
conservatives' view of, 17-18
Pike's Peak gold region, 81
Platonist, diarist as, 128, 141, 155, 192
Polk, James K., 92*n*21
Pope, John, 166
popular sovereignty. *See* new territories
Porter, David D., 157
Pratt, Henry, 122
The President's Proclamation of September 22, 174
press. *See also specific publication*
business interests controlling, 54
Prince of Wales, favorable opinion towards, 47-49
Princeton College, 142
prisoners of war
Butler, Pierce, as, 108-9
Confederate, Antietam, 172
Confederate, crew of *Savannah*, 99
Confederate, Gettysburg, 197
Confederate, Moorefield, 235
The Privilege of the Writ of Habeas Corpus under the Constitution (Binney), 166
Purviance, Emily Atherton, 53
Purviance, George D., 53

quack medicine vendors, 50
Quakers, 168, 272
in diarist's ancestry, 244

race relations. *See* abolitionists; Negroes; rioting; slavery
railroad companies
Baltimore & Wilmington Railroad, 73, 86, 143
government controlled by, 21, 158
Heckscher's interest in, 130-31
Little Schuylkill Navigation, Railroad, and Coal Company, 138, 148
Northern Central burnt, 86
Pennsylvania Railroad, 172-73
Philadelphia Railroad burnt, 86*n*15
Reading Railroad, 132
Read, John M., 207

Read, T. Buchanan, 121
Recollections, Historical, Political, Biographical, and Social (Ingersoll, C.J.), 150–51
Reconstruction, 250
Reed, Thomas Buchanan, 121
Reed, William B., 26, 132
refugees' postwar plot, 258
Republican Party
  Binney, 23–24
  Democratic party v., 38
  Democrats' excesses as beneficial to, 11, 23, 54, 187, 190
  McMichael, 26
  moderate views of, 61
  Read, 207
Rhode Island
  regiments of, 88, 104–5
  Sprague, governor of, 88
Richfield, New York, 238–39, 265–66
Richmond, Virginia, battle of, 152–54, 223, 226
Richmond Whig, 26
Riethmuller, Christopher James, 233
rioting
  anti-Conscription Act, 200
  anti-Negro, in New York, 199
  Democrats inciting, 193
  Irish against Negroes, 2n4, 169
Rising Sun Inn, 47, 87, 245
Rives, William C., 19, 26
Robert's Mill, 168
Rush, Benjamin, 62, 118
Rush, James Murray, 118, 127–28
Rush, Richard, 62n84, 99
Rush, William, wood statues by, 28n34
Russell, William Howard, 105
Russia, Cameron as minister to, 103, 131

Sanitary Commission, 217, 221, 222n10, 224–26
Saturday Review & Spectator, 265
Saulsbury, Willard Sr., 183
Savannah (privateer), 99n32
Saxon ethnicity, superiority of, 88
Schooley's Mountain, 39
Schwegler, Albert, 192
Scott, Winfield, 76
secession, 115–16
  Baltimore secessionists, 158
  banks threatened by, 58–59, 81
  businesses influenced by, 58–59, 81
  Butler favoring, 161–62
  Constitution on, 78–79
  Dallas against, 115–16
  diarist's argument against, 63
  inevitability of, 64, 69
  Ingersoll, Charles, favoring, 117
  Jones favoring, 202
  legalized, 82–83
  Mason favoring, 31
  South Carolina's, 72
Second Battle of Bull Run, 166, 182
Sedgley estate, 121–22
Semmes, Raphael, 230
Sergeant, John, 154
Seward, William H., 212
  assassination attempt against, 251
  Fisher, Joshua Francis, opposed to, 186
  at Gettysburg, 208–9
  governor/senator/secretary of state, 27
  on Mason and Slidell affair, 128
  on new territories, 27
  on slavery, 27
sewing machine, 59
Seymour, Horatio, 172, 199
Sharon springs, 200–201, 227
Sharswood, George, 112
Sheridan, Philip H., 235–36
Sherman, William Tecumseh, 216, 223, 246
Sinkler, William, 72
slavery, 3–9, 18, 39. *See also* abolitionists; Negroes; new territories
  actual emancipation of slaves, 245
  anecdote about cruelty of, 158–59
  Bible interpreted as favoring, 207
  The Bible & Slavery, 211
  Bible View of Slavery, 209
  Breckinridge on, 39
  Civil War as war against, 98
  concubines as victims of jealous wives, 202
  Congress' plans for managing, 124–25
  conservatives' view of, 17–18
  decent civilization v., 19
  democracy v., 3
  Dred Scott decision, 7n17
  Emancipation Proclamation, 174
  fugitive slave law, 87

Journal of a Residence on a Georgian Plantation, 197
mixture of races anecdote, 18-19
New York Times advocates emancipation, 107
northern sentiment toward, 61
Pennsylvania Anti-Slavery Society, 202*n*44
Seward on, 27
white supremacist doctrine, 53*n*79
world opinion turning against, 6
Slidell, John, 122, 125-26, 127, 128
    Mason and Slidell question, 122, 125-26, 127, 128
Slocum, John S., 104
Smith, Charles Ross, 105-7
Smith, Esther "Hetty" Fisher, 177, 178*n*69
Smith, George R., 138, 229, 264
Smith, Goldwin, 207, 246-47*n*34
Smith, Rebecca, 123
soldier
    discharged, seeking work, 250
    former U.S. officers turned Confederate, 97-98
    Negro, 198, 200
    Our Black Army, 200
    professed "pleasant life" of, 105
    Rebel refugees' postwar plot, 258
    right to vote, 116
Somerville country seat, 101*n*36, 214, 280
South. *See also* slavery
    1864 accounts of Mississippi/Louisiana, 214-15
    abuse of power by, 20, 24, 33
    caste system of, 98
    Dred Scott decision, 7*n*17
    England's relationship with, 126, 230
    England & the South, 126, 127
    excesses of, as beneficial to North, 7*n*17, 11, 23, 54, 187, 190
    Gilpin on power of, 88
    Northern interests v., 4-8
    Northern power overwhelming to, 69, 96
    Sherman's devastation of, 246
South Carolina, 12
    beyond reach of reason, 109
    Charleston in flames, 84
    declaration of sovereignty by, 67-68

du Pont takes Beaufort, 121
factious nature of, 65
Fort Sumter, 83, 84
secession of, 72
Spain. *See also* Europe
    claims in Mexico of, 129
    landing at Vera Cruz, 129,
    slaveholding nation, 43
sperm candles, coal oil v., 59
Sprague, William, 88, 104-5
Stanton, Edward M., 131-32, 200
Star of the West (ship), 71*n*1
Stenton country seat, 23*n*17, 280
    1860 visits to, 23, 40-44
Stephens, Alexander II, 62, 74, 164
Stillé, Charles J., 181-82
St. John (steamship), 236
St. Peter's Church, Philadelphia, 119
streetcar, 158, 159
Strong, William, 207
Stroud, George, 112
suffrage, Negro, 12, 211*n*1, 212, 250-51, 262
Sumner, Charles, 211*n*1, 212
The Sunday Despatch, 128
Sverson, Thomas, 100, 112, 232
Swarthmore College, 168

Taney, Roger B., 94-95
telegraph, election results via, 57
Tennyson, Alfred, 136
Texas, annexation of, debated, 4
Thomas, George H., 134-35
Thompson, James, 207
Tod, David, 228
transcendentalist, diarist as, 128
Trent (British ship), 122*n*66
The Trial of the Constitution (Fisher, S. G.), 9, 10
    announced publication of, 174-75
    suspension of habeas corpus presaged in, 204
Trollope, Anthony, 135-37
The True Interest of the Border States, 72-73
tuberculosis, 203-4
Tucker, John, 132-33

Union Army. *See also* Army of Potomac; soldier; *specific person; specific place*

Gettysburg, Meade v. Lee, 196-97
  inactivity of, 130-31
  Malvern Hill, 164
  Our Black Army, 200
  retreating from Sherman's advance, 223
Union League Club
  founding of, 179
  Henry, Thomas Charlton, of, 217
  promoting re-election of Lincoln, 221
  re-election of Lincoln address, 241
  success of, 185-86
Union Party
  1860 Baltimore convention, 34-35
  1863 Pennsylvania election victory, 206
  slavery issue bypassed by, 34-35
University of Pennsylvania, 98n30
Utah, Kane expedition to, 92

Vallandigham, Clement L., 135, 192
Van Buren, John, 172
Van Buren, Martin, 22
Vermont, pro-slavery bishop in, 209
Verree, John Paul, 130
Vicksburg, Mississippi, battle of, 198
Virginia
  exhausted, 166
  former U.S. officers turned Confederate, 97-98
  Northern troops enter, 93-94
  Richmond Whig, 26, 26n25
  slaveholder's opinion of *The Law of the Territories*, 19
  Stonewall Jackson in, 151, 195
  West Virginia's statehood, 176
Volunteer Refreshment Saloon, 250

Wadsworth, James S., 115, 222-23
Wainwright, Nicholas B., 2
Wakefield country seat, 96, 280
  antiques/relics from, 223
  ice skating at, 212-13
  Lucretia Mott/Deborah Wharton at, 168

Waln, S. Morris, 91
Warren, Anna, 277
Warren, Fort, 164
Warren, Phoebe, 277
Warren, Stephen, 277
Warrior (steamship), 126
Washington, D.C.
  garrisoning of, 73
  troops forwarded to, 88, 96
  Wadsworth as governor of, 115, 222-23
Watmough, William Nicklin, 152-54, 223, 226
Webster, Daniel, 150
Welles, Eli, 163
Wells Coverly's hotel, 174
West Virginia
  Harper's Ferry, 18, 88
  statehood, 176
Wharton, Annie, 203-4, 210
Wharton, Deborah, 168, 273
Wharton, George M., 257
Wharton, Joseph, 203n47
Wharton, Mary, 223
Wharton School, 203n47
Wharton, William, 203
white supremacy, 53n79. *See also* Negroes; slavery
Whittier, John Greenleaf, 206n51
Wilcocks, Ann, 278
Wilcocks, Mary, 277
Wilcocks, Samuel, 230
Winslow, Jeremiah, 142
Wister, Charles J., 29
Wister, Langhorne
  Duncannon estate, 173-74
  firsthand accounts of war from, 164
Wister, Owen J., novelist, 39-40
Wister, Sarah Butler, 217
Wister, William, 118n59
  mob violence advocated by, 101
Woodward, George W., 205, 207
Wool, John Ellis, 157
working class, post-Civil War, 268

Zouaves, New York, 93-94

THE NORTH'S CIVIL WAR SERIES
Paul A. Cimbala, series editor

1. Anita Palladino, ed., *Diary of a Yankee Engineer: The Civil War Story of John H. Westervelt, Engineer, 1st New York Volunteer Engineer Corps.*
2. Herman Belz, *Abraham Lincoln, Constitutionalism, and Equal Rights in the Civil War Era.*
3. Earl J. Hess, *Liberty, Virtue, and Progress: Northerners and Their War for the Union.* Second revised edition, with a new introduction by the author.
4. William L. Burton, *Melting Pot Soldiers: The Union's Ethnic Regiments.*
5. Hans L. Trefousse, *Carl Schurz: A Biography.*
6. Stephen W. Sears, ed., *Mr. Dunn Browne's Experience in the Army: The Civil War Letters of Samuel W. Fiske.*
7. Jean H. Baker, *Affairs of Party: The Political Culture of Northern Democrats in the Mid-Nineteenth Century.*
8. Frank L. Klement, *The Limits of Dissent: Clement L. Vallandigham and the Civil War.* With a new introduction by Steven K. Rogstad.
9. Lawrence N. Powell, *New Masters: Northern Planters during the Civil War and Reconstruction.*
10. John A. Carpenter, *Sword and Olive Branch: Oliver Otis Howard.*
11. Thomas F. Schwartz, ed., *"For a Vast Future Also": Essays from the* Journal of the Abraham Lincoln Association.
12. Mark De Wolfe Howe, ed., *Touched with Fire: Civil War Letters and Diary of Oliver Wendell Holmes, Jr.* With a new introduction by David Burton.
13. Harold Adams Small, ed., *The Road to Richmond: The Civil War Letters of Major Abner R. Small of the 16th Maine Volunteers.* New introduction by Earl J. Hess.
14. Eric A. Campbell, ed., *"A Grand Terrible Dramma": From Gettysburg to Petersburg: The Civil War Letters of Charles Wellington Reed.* Illustrated by Reed's Civil War Sketches.
15. Herbert Mitgang, ed., *Abraham Lincoln: A Press Portrait.*
16. Harold Holzer, ed., *Prang's Civil War Pictures: The Complete Battle Chromos of Louis Prang.*
17. Harold Holzer, ed., *State of the Union: New York and the Civil War.*
18. Paul A. Cimbala and Randall M. Miller, eds., *Union Soldiers and the Northern Home Front: Wartime Experiences, Postwar Adjustments.*
19. Mark A. Snell, *From First to Last: The Life of Major General William B. Franklin.*

20. Paul A. Cimbala and Randall M. Miller, eds., *An Uncommon Time: The Civil War and the Northern Home Front.*

21. John Y. Simon and Harold Holzer, eds., *The Lincoln Forum: Rediscovering Abraham Lincoln.*

22. Thomas F. Curran, *Soldiers of Peace: Civil War Pacifism and the Postwar Radical Peace Movement.*

23. Kyle S. Sinisi, *Sacred Debts: State Civil War Claims and American Federalism, 1861–1880.*

24. Russell L. Johnson, *Warriors into Workers: The Civil War and the Formation of Urban-Industrial Society in a Northern City.*

25. Peter J. Parish, *The North and the Nation in the Era of the Civil War.* Edited by Adam I. P. Smith and Susan-Mary Grant.

26. Patricia Richard, *Busy Hands: Images of the Family in the Northern Civil War Effort.*

27. Michael S. Green, *Freedom, Union, and Power: The Mind of the Republican Party During the Civil War.*

28. Christian G. Samito, ed., *Fear Was Not In Him: The Civil War Letters of Major General Francis S. Barlow, U.S.A.*

29. John S. Collier and Bonnie B. Collier, eds., *Yours for the Union: The Civil War Letters of John W. Chase, First Massachusetts Light Artillery.*

30. Grace Palladino, *Another Civil War: Labor, Capital, and the State in the Anthracite Regions of Pennsylvania, 1840–1868.*